Higher Education and the Future of Graduate Employability

Higher Education and the Future of Graduate Employability

A Connectedness Learning Approach

Edited by

Ruth Bridgstock

Professor of Teaching and Curriculum Innovation in The Centre for Learning Futures, Griffith University, Australia

Neil Tippett

Post-Doctoral Research Fellow in the Division of Education Arts and Social Sciences, University of South Australia

Edward Elgar
PUBLISHING

Cheltenham, UK • Northampton, MA, USA

Published by
Edward Elgar Publishing Limited
The Lypiatts
15 Lansdown Road
Cheltenham
Glos GL50 2JA
UK

Edward Elgar Publishing, Inc.
William Pratt House
9 Dewey Court
Northampton
Massachusetts 01060
USA

A catalogue record for this book
is available from the British Library

Library of Congress Control Number: 2019935386

This book is available electronically in the **Elgar**online
Social and Political Science subject collection
DOI 10.4337/9781788972611

MIX
Paper from
responsible sources
FSC   FSC® C013056
www.fsc.org

ISBN 978 1 78897 260 4 (cased)
ISBN 978 1 78897 261 1 (eBook)

Printed and bound in Great Britain by TJ International Ltd, Padstow, Cornwall

Contents

Figures

Tables

Contributors

Wajeehah Aayeshah is a researcher of Media Studies and Educational Design. She is a third space academic at the University of Melbourne, designing curriculum and investigating learning and teaching in higher education. Her PhD explored games for journalism education. Her research interests include representations of Muslims in media, indigenous pedagogies, educational games, teaching and learning spaces, and student wellbeing. She is an academic geek who loves traveling, photography, drinking tea and collecting stories.

Kay Are is a writer of multimodal, multi-species and site-responsive poetry, and an environmental humanities researcher with interests in posthumanist, decolonising and post-Cartesian pedagogies. Kay has recently published in the areas of touch as a learning modality; on conceptualising learning environments through quantum field theory; and on feminist-materialist teaching strategies, as well as various creative works.

Peter Ayriss is a program development consultant in a centralised learning and teaching unit with over 20 years' experience in higher education. His current role is to provide learning and teaching support for programs. Research interests include the student role in assessment, how academics cope in times of stress, and making the transition from content expert to a teaching academic.

Timothy Barraud is an Associate Principal – Junior Secondary at Indooroopilly State High School and a proud educational leader. He collaborated with Natalie Wright and Jeremy Kerr to develop a social entrepreneurship program focused on design thinking and human-centred design and innovation at Indooroopilly SHS. As a member of Queensland Student Innovation and Entrepreneurs Alliance he assists the leadership of the gen[in] project, an innovation challenge across Queensland to prepare students for a future through ideation and collaboration.

Marita Basson is a Senior Lecturer in Urban Planning and Design at the University of Southern Queensland. Her research interests cover urban and regional development and social sustainability, online engagement and active learning. She has published scholarly book chapters, reviewed journal articles and refereed conference papers on these subjects.

Beata Batorowicz is an Associate Professor in Sculpture and Creative Arts Coordinator at the University of Southern Queensland. As a contemporary artist and researcher, Batorowicz holds substantial experience in cross-university collaborations. Her projects such as *Dark Rituals* (2018), *Antipods* (2015), *Tales Within Historical Spaces* (2012), received a *USQ Citation for Outstanding Contributions to Student Learning, Arts Queensland Project Development grant* and an *ICCC Linking Fellowship*.

Simon Bedford is the Director of Learning Transformations at Western Sydney University where he develops professional learning programs, promotes connected pedagogies, and delivers twenty-first century curricula within future learning spaces. Simon's research draws on a range of conceptual frameworks, methodologies and methods in the areas of learning analytics, assessment literacies, and curriculum design. Simon is leader of the Higher Education Research and Development Society of Australasia (HERDSA) group looking at assessment quality.

Kenton Bell is a postgraduate student at the University of Wollongong. Kenton's primary research focus is on ways to engage men in preventing violence against women. Recently, the public report from his 'Case Study of White Ribbon Australia's Ambassador Program' was released. Bell's professional objectives are improving the teaching and learning of applied sociology focusing on men and masculinities and law and society while researching solutions-oriented approaches to preventing violence. Additionally, he is the editor of the *Open Education Sociology Dictionary* (http://SociologyDictionary.org).

Ruth Bridgstock is Professor of Curriculum and Teaching Transformation in the Centre for Learning Futures at Griffith University. She is interested in how we can develop and support 'future capable' learners, teachers and educational institutions. Ruth is Principal Fellow of the Higher Education Academy, and Australian National Senior Teaching Fellow for *Graduate Employability 2.0*, which is concerned with how students, teachers and educational institutions can build and use social networks for innovation, career development, and learning. Her blog is futurecapable.com.

Jason L. Brown is Head of Careers and Employability at La Trobe University and a doctoral student at the University of Southern Queensland's Australian Collaboratory for Career, Employability, and Learning for Living. Jason's practice and research is in the design and delivery of innovative curricula and co-curricular programs that aim to enhance student employability. He has been recognised for his work through receipt of the Career Development of Australia's Excellence in Leadership Award in 2018.

Simon Buckingham Shum is Professor of Learning Informatics at the University of Technology Sydney (UTS), and Director of the Connected Intelligence Centre. His Human-Centred Informatics approach has been developed in fields including Scholarly Hypertext, Collective Intelligence and Learning Analytics. He has co-edited/authored *Visualizing Argumentation* (Springer, 2003), *Knowledge Cartography* (Springer, 2008, 2014), and *Constructing Knowledge Art* (Morgan & Claypool, 2015). He is a co-founder of the Society for Learning Analytics Research, and has served twice as Program Chair of the International Conference on Learning Analytics and Knowledge.

Sam Byrnand lectures in Political and Legislative History at the University of Canberra, specialising in Indigenous participation in the Australian political process. His research into the 1967 Referendum has recently been recognised as a vital component in the demystification of this significant national event. His other areas of research are in visual communications and trauma therapy of returned military service personnel.

Peter Copeman is Senior Teaching Fellow in the University of Canberra's Teaching and Learning Directorate, convening the Graduate Certificate in Tertiary Education course, co-facilitating the Centre for Excellence in Learning and Teaching Scholarship, and helping drive the university's Indigenising the Curriculum project. He is a Senior Fellow of the Higher Education Academy with multi-award-winning teaching credentials in academic staff development, student learning support English language teaching, and theatre. His research interests include Indigenous epistemologies and pedagogies, teaching induction for new academics, and research communication.

Gail Crimmins is the Program Area Coordinator for Communication and First Year Experience Lead within the School of Communication and Creative Industries, University of the Sunshine Coast. Her research interests include gender in higher education, gender inequity in organisational structures, and learning and teaching in higher education.

Julieanne Cutrupi is the current Manager of Careers at UTS, with almost 17 years' experience in Higher Education and graduate recruitment in Australia and the UK. She is a former member of the NAGCAS Management Committee, Chairing Institutional Representatives across Australia. Julieanne is a member of ACEN, AAGE and The Careers Leadership Collective. Recently Julieanne has been involved in a range of research projects including an ATN project with the aim to help International Students succeed in Work Integrated Learning.

Margarietha J. de Villiers Scheepers is the Program Coordinator for the BBus Entrepreneurship program at the University of the Sunshine Coast. Her research interests include start-up entrepreneurial experiences, entrepreneurship ecosystems and corporate entrepreneurship. Her learning and teaching publications focus on cultivating an entrepreneurial mindset and employability in higher education.

Jo Devine is a Senior Lecturer in Construction Engineering and Management at the University of Southern Queensland. She has extensive industry experience as an engineer prior to joining USQ. Her research interests are in student diversity and engineering education.

Neal Dreamson is a Senior Lecturer in the Faculty of Education, Queensland University of Technology. He earned a PhD in intercultural education in 2016 and a DDES in interactive user experience design in 2007. His research expertise is a socio-cultural–philosophical approach to technology integration, cultural diversity, and digital citizenship. His recently published books are *Reinventing Intercultural Education* (Routledge, 2016) and *Pedagogical Alliances Between Indigenous and Non-Dualistic Cultures* (Routledge, 2018). His current work is to pedagogicalise *inter-connective experiences*.

Brian Egloff is an Adjunct Professor at the University of Canberra and an Honorary Associate Professor at The Australian National University. Brian is currently lecturing in Indigenous Heritage and Landscapes following on from four decades of work fostering Aboriginal Land Rights with the Yuin nation of the south coast of New South Wales.

Peter English is Lecturer in Journalism at the University of the Sunshine Coast, where his work focuses on journalism in traditional and social media, with an emphasis on sport.

Melissa Forbes is a Senior Lecturer in Music at the University of Southern Queensland in Toowoomba, Australia. Her PhD research examined the use of collaborative learning for first year music practice courses at USQ. Current research interests include collaborative learning and creativity, contemporary commercial music vocal pedagogy and alternative pathways to, through and beyond higher music education.

Gabrielle Gardiner has worked at the University of Technology Sydney (UTS) in a variety of project and management roles, including development of the 'Data Intensive University' strategy, now established as the Connected Intelligence Centre. With a background in communication, information and knowledge management, Gabrielle has administrative responsibility for cementing CIC's reputation as a world-leading hub for analytics research and learning. Gabrielle also has experience in research data management and curation, and ethics, having led the team that established the NSW node of the Australian Data Archive and the Aboriginal and Torres Strait Islander Data Archive.

Moein Ghodrati works as an Enterprise Architect to build best practice solutions for leading higher education institutions across Australia. Harnessing technology to deliver strategic business value and improving the society has always been the first priority in his career. He has been playing a pivotal role in major transformational projects including the E4Kids and eResource at the University of Melbourne, the Inspired Learning Initiative at UNSW Sydney, and is currently leading the design of the Digital Learning Ecosystem at UTS as part of the LX transformation project.

Mitch Goodwin is a media artist and academic with a research interest in emergent media ecologies and digital aesthetics. An interdisciplinary academic, Mitch has presented at SXSW Interactive (Austin, TX), the Art Association of Australia (GOMA, Brisbane), the David Bowie symposium (ACMI, Melbourne) and at the Australian Anthropology Society in which he interrogated the ethics of drones and autonomous systems. His media work has screened widely, including the IEEE VISAP (Baltimore, MD), The Lumen (Cardiff), MADATAC (Madrid) and the WRO Media Arts Biennale (Poland). http://mitchgoodwin.com.

Bryonny Goodwin-Hawkins is a postdoctoral research associate at Aberystwyth University, Wales. Her research focuses on rural development and EU policies, and she works in collaboration with the Welsh Local Government Association and partners across Europe. Bryonny was formerly a founding member of the University of Melbourne's Faculty of Arts Curriculum Design Lab. As a socio-cultural anthropologist, she is particularly interested in creating connected undergraduate curricula in the social sciences.

Sara Hammer leads a small program quality enhancement support team within a centralised learning and teaching unit at the University of Southern Queensland. Her notable research has focused on the conceptualisation and development of graduate learning outcomes such as graduate attributes. Her most recent work has focused on the use of capstone units for quality assurance purposes.

Michael Healy is a careers and employability educator and doctoral student at the University of Southern Queensland. In his practice and research, he is focused on exploring methods of promoting transformational careers and employability learning for university students, particularly using career writing and connectedness learning methods. He is a member of the Australian Collaboratory for Career, Employability, and Learning for Living, a research group based at USQ and focused on the psychology of working and careers.

Scott Heyes is an Associate Professor of Landscape Architecture at the University of Canberra, and holds research associate positions at the Smithsonian Institution's Arctic Studies Center in Washington, DC and at Trent University's Frost Centre for Canadian and Indigenous Studies. His research and teaching interests centre on Indigenous knowledge systems and heritage issues in Indigenous Australia, Fiji, and the Inuit homelands of Arctic Canada, involving several collaborative projects with Indigenous communities and industry partners using ethnographic and participatory methods, spanning more than fifteen years, and leading to research outputs both in traditional forms like co-publications and conference papers, and creative outputs such as short films, design studios, design works, maps, and major exhibitions.

Denise Jackson is the Director of Work-Integrated Learning (WIL) in the ECU School of Business and Law. She is a National Board Director and WA State Chair for the Australian Collaborative Education Network, the national association for WIL. Denise has received a number of research and teaching awards, most recently a national Citation for Outstanding Contribution to Student Learning. Her research spans student transition from university to the workplace, career development learning, professional identity development and work integrated learning.

Brianna L. Julien is a Lecturer in Human Physiology in the School of Life Sciences at La Trobe University, with a PhD on factors influencing postural reflex activity and a Graduate Certificate in Higher Education. Brianna, a Fellow of the Higher Education Academy, is dedicated to meeting the challenges facing science educators in preparing students for an uncertain future and to developing innovative and engaging learning experiences that will stimulate a love of science and lifelong learning in the next generation of scientists. Brianna's research interests are scientific skill development through authentic learning activities, use and development of open access educational resources, and embedding employability skills into science curricula.

Jeremy Kerr is a Senior Lecturer at the Queensland University of Technology and coordinator for the Visual Communication program. His research centres on applying co-design and participatory design frameworks to foster community capacity-building and self-advocacy. Jeremy works in the areas of intercultural design, mental health and cross-institutional education, with current projects including the Diverse Learners Hub, an online resource translating autism research for wider implementation, and CARE International's Pikinini Kisim Save (PKS) Project.

Alexander Kist is an Associate Professor in Telecommunications and the School Coordinator (Learning and Teaching) with the School of Mechanical and Electrical Engineering. His research interests include teletraffic engineering, performance modelling, remote access laboratories, and engineering education. He is the author of more than 130 scientific articles, an executive member of the International Association of Online Engineering.

Kirsty Kitto is a Senior Lecturer in Data Science in the Connnected Intelligence Centre at the University of Technology Sydney (UTS). She models the ways in which humans interact with complex information environments, paying special attention to the interdependencies between language, attitudes, memory and learning. This theoretical work has led her to an ongoing interest in the contextuality inherent in lifelong learning and how we might build smart IT infrastructure that puts people in control of their data.

Elizabeth Lakey is an academic in the Graduate School of Humanities and Social Sciences in the Faculty of Arts at the University of Melbourne. Her disciplinary background is in Development Studies, Migrant Cultural Studies, Community Development and several languages. Elizabeth is the Work Integrated Learning (WIL) Coordinator in the Faculty of Arts. In this role she teaches several subjects that integrate WIL into arts curricula, facilitated through avenues such as internships, global volunteering and project-based learning.

Louise Lexis is a Senior Lecturer in Human Physiology in the School of Life Sciences at La Trobe University, and a fellow of the Higher Education Academy. Louise has a Master of Science in Exercise and Sport Sciences from the University of Florida and a PhD from the University of Queensland. Louise is committed to designing and delivering innovative and authentic scientific and employability curricula that are designed to help educate our next generation of science professionals. Louise's research interests include evaluating the acceptance and effectiveness of custom-designed open access resources, Students as Partners projects, and authentic scientific and employability curricula.

Kate Lloyd is the Academic Director of Learning, Teaching and Research for the Professional and Community Engagement (PACE) program at Macquarie University. Kate's research focuses on several projects which take an applied, action-oriented and collaborative approach to research characterised by community partnerships, co-creation of knowledge and an ethics of reciprocity. Kate holds an ARC Discovery Grant and recently received on behalf of PACE, the AAUT award for programs that enhance student learning.

Mandy Lupton is a Senior Lecturer in the Centre for Learning Futures at Griffith University. She has taught online subjects in teacher-librarianship, connected learning and inquiry learning. She uses a suite of social media tools and platforms for teaching and learning and requires her students to create a range of web-based artefacts for their assignments. Her research interests include inquiry learning, connected learning, information literacy and digital literacies.

Tessa McCredie is the Associated Director of the Careers and Employability service at the University of Southern Queensland. Tessa's research has focused on the role of the Career Development Practitioner in the employability agenda in higher education and leads a team of professional staff in supporting the embedding of employability into curriculum.

Amanda McCubbin is a program development consultant who provides advice to academic staff on issues of program quality enhancement at the University of Southern Queensland. Her research interests include academic development, quality assurance and quality enhancement with her most recent work focusing on benchmarking attributes that contribute to the higher education accreditation process in Australia.

Joanna McIntyre is the Program Area Coordinator for Creative Industries within the School of Communication and Creative Industries, University of the Sunshine Coast. Her research interests include celebrity, cinema and television, queer and transgender representation, and Australian culture.

Kay Oddone is a lecturer in the Faculty of Education, Queensland University of Technology. Her research explores the experience of school teachers who use personal learning networks for professional learning. She has twenty years' experience in education and information management. She has presented nationally and internationally, and her research interests are networked and connected learning, digital literacy and the use of social technologies in learning.

Mark Philips is an analyst at Caltex Australia. Prior to this he worked in data analytics at the University of Technology Sydney (UTS) where his research focused on understanding the key drivers of student employability. He is undertaking a Master of Data Science at UTS.

Peter Radoll is Professor of Information Technology, inaugural Dean of Aboriginal and Torres Strait Islander Leadership and Strategy, and Director of the Ngunnawal Centre at the University of Canberra. He is a descendant of the Anaiwan People of northern New South Wales. Previously Peter held various university roles including Dean and Director of the Wollotuka Institute at the University of Newcastle, Director of the Tjabal Centre and Associate Lecturer in Information Systems at the Australian National University. He is a leading academic in the area of diffusion of ICTs in Aboriginal communities, and Visiting Research Fellow at the Centre of Economic Policy Research at the ANU.

Michael 'Maxx' Schmitz is a third space academic, curriculum designer and ancient historian specialising in military history. In his capacity as a curriculum designer Maxx has worked in the academic, government and private sectors and is particularly interested in experiential learning, diversification of assessment, the use of technology in teaching and has been closely involved in several digital learning projects including VR and Object-based learning (OBL) initiatives.

Neil Tippett is a postdoctoral research fellow at the University of South Australia. As a multi-disciplinary researcher, his research interests span child behaviour, school bullying, health and wellbeing, and more recently, graduate outcomes. Through his work with Ruth Bridgstock, Neil has developed a strong interest in supporting students throughout university and has recently conducted research projects which investigate orientation and the first-year experience, study tours, and student perceptions of online learning.

Matalena Tofa is a postdoctoral researcher at Macquarie University. She has a PhD in human geography and a Masters of Education. Her research interests include social networks, curriculum development, and collaborative and participatory research methods.

Bill Wade has over 18 years of higher education experience in key leadership roles and also benefits from over 10 years of direct creative industry experience. He has been instrumental in working closely with the creative arts industries to enhance connectedness, project-based and work integrated learning within the programs he has been responsible for leading.

Mary Walsh lectures in Politics at the School of Politics, Economics and Society, University of Canberra. She is the Program Director of the Bachelor of Politics and International Relations degree and Founding Patron of the Politics, International Relations and National Security student association (PIRaNaS). Her most recent publications appear in *Contemporary Political Theory*, *The Review of Politics*, *The Australian Journal of Political Science* and *Democratic Theory*. She currently mentors Indigenous students on the topic of Constitutional Recognition.

Natalie Wright lectures in Interior Design in the QUT School of Design. Her community-engaged research explores design thinking and design-led innovation in secondary, tertiary and institutional education contexts, as a framework to prepare a twenty-first century-ready workforce. Her PhD developed a Design-led Educational Innovation Model, tested through an informal design immersion program delivered in regional/rural high schools. Current work is focused on building capacity for school teachers to teach design and utilise design thinking for learner-centred curriculum design and delivery.

1. A connected approach to learning in higher education

Ruth Bridgstock and Neil Tippett

INTRODUCTION

Connectedness has always been central to peoples' lives and careers. Terms such as co-operation, collaboration, communication, and persuasion refer to specific aspects of connectedness, which encapsulate the spectrum of person-to-person interactions that shape our daily lives. A substantial body of literature spanning the last 70 years documents the individual, social and cultural benefits that connecting with others brings (Lewis, 1953; Manderson, 1948; Reis, 1984), improving our life satisfaction, and enhancing wellbeing. Equally, connectedness allows us to prosper in our career pathways by boosting productivity, improving our confidence, finding us opportunities, and supporting our skill and knowledge development (Argyle, 1981; Friend and Cook, 1992).

Seminal work by educational theorists such as Berger and Luckmann (1966) explored the social construction of knowledge and learning, investigating how a more social approach to teaching could support educational outcomes; however, the development of social capabilities remained largely implicit in higher education curricula until the early 1990s (Johnson and Johnson, 1990). The last two decades have seen a greater recognition of the importance of social interaction to learning in higher education, evidenced by universities' increasing focus on developing their learners' social capabilities. Curriculum emphases have shifted towards promoting not only disciplinary and technical capabilities, but also transferable skills that can be applied in many different contexts (Clanchy and Ballard, 1995). Capabilities such as communication, collaboration and teamwork have become ubiquitous in university courses, emerging as some of the most valuable, and yet tacit and often difficult to teach, skills that learners from every discipline develop during their time at university.

Extending from several decades of research into social learning in formal educational environments, in the 1990s scholars started to explore learning that occurred through informal and networked social mechanisms. Lave and Wenger's (1991) seminal work on communities of practice contributed significantly towards a broad recognition of learning processes that occur through informal participation in shared practice. By the early 2000s, with the rise of social media, educators started to acknowledge the roles that digital networks play in learning, and the importance and distinctiveness of communication and collaboration in digital contexts. For connectivist learning theorists (Downes, 2005; Siemens, 2005), knowledge is distributed across a network of connections, and learning consists of the ability to navigate and make sense of those networks.

This book acknowledges that all contemporary universities appreciate the importance of developing learners' social capabilities, and that all universities teach using social methods to some extent. However, we argue that higher education social teaching practice is hindered by the bounded nature of institutional policies and structures, which preclude wider partner interaction, and traditional approaches to teaching, which emphasise content knowledge and transmissive pedagogies. It is very hard for us to collaborate across disciplines, with researchers or with other organisational units inside the institution, let alone move beyond institutional boundaries to engage with professional, industry and community connections for teaching. We are doing ourselves and our learners a disservice by not doing so.

Learning is something that naturally and optimally happens in ecologies and informal communities (Bridgstock, 2017; Mitchell and Sackney, 2011). In the digital age, learning is also highly networked, occurring through extended and diverse connections with people, systems and information (Siemens, 2005). As educators, we need to be fostering both communities and networks for learning, and the capabilities that learners will need in order to make the most of these in their lives and work. If we are to achieve this, teachers must become much better connected, and so must our institutions.

Building upon existing knowledge and practices, this volume encourages a step-change in the way that we think about teaching in higher education by introducing the Connectedness Learning Approach. The Connectedness Learning Approach was developed by the first author in conjunction with a large number of university educators, industry and community partners, and students/graduates during the course of an Australian National Senior Teaching Fellowship. The Connectedness Learning Approach argues that by using socially networked, connected activities such as mentoring, collaborative problem-solving, crowdsourcing and networked learning, in partnership with industry and community where relevant, we have the potential to achieve far more in education than we could by 'going it alone'. Through ten cases of practice, this volume examines empirically how higher education can foster learner and institutional connectedness, exploring organisational structures, processes and practices, pedagogical approaches, and the capabilities themselves which can best help learners succeed in their learning and beyond.

This introductory chapter presents a background to the Connectedness Learning Approach, focusing on how connectedness can benefit us in our lives and work roles. It examines how twenty-first century influences, such as globalisation, super-complexity, the innovation economy and the digitally networked world necessitate the development of new capabilities to meet ever changing workplace demands. The chapter then discusses the role that connectedness plays in current teaching practice, and the reasons that development of connectedness learning in higher education is necessary.

Against this background, the second half of this chapter sets out how the Connectedness Learning Approach can be used in higher education to support learners in building, maintaining and making the most of their networks and social relationships for life and career. The approach takes a systems perspective, describing learners' connectedness capabilities, and then exploring associated pedagogic approaches and institutional-enabling strategies that facilitate their development. The background and phases of research that have guided the development of this approach are outlined, accompanied by a brief description of the process through which this volume has been prepared. Finally, the chapter briefly introduces ten conceptual and empirical investigations, employed across a variety of higher education contexts. These investigations emphasise how different elements of the approach can be used by universities to foster connectedness. Through these chapters, the volume presents an authentic and relevant account of how we can embed connectedness into learning and teaching.

WHY IS CONNECTEDNESS IMPORTANT?

The ways in which we interact with others can have a profound impact on our daily lives, affecting our individual and community health and wellbeing, our potential to enact social change, our learning and career development, and our productivity at work (Bridgstock, 2019a). It is worth noting up front that in recent times, the shape, functioning and use of social networks have all shifted dramatically under the influence of digital tools and social media. Strong ties have seen the least change in the digital age; most people still typically have 7–12 individuals with whom they interact in an ongoing manner, and with whom they maintain high levels of trust and intimacy. However, our ability to develop weak and indirect ties has expanded greatly through digital networks, potentially increasing the social sphere of influence. These digital networks offer us the potential to connect with hundreds, and in some cases, thousands more people, generating an expansive network of weak ties which allow for greater flow of information and resources (Kaplan and Haenlein, 2010).

Connectedness and Health and Wellbeing

Maintaining strong social connections is predictive of positive health and well-being outcomes (Gadermann et al., 2016; Power et al., 2015). Connectedness is strongly linked to better mental health outcomes across the lifespan (Haslam et al., 2017); it has the potential to improve confidence, positive feelings, and life satisfaction (Jose, Ryan and Pryor, 2012), but can also insulate people from potentially harmful life experiences, including poverty and displacement as a refugee or asylum seeker (Mahoney and Siyambalapitiya, 2017).

With the advent of social media, it could be expected that social connectedness has increased, making us happier and healthier than ever before. However, studies suggest the relationship between social media use, social connectedness and wellbeing is more complex. While social media can make it easier to connect with others and create groups and communities, it can also become a source of alienation and ostracism for young people (Allen et al., 2014), providing a platform for negative online behaviours such as cyberbullying, which can negatively impact on our physical and mental health (Best, Manktelow and Taylor, 2014). Several studies have demonstrated a relationship between social media use, loneliness and depression (Utz and Breuer, 2017; Verduyn et al., 2017), however, the direction of causality is unclear. Negative experiences on social media have the potential to cause loneliness or depression, yet at the same time, lonely and depressed people may also be more inclined to seek social support online (Song et al., 2014).

Considering connectedness from a socio-cultural rather than individual perspective, an accompanying body of literature has explored the positive impact of social networks upon community wellbeing. Community wellbeing is described as "a state of being with others and the environment that arises where human needs are meet, where individuals and groups can act meaningfully to pursue their goals, and where they are satisfied with their way of life" (Armitage et al., 2012, p. 17). Social connectedness acts as a key driver of community wellbeing, with factors such as community spirit and cohesion, shared values, and social interaction each contributing towards the wellbeing of a community. In a connected community, people are more likely to volunteer, participate and share resources, and correspondingly, those communities will be more resilient in the face of natural disasters and other rapid changes (McCrea, Walton and Leonard, 2016). Communities that are cohesive and well-connected offer greater levels of support, sharing of resources, and the potential to restore and maintain a state of positive wellbeing for all community members.

Connectedness and Social Change

Social connectedness can also be an effective vehicle for social change. Social networks have the potential to fulfil collective interests by catalysing purposive action (Coleman, 1990). Often termed civic participation or engagement, purposive action is co-operative behaviour undertaken by multiple members of a social network in unison. This type of action usually has a far greater impact than solitary actions taken by one individual. Whether purposive action occurs at the level of the community or as a social movement, this form of change is usually initiated through communication between individuals with a shared desire to enact social change. With the advent of the Internet, opportunities to communicate and connect with others who share the same beliefs have expanded exponentially, leading to rapid spread across communities, and inspiring global movements, such as the prolonged protests that occurred during the Arab Spring (Castells, 2015). Despite this, social media alone is not a panacea for social movements – it has also given rise to so-called 'slacktivism', where people support an organisation or movement on social media without taking any action beyond this.

Connectedness for Career Development

The positive effects of social capital and networking behaviour on different aspects of career development are well documented. For instance, Jackson (2014) demonstrated, using national modelling of graduate destinations statistics, that graduates who used social capital-based approaches to acquire work had far more positive initial graduate outcomes than those who did not. Networking comprises the acquisition and strengthening of ties. Its long-acknowledged benefits include increased access to resources, information, career opportunities, sponsorship and support (Duncan and Dunifon, 2012; Seibert, Kraimer and Liden, 2001). With changes to the structure of the labour market, the 'gig economy' and the decline of the traditional organisational career, networking is arguably more important for one's career development now than it ever has been. Many people are now engaging in portfolio careers, using their networks and social capital to recurrently seek out new career opportunities. In the current era of LinkedIn and SEEK, many of these career development functions have moved online. Employers and recruiters now routinely screen potential employees using social media and search engines. In a survey of American recruiters, Lancaster (2016) found 91 per cent had used social media as an applicant screening tooling, and 7 in 10 had made positive recruitment decisions based on information posted on social networking sites.

Connectedness also fosters productivity at work. As one example, advanced economies are increasingly finding value in the creation and production of new knowledge. Innovation and enterprise are fuelled through social interactions, benefitting from collaborative, complex social environments which offer an active combination of people, knowledge and resources (Mascia, Magnusson and Björk, 2015). Creativity can be fostered through exposing individuals to new ideas and processes, particularly those that span disciplinary, institutional or geographical boundaries (Granovetter, 2005), with social networks acting as mechanisms through which creative ideas can be integrated, implemented, and brought to fruition (Tocher, Oswald and Hall, 2015). Social networks also provide opportunities for individual enterprise, opening access to new markets or resources. In contrast to the closed, organisationally-based knowledge production of previous times, innovation is becoming more and more 'open' (Chesbrough, Vanhaverbeke and West, 2006), that is, autonomous, diverse and decentralised.

Connectedness for Learning

Much of learning is inherently social, and the roles that social relationships and networks play in professional and lifelong learning are of great relevance to universities that wish to strengthen the employability of their graduates (Field, 2009). Valuable learning is achieved through situated practice that is embedded into an informal framework of social support and development. Informal social learning processes include expert modelling, mentoring, explicit instruction, advice and feedback. In the workplace, these processes are all-pervasive, fostering ongoing professional learning and organisational acculturation (Billett, 2008; Boud and Middleton, 2003; Lave and Wenger, 1998). Face-to-face learning strategies tended to be employed along the lines of a community of practice or enquiry (Lave and Wenger, 1998), involving active relationship building between individuals with similar interests. Communities of practice often rely on strong ties and involve repeated and extended reciprocal interactions.

We all learn from 'weak tie' connections outside our communities of practice as well. Social media and digital networks have become central to our lives over the last few years, and for many these have helped to expand the reach of wider networks in helping people learn new capabilities and keep up to date with trends of interest (Bridgstock, 2017). Online modes of social informal learning can take the form of a distributed learning network of professionals and other interested people (Albors, Ramos and Hervas, 2008), in which people may not even know the people with whom they are interacting, or know them only slightly. Networked informal learning through social media can be used to obtain on-demand, 'just in time' quick-turnaround information.

Professionals obtain the information quickly, and then pass it along by sharing or retweeting. The power of digital networks for informal, personalised learning can be considerable. In order to take advantage of this power, learners must possess the critical capacity to (a) select where and how to go online to learn; (b) filter data for credibility and usefulness; and (c) synthesise it with existing knowledge (Bridgstock, 2017).

Digital networks can also be used for other forms of learning which rely on weak or indirect ties, such as collective intelligence, and crowdsourced approaches to learning (Leimeister, 2010), the most prominent example of which is Wikipedia. Social media has now made it possible to draw upon the collective expertise of an entity ('the crowd') comprising many diverse individuals with many different capabilities, to solve complex problems which could not be answered individually (Albors, Ramos and Hervas, 2008). This kind of networked learning allows for the creation of group-based socially constructed skills and knowledge that develop and evolve over time. Each individual in the network draws from their own perspectives, capabilities and approaches, and in turn adapts to, and learns from, their circumstances and contexts (see for instance Engestrom, 2001; Lave and Wenger, 1998). As a result, such larger networks represent a confluence of varying skills, experiences and perspectives, fostering knowledge and capabilities which are broader and more adaptable than the skills we would be able to develop as individuals. As an example of this, the Foldit multiplayer online game harnessed the complementary abilities of many thousands of players, who worked collaboratively to develop an assortment of new strategies and algorithms to predict complex protein structures (Cooper et al., 2010). Through the online game, gamers were able to solve a puzzle in less than three weeks that had eluded scientists using conventional methods for more than a decade.

EMPLOYABILITY PLUS: WHERE DOES CONNECTEDNESS FIT IN HIGHER EDUCATION?

Universities across the world are being tasked with preparing their students for the world of professional work. This enterprise has become increasingly difficult over recent years due to widespread labour market uncertainty and the massification of the higher education system in many Western countries (Tomlinson, 2012). In contrast to the previous era, in which ongoing professional work was virtually guaranteed for university-qualified individuals, contemporary graduates must be proactive and flexible, and have the capacity to adapt to a job market with continually shifting requirements (Clarke, 2008). It is said that rather than seeking security in employment, graduates must now seek security in employability.

In this volume we take a pragmatic stance to the graduate employability agenda, accepting that learners, education institutions and policy makers alike are highly motivated for graduates to obtain positive employment outcomes. Employability is often operationalised as a graduate's ability to gain employment within a few months of course completion, a view which aligns with many national graduate outcomes survey measures. Instead we choose to take a broader conceptualisation of employability as encompassing a graduate's ongoing capacity to live and work productively and meaningfully in an increasingly dynamic and complex society (see also Fullan, 1993). Thus, we move beyond overly restrictive and often short-term definitions of employability which are limited to employment within a few months of course completion. For us, employability is the capacity to 'employ' one's 'abilities' – that is, the ability to harness one's skills, knowledge and other attributes in order to add value across a range of different contexts across the life course, including employment and career, as well as community and civic engagement.

Nearly all contemporary educational activity, including learning theory and research, is focused on developing the skills and capabilities of the individual person. This perspective is congruent with human capital theory, which considers the economic implications of the knowledge, skills and competences embodied within us as individuals, arguing that the more educated a population is, the more productive they will be (Olaniyan and Okemakinde, 2008). Traditionally, universities have sought to foster graduate employability primarily by developing their students' 'employability skills', 'graduate attributes' or 'graduate capabilities' through the curriculum (Yorke, 2006). Employability skills can be most commonly categorised into discipline-specific skills and knowledge, and transferable skills (skills and knowledge that can be transferred from one context to another). University policy documents often accompany these lists of employability skills with additional desirable qualities or attributes that employers may look for, including resilience, initiative, and grit/ determination.

Over the last five years, scholars have begun to acknowledge the importance of capital influences on employability. These capital influences can be thought of as the resources that the graduate brings to their employability journey, and have been suggested to include cultural, identity and social capital, as well as human capital (skills and knowledge) (Holmes, 2013; Tomlinson, 2017). Cultural capital refers to culturally valued knowledge, behaviours and dispositions aligned to the workplace. Identity capital relates to the graduate's ability to draw upon their experiences to develop a career self-concept and articulate a fruitful personal narrative relating to work (Tomlinson, 2017). Strongly related to connectedness, social capital represents the social relationships and networks that help graduates develop and mobilise their human capital for employability.

Universities do acknowledge that socially-based activities, such as group or team work, are an important source of learning, and these are commonly incorporated into degree programs. Where used appropriately, group work can assist students in developing their capabilities for employability, including interpersonal communication skills, teamwork, negotiation, professionalism and self-regulation (Rossin and Hyland, 2003). However, in practice this approach often lacks authenticity. Assigning students from the same course to small groups to work on a problem in class is in many ways unrepresentative of how a group would function in the true working environment. Teamwork in the real world involves interacting with people from different disciplinary backgrounds, with different agendas and perspectives. In the real world, the problem is rarely presented neatly, with people assigned to roles, but can be highly emergent and both the aims and roles contested.

Recently, higher education has also started to embrace work integrated learning, service learning and other complex experiential learning approaches as a means of fostering and applying these capabilities and others (such as metacognitive self-regulation, emotional intelligence, and workplace cultural knowledge and skills) within an authentic environment. This is a very important step in fostering graduate employability more effectively. However, what is missing from the commentary of the benefits of these complex learning approaches is that they also offer the opportunity to connect with people beyond the classroom and university. Through the learning experience, students interact with others in productive ways, acquire new perspectives, build trust, and develop authentic professional and interest-based communities and networks. These relationships are just as important to their future lives as the individual skills the students acquire.

Digital networks can expand the reach of career development activities, with online social networking behaviour in particular having an enormous and increasing impact on the employability of graduates (Nikitkov and Sainty, 2014). While many graduates are well versed in the use of digital networks in their personal lives, studies suggest that relatively few at present possess the capabilities to exploit the opportunities for career development afforded through social media platforms, such as LinkedIn (Benson, Morgan and Filippaios, 2014; Bridgstock, 2019a). Many undergraduate students do not even think of digital networks as a valuable source of learning (Madge et al., 2009).

As an alternative and complementary perspective to the traditional skills-based approach used throughout higher education, the connected approach to learning outlined in this volume foregrounds the central roles of partnerships, groups, communities, and networks in order to better prepare students for their future lives and work. Addressing dimensions of learning and behaviour such as work integrated learning, learning through networks, and career development learning using authentic tools, The Connectedness Learning Approach considers the social and relational dimensions of learning, work and career, and how these can be successfully applied across higher education. With the increasing influence of social media, it also considers how these dimensions involve interactions and activities occurring within the digital space, both in addition to, but also instead of, face-to-face.

HOW THIS VOLUME CAME TO BE: A CONNECTEDNESS LEARNING-BASED PROCESS

This edited volume has its inception in an Australian National Senior Teaching Fellowship, *Graduate Employability 2.0*, undertaken in 2015–2016 at Queensland University of Technology by Ruth Bridgstock (see Bridgstock, 2019b). The fellowship sought to support the Australian higher education sector in fostering the capabilities of learners so that they were able to capitalise upon the affordances of digital and analogue social networks, both in life and work. The fellowship was constructed around four overlapping phases which together set out to: increase sectoral awareness of the importance of social network capabilities to graduate employability; increase knowledge of effective ways to develop these skills; and, increase inclusion of social network capability development in higher education learning and teaching.

Phase 1: Research

The initial phase of the fellowship offered the opportunity to empirically establish a connectedness learning approach in higher education. It asked which learning and teaching approaches were best suited to fostering students' capabilities and networks, and which institutional-enabling strategies were fundamental to supporting better networked learning and teaching. Additionally, by engaging with learning stakeholders across the higher education sector in Australia and beyond, the fellowship afforded the opportunity to increase understanding and adoption of connectedness learning and provide capacity-building opportunities and resources to support this. The fellowship commenced with a literature, policy and environmental scan to confirm the roles that digital and face-to-face relationships, networks and social capital play in graduate careers. Current higher education practice relating to this was examined using a combination of student surveys, interviews and case studies with educators, alumni and industry/community representatives. Together, this allowed for an assessment of the current 'state of play' concerning the connectedness of learners, programs and higher education institutions in Australia.

The findings from these Phase 1 activities offered a consistent picture around the connectedness of students, programs and universities, revealing a current oversight, but also a significant opportunity for higher education. The most apparent finding centred around the professional networks of undergraduate students and early graduates, which could be described as embryonic at best. Students appeared to lack confidence in their connectedness capabilities, particularly when it came to establishing and growing professional connections, and also struggled in negotiating networked behaviour online. Based upon the empirical work conducted as part of the Fellowship, connectedness learning seemed to remain a tacit and largely post-graduation process. Although alumni and industry interviewees both emphasised the importance that social networks and social network capabilities were able to bring to graduates' professional lives, connectedness learning was either lacking or entirely absent in many Australian higher education programs. Interviews and case studies with teachers and institutional leaders identified the difficulties that educators faced in developing effective and sustainable networks or collaborations with industry stakeholders, as well as with other learning and teaching partners. In part, these difficulties were often attributed to the strongly entrenched legacies of organisational structures, processes, cultures and philosophies that beset higher education institutions.

Students' social networks were found to largely be formed through socialising with peers (Madge et al., 2009), part-time employment, internships, extra-curricular activities, school networks and family members' contacts (Clark et al., 2015). While the interviews unearthed a few cases of exemplary connectedness learning practice, this was not widespread among participants nor universities, and was not systematic or integrated within institutions. Exemplary practice included work integrated learning programs (such as internships or industry projects), and to a lesser extent, alumni engagement initiatives, industry guest teaching, development of LinkedIn profiles and co-curricular leadership and recognition programs. When asked why the prevailing approaches to learning and teaching showed such an apparent disconnect, participants indicated: (1) a lack of top-of-mind awareness of the value of social networks to graduate success, including the absence of related concepts from institutional and course learning outcome lists; (2) the idea that teaching involving industry/community partnerships and connections beyond the university tends to be resource-intensive and associated with higher risk than classroom-based teaching; and lastly (3) because of large bureaucratic organisational structures and processes, which mean that universities were generally not set up to connect effectively with external or internal stakeholders for learning and teaching.

Participants often described these challenges in terms of two metaphors: the university as a 'walled garden', with teachers, learners and learning on the inside, and work, career and life on the outside; or alternatively, the university as a series of 'silos', with minimal exchange of knowledge or ideas and limited collaboration between organisational areas. Unlike university research and commercialisation activities, for learning and teaching there seems to be much less strategic or systematic development and management of external engagement and partnerships, such as client relationship management approaches.

Phase 2: Developing the Connectedness Learning Approach

The analysis and synthesis of the Phase 1 activities informed the development of a connected approach to university teaching and learning which could be applied across a variety of higher education contexts. Three outputs were developed: (1) a set of key principles that universities can use to implement connectedness learning; (2) a Connectedness Learning Model which summarises the individual capabilities, learning and teaching approaches, and institutional enabling strategies which support connectedness learning; and (3) a connectedness learning toolkit for educators. The initial prototype of the principles and Connectedness Learning Model were developed and progressively refined over the course of the fellowship, using input from all participants. In developing and refining these tools, the fellowship took a 'mind hive', socially networked approach. Essentially acting as a digitally-based crowdsourcing process, the mind hive approach utilised participants' collective expertise, enthusiasm and professional contacts by involving them in all aspects of the fellowship and offering each of them multiple routes through which to engage and contribute. As a result, the principles and Connectedness Learning Model are a representation of their combined knowledge and expertise, gathered over the course of the entire fellowship.

The 18 key principles offer a template which higher education institutions can use to effectively implement the Connectedness Learning Model. These principles form the basis of the analytical and evaluative elements of the practical connectedness toolkit for educators (www.graduateemployability2-0.com) which was employed across varying higher education contexts in the capacity building phase of the fellowship. Developed according to the findings from Phase 1 of the fellowship, the 18 key principles for connectedness learning are:

Connectedness capabilities
1. Students have the opportunity to develop social connections and relationships.
2. Students develop one or more of the connectedness capabilities, particularly building a connected identity and identifying and growing new connections.

3. Students develop skills in terms of career development learning, networked learning and/or collaboration for problem-solving or creating new knowledge.

Connectedness pedagogies

1. The learning is authentic and occurs in real professional contexts, involving professional activities and interactions with professionals. This could involve the use of open, industry-authentic tools and technologies.
2. Students co-design a learning experience that is meaningful for them.
3. Industry/community partners provide input into designing a learning experience that is meaningful for them.
4. Partners are carefully selected for alignment with student and program needs and will benefit from/find value in the partnership themselves.
5. Appropriate just-in-time resources and learning activities are provided to help students connect with networks effectively.
6. The program is tailored to partner, learning context and specific student needs.
7. Students maintain the connections they have made and continue to benefit from them, including having ongoing engagement with the program (e.g. as alumni).

Enabling strategies

1. The program is 'plugged in' to wider professional, industry and interest groups and networks.
2. The program seeks out and develops new relationships in a strategic way, according to principles of reciprocity.
3. The program deepens the relationships it has in effective ways, including through valuing its connections.
4. Interactions and communications are straightforward and effective.
5. Processes are simple and straightforward, with 'red tape' minimised.
6. Partnerships and networks within the university (intra-university connections) are present and optimised.
7. There are enough resources (people, workload, funding) to foster sustainable connectedness.
8. There is an evaluation plan in place that covers the above dimensions.

The second output of this phase was the Connectedness Learning Model (see Figure 1.1). This model summarises: (1) the capabilities that individuals require to make the most of their social connections; (2) the core learning and teaching approaches that were found to be most effective in developing student connectedness capabilities at the present time; and (3) the institutional-enabling strategies that helped to ensure the sustainable success of connectedness initiatives, and that the university itself was well 'networked'. The Connectedness

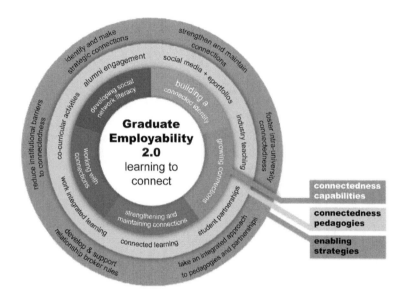

Figure 1.1   *The Connectedness Learning Model*

Learning Model is unpacked and explored in more detail in Chapters 2, 6 and 11 of the present volume.

The final output from Phase 2 was the connectedness learning toolkit for educators. The toolkit comprises reflective and evaluative tools that can be used to characterise and analyse the connectedness of students and programs; action-planning tools which can help educators to prioritise and strategize the development of connectedness in their programs; and a range of supporting resources, including capability frameworks, practice case studies and links to external resources and references.

Phase 3: Capacity Building

The final phase of the fellowship aimed to disseminate the research findings and share the principles, Connectedness Learning Model and toolkit across the higher education sector. By doing this, connectedness learning approaches were embedded at different levels of educational practice and policy across 18 Australian universities. Thirty-four engagement activities (including workshops, seminars, consultation and roundtables) were conducted across these 18 higher education contexts during the latter half of 2016, with nearly 1,200 tertiary educators joining the connectedness learning online network.

Educators identified many opportunities through which they had been able to implement the Connectedness Learning Approach in their practice, including through curriculum design, reflective processes and strategic planning. The fellowship provoked a clearly identifiable change in the higher education sector. When surveyed a few months after the capacity building phase, more than eight in ten (81.5 per cent) participants had implemented some element or elements of the Connectedness Learning Approach in their institution. Furthermore, about 70 per cent of participants wanted to adopt connectedness learning more deeply, such as by enacting systemic and curricular changes, but required more time than the 12-month fellowship period to do so.

Phase 4: Connectedness Learning Mentoring

This volume is the culmination of a response to educators' requests that they needed more time and developmental support in order to embed the principles, Connectedness Learning Model and toolkit into their learning and teaching. In March 2017, a call for expressions of interest was sent out to educators and scholars through the connectedness learning online network, as well as via other scholarly distribution lists. The call asked for brief abstracts from teams in higher education institutions who wished to explore aspects of the Connectedness Learning Model in depth within their educational contexts and contribute their results towards an edited collection. More than 40 abstracts were received, with successful submissions chosen for diversity in subject matter, elements of the Connectedness Learning Model with which they had engaged, the quality of the submission, and the commitment of the team towards the volume development process.

Unlike typical edited volumes, this manuscript started development before any of the empirical work reported in the chapters commenced. A connectedness learning approach was taken throughout the process. All teams agreed to participate in mentoring and peer collaboration which covered their in-depth explorations and the writing up of results. Ruth Bridgstock visited each team in person at least once so they could share, develop and refine their work, and this was followed up with at least one or more online meetings with each team during the fieldwork. Once teams had findings to share, a Connectedness Learning Roundtable was hosted in December 2017. Each team attended and presented their work, then began the process of preparing their chapters, aided with mentoring from the editors, as well as each other. During the write up and editing phase, the editors met with each team twice via Skype, and also arranged a whole-of-group get-together to discuss shared challenges with development and writing. Chapter contributors worked developmentally in an ongoing way with other contributors to review and edit chapters, and we also called upon members of the wider network to provide fresh eyes on contributions where they were needed. Throughout the process, contributors, editors and viewers alike were invited actively to speak back critically and constructively to the principles and Connectedness Learning Model, and to share their experiences of this within their chapters.

This volume ultimately provides the fruits of this labour: thirteen chapters, organised to correspond with the elements of the Connectedness Learning Model that they emphasise, moving from the inside of the Connectedness Learning Model towards the outside. The first section of this volume examines the individual capabilities required to connect with others for success in life and work, and how students can develop them. The second section engages with the learning and teaching approaches that lend themselves to enhancing the connectedness of learners, including work integrated and community-connected learning approaches. The third section engages with the institutional enabling strategies that universities can adopt to foster fruitful learning partnerships and networks with external and internal learning stakeholders, including industry, community, alumni, students, other organisational areas within the institution, and other educational providers. Together, these accounts, which span a wide variety of higher education contexts, set forth an authentic and relevant account of how higher education institutions can embed connectedness into their learning and teaching, and support their learners to acquire the knowledge, skills and capabilities to succeed in work and life.

REFERENCES

Albors, J., Ramos, J. C. and Hervas, J. L. (2008). New learning network paradigms: Communities of objectives, crowdsourcing, wikis and open source. *International Journal of Information Management, 28*(3), 194–202.

Allen, K. A., Ryan, T., Gray, D. L., McInerney, D. M. and Waters, L. (2014). Social media use and social connectedness in adolescents: The positives and the potential pitfalls. *The Educational and Developmental Psychologist, 31*(1), 18–31.

Argyle, M. (1981). *Social Skills and Work*. London: Routledge and Kegan Paul.

Armitage, D., Béné, C., Charles, A. T., Johnson, D. and Allison, E. H. (2012). The interplay of well-being and resilience in applying a social-ecological perspective. *Ecology and Society, 17*(4), 15–32.

Benson, V., Morgan, S. and Filippaios, F. (2014). Social career management: Social media and employability skills gap. *Computers in Human Behavior, 30*, 519–525.

Berger, P. and Luckmann, T. (1966). *The Social Construction of Reality: A Treatise in the Sociology of Knowledge*. Garden City, NY: First Anchor.

Best, P., Manktelow, R. and Taylor, B. (2014). Online communication, social media and adolescent wellbeing: A systematic narrative review. *Children and Youth Services Review*, *41*, 27–36.

Billett, S. (2008). Learning throughout working life: A relational interdependence between personal and social agency. *British Journal of Educational Studies*, *56*(1), 39–58.

Boud, D. and Middleton, H. (2003). Learning from others at work: Communities of practice and informal learning. *Journal of Workplace Learning*, *15*(5), 194–202.

Bridgstock, R. (2017). The university and the knowledge network: A new educational model for 21st century learning and employability. In M. Tomlinson (ed.), *Graduate Employability in Context: Research, Theory and Debate* (pp. 339–358). London: Palgrave Macmillan.

Bridgstock, R. (2019a). Graduate Employability 2.0: Education for work in a networked world. In J. Higgs, G. Crisp and W. Letts (eds), *Education for Employability: The Employability Agenda*. Rotterdam: Sense-Brill Publishers.

Bridgstock, R. (2019b). *Graduate Employability 2.0: Enhancing the Connectedness of Learners, Teachers and Higher Education Institutions. Final Report of the National Senior Teaching Fellowship*. Canberra: Department of Education and Training.

Castells, M. (2015). *Networks of Outrage and Hope: Social Movements in the Internet Age*. Malden, MA: John Wiley and Sons.

Chesbrough, H., Vanhaverbeke, W. and West, J. (2006). *Open Innovation: Researching a New Paradigm*. Oxford: Oxford University Press.

Clanchy, J. and Ballard, B. (1995). Generic skills in the context of higher education. *Higher Education Research and Development*, *14*(2), 155–166.

Clark, G., Marsden, R., Whyatt, J. D., Thompson, L. and Walker, M. (2015). 'It's everything else you do…': Alumni views on extracurricular activities and employability. *Active Learning in Higher Education*, *16*(2), 133–147.

Clarke, M. (2008). Understanding and managing employability in changing career contexts. *Journal of European Industrial Training*, *32*(4), 258–284.

Coleman, J. S. (1990). *Foundations of Social Theory*. Cambridge, MA: Harvard University Press.

Cooper, S., Khatib, F., Treuille, A., Barbero, J., Lee, J., Beenen, M. … Popović, Z. (2010). Predicting protein structures with a multiplayer online game. *Nature*, *466*(7307), 756–760.

Downes, S. (2005). *An introduction to connective knowledge*. Paper presented at Media, Knowledge and Education: Exploring New Spaces, Relations and Dynamics in Digital Media Ecologies, Innsbruck.

Duncan, G. J. and Dunifon, R. (2012). 'Soft-skills' and long-run labor market success. *Research in Labor Economics*, *35*, 313–339.

Engestrom, Y. (2001). Expansive learning at work: Toward an activity theoretical reconceptualization. *Journal of Education and Work*, *14*(1), 133–156.

Field, J. (2009). Learning transitions in the adult life course: Agency, identity and social capital. In B. Merrill (ed.), *Learning to Change? The Role of Identity and Learning Careers in Adult Education* (pp. 17–32). Frankfurt: Peter Lang.

Friend, M. and Cook, L. (1992). *Interactions: Collaboration Skills for School Professionals*. New York: Longman Publishing Group.

Fullan, M. (1993). *Change Forces: Probing the Depths of Educational Reform*. London: Falmers Press.

Gadermann, A. M., Guhn, M., Schonert-Reichl, K. A., Hymel, S., Thomson, K. and Hertzman, C. (2016). A population-based study of children's well-being and health: The relative importance of social relationships, health-related activities, and income. *Journal of Happiness Studies*, *17*(5), 1847–1872.

Granovetter, M. (2005). The impact of social structure on economic outcomes. *The Journal of Economic Perspectives*, *19*(1), 33–50.

Haslam, C., Cruwys, T., Haslam, S. A. and Jetten, J. (2017). Social connectedness and health. In N.A Pachana (ed.), *Encyclopedia of Geropsychology*, (pp. 2174–2182). Singapore: Springer Verlag.

Holmes, L. (2013). Competing perspectives on graduate employability: Possession, position or process? *Studies in Higher Education*, *38*(4), 538–554.

Jackson, D. (2014). Factors influencing job attainment in recent bachelor graduates: Evidence from Australia. *Higher Education*, *68*(1), 135–153.

Johnson, D. W. and Johnson, R. T. (1990). Social skills for successful group work. *Educational Leadership*, *47*(4), 29–33.

Jose, P. E., Ryan, N. and Pryor, J. (2012). Does social connectedness promote a greater sense of well-being in adolescence over time? *Journal of Research on Adolescence*, *22*(2), 235–251.

Kaplan, A. M. and Haenlein, M. (2010). Users of the world, unite! The challenges and opportunities of social media. *Business Horizons*, *53*(1), 59–68.

Lancaster, T. (2016). Teaching students about online professionalism: Enhancing student employability through social media. In V. Benson and S. Morgan (eds), *Social Media and Networking: Concepts, Methodologies, Tools, and Applications* (pp. 1784–1805). Hershey: IGI Global.

Lave, J. and Wenger, E. (1991). *Situated Learning: Legitimate Peripheral Participation*. Cambridge: Cambridge University Press.

Lave, J. and Wenger, E. (1998). *Communities of Practice: Learning, Meaning, and Identity*. Cambridge: Cambridge University Press.

Leimeister, J. M. (2010). Collective intelligence. *Business and Information Systems Engineering*, *2*(4), 245–248.

Lewis, A. (1953). Health as a social concept. *The British Journal of Sociology*, *4*(2), 109–124.

Madge, C., Meek, J., Wellens, J. and Hooley, T. (2009). Facebook, social integration and informal learning at university: 'It is more for socialising and talking to friends about work than for actually doing work'. *Learning, Media and Technology*, *34*(2), 141–155.

Mahoney, D. and Siyambalapitiya, S. (2017). Community-based interventions for building social inclusion of refugees and asylum seekers in Australia: A systematic review. *Journal of Social Inclusion*, *8*(2), 66–80.

Manderson, L. (1948). The social context of wellbeing. In L. Manderson (ed.), *Rethinking Wellbeing* (pp. 1–25). Netley, South Australia: Griffin Press.

Mascia, D., Magnusson, M. and Björk, J. (2015). The role of social networks in organizing ideation, creativity and innovation: An introduction. *Creativity and Innovation Management*, *24*(1), 102–108.

McCrea, R., Walton, A. and Leonard, R. (2016). Developing a model of community wellbeing and resilience in response to change. *Social Indicators Research*, *129*(1), 195–214.

Mitchell, C. and Sackney, L. (2011). Building and leading within learning ecologies. In T. Townsend and J. MacBeath (eds), *International Handbook of Leadership for Learning* (pp. 975–990). Dordrecht: Springer.

Nikitkov, A. and Sainty, B. (2014). The role of social media in influencing career success. *International Journal of Accounting and Information Management*, *22*(4), 273–294.

Olaniyan, D. and Okemakinde, T. (2008). Human capital theory: Implications for educational development. *Pakistan Journal of Social Sciences*, *5*(5), 479–483.

Power, J., Schofield, M. J., Farchione, D., Perlesz, A., McNair, R., Brown, R. ... Bickerdike, A. (2015). Psychological wellbeing among same-sex attracted and heterosexual parents: Role of connectedness to family and friendship networks. *Australian and New Zealand Journal of Family Therapy*, *36*(3), 380–394.

Reis, H. T. (1984). Social interaction and well-being. *Personal Relationships*, *5*(1984), 21–45.

Rossin, D. and Hyland, T. (2003). Group work-based learning within higher education: An integral ingredient for the personal and social development of students. *Mentoring and Tutoring*, *11*(2), 153–162.

Seibert, S. E., Kraimer, M. L. and Liden, R. C. (2001). A social capital theory of career success. *Academy of Management Journal*, *44*(2), 219–237.

Siemens, G. (2005). Connectivism: A learning theory for the digital age. *International Journal of Instructional Technology and Distance Learning*, *2*(1) (online).

Song, H., Zmyslinski-Seelig, A., Kim, J., Drent, A., Victor, A., Omori, K. and Allen, M. (2014). Does Facebook make you lonely? A meta analysis. *Computers in Human Behavior*, *36*, 446–452.

Tocher, N., Oswald, S. L. and Hall, D. J. (2015). Proposing social resources as the fundamental catalyst toward opportunity creation. *Strategic Entrepreneurship Journal*, *9*(2), 119–135.

Tomlinson, M. (2012). Graduate employability: A review of conceptual and empirical themes. *Higher Education Policy*, *25*(4), 407–431.

Tomlinson, M. (2017). Forms of graduate capital and their relationship to graduate employability. *Education+Training*, *59*(4), 338–352.

Utz, S. and Breuer, J. (2017). The relationship between use of social network sites, online social support, and well-being: Results from a 6-wave longitudinal study. *Journal of Media Psychology*, *29*(3), 115–125.

Verduyn, P., Ybarra, O., Résibois, M., Jonides, J. and Kross, E. (2017). Do social network sites enhance or undermine subjective well-being? A critical review. *Social Issues and Policy Review*, *11*(1), 274–302.

Yorke, M. (2006). *Employability in Higher Education: What It Is – What It Is Not*. York: The Higher Education Academy.

PART I

Connectedness capabilities

2. Connectedness capabilities

Ruth Bridgstock and Neil Tippett

INTRODUCTION

Connectedness capabilities comprise the knowledge, skills and attributes that individuals require to build, maintain and make the most of their networks and social relationships for life and career (Bridgstock, 2019a; Forret and Dougherty, 2001). As Chapter 1 illustrated, a university education that focuses predominantly on developing learners' disciplinary and transferable skills is no longer a guarantee of positive career outcomes. In part, this is because of the far greater numbers of students moving into the graduate labour market than ever before. In both Australia and the United Kingdom, graduates from many fields now face a highly competitive short-term job market (Karmel and Carroll, 2016). Once they surmount the initial challenges involved in transitioning to the world of work, graduates will continue to be tested as they learn how to live and work productively and meaningfully in an increasingly dynamic and complex society.

Higher education plays an important role in preparing students for both short-term job outcomes and their broader career and life journeys. It is widely agreed that upon leaving university, students should be equipped with the foundational capabilities to enable them to build and manage their careers, add economic and social value to their work, and continue learning (Barnett, 2006; Becker et al., 2017; Oliver and Jorre de St Jorre, 2018). One critical aspect of these activities is the students' ability to build, maintain and make the most of mutually beneficial relationships over time, including via digital platforms and social media. This chapter explores this capacity, considering why it is important and how it is currently being addressed in higher education. The chapter then outlines five connectedness capabilities drawn from research that will enable graduates to forge and make the most of meaningful social relationships and networks. Finally, three empirical studies (covered in Chapters 3–5 of this volume) are introduced. In different ways, each study explores how these connectedness capabilities are being integrated into higher educational curricula, and the impact they are having on graduates' lives and careers.

CAPABILITIES FOR GRADUATE EMPLOYABILITY

Over the past two decades, universities have increasingly engaged with the concept of graduate employability, mapping and modifying curricula and pedagogic practice, and developing co-curricular programs to help maximise the success of their graduates in a congested labour market. Efforts have largely concentrated on developing students' 'employability skills' (Yorke, 2006), most commonly conceptualised as a combination of discipline-specific and transferable skills, which are underpinned by a range of additional qualities that employers desire such as proactiveness, resilience, determination, and adaptability. Discipline-specific skills represent the skills and knowledge that are relevant to a particular domain, discipline or subject area, and are often incorporated into curricula to address specific professional or occupational needs, including meeting the requirements of industry accreditation bodies. Transferable skills include broader capabilities that can be applied across contexts or disciplines, such as written communication or digital literacy. There is some divergence in the literature with respect to which transferable skills are important to graduate employability, as evidenced by the variety of disparate conceptual frameworks which define such skills (Suleman, 2016), however, social skills such as communication and teamwork are commonly agreed to be of value because they enable graduates to work effectively with others (Tymon, 2013).

Some scholars have questioned the efficacy of the employability skills approach in preparing students for life and work, with many pointing out the difficulty of measuring skills and their impact on graduate outcomes (Cranmer, 2006; Duncan and Dunifon, 2012). Others have commented on the artificiality of the transferable skills construct. Because they are acquired and applied in disciplinary and other highly contextually specific circumstances, transferable skills cannot simply be 'transferred' from university to professional work, or between professional roles as the label implies (Barrie, 2006; Jones, 2009). Rather, they must be 'translated' and re-contextualised, which often requires significant additional learning. A considerable tranche of literature over the last decade documents the fact that employers continue to report that graduates are not employment-ready, and lack some of the simplest skills needed for successful employment. Despite attempts to build ongoing dialogues between employers, professional associations and universities about skill requirements, employers in all fields continue to report dissatisfaction with graduates' disciplinary and transferable skill sets (Shah, Grebennikov and Nair, 2015).

It is clear that the employability skills usually emphasised in higher education represent only one small segment of the broad set of influences and capabilities that impact on graduate outcomes (Nagarajan and Edwards,

2014). Many of these are not under the control of the graduate, nor can they be easily influenced by higher education, such as the extent to which suitable job opportunities are available in the labour market (Jackson and Bridgstock, 2018). There are also non-capability 'supply-side' factors that have an impact on graduate employment outcomes, such as institutional reputation, and bio-graphical/demographic characteristics of the graduate (Karmel and Carroll, 2016).

Despite the restrictive nature of many official graduate outcome measures (Jackson and Bridgstock, 2018), thinking around graduate employability has started to expand beyond notions of short-term employment outcomes to start to address graduates' lifelong and 'life wide' experiences in building lives and careers, including how to add value in different ways across different domains. So too, thinking about the capabilities and experiences from which graduates will benefit has started to expand. For instance, the literature has started to embrace the idea that each graduate will develop a unique personal capability set which forms the basis and expression of their distinctive graduate identity (Hinchliffe and Jolly, 2011; Tomlinson, 2017). Through learning experiences within and outside higher education, students develop personal ethical values and social awareness, skills and knowledge, and the ability to engage and apply their capabilities in different contexts. Thus, over time the graduate develops a self-concept that helps them make sense of their learning experiences, beliefs and capabilities, and directs their behaviour.

The formation of graduate identities and self-concept are tied to the development and use of metacognitive capabilities. A critical awareness and understanding of thinking and learning processes means that students can self-manage learning and career development in an ongoing way. This includes the ability and propensity to continue learning and adapt to make the most of employment opportunities, as well as the capacity to find ways to add value through work and social engagement (Bridgstock, 2009). In the context of the contemporary world of work, many graduates will need to be enterpris-ing and continually identify or create opportunities for themselves, whether through self-employment, work as an employee, or through other contributions (Bell, 2016; Rae, 2007).

CONNECTEDNESS CAPABILITIES

The ability to foster connections with others, to work productively with them to achieve desired outcomes, and to contribute to/benefit from wider networks is another important set of capabilities. More than teamwork, interpersonal or communication skills, connectedness capabilities are concerned with making the most of the inherently social world in which we live (Bridgstock, 2019a; Forret and Dougherty, 2001). As discussed by Bridgstock and Tippett in

Chapter 1, through social and networked processes, connectedness capabilities facilitate many of the activities involved in graduate employability, including identity development (Field, 2009), career development, enterprise and entrepreneurship, lifelong learning, and productivity at work.

The five connectedness capabilities described in the Connectedness Learning Model represent the individual (and also programmatic and organisational) capabilities required to develop and connect with social networks, and to work productively with, and through, them. These connectedness capabilities are:

1. *Building a connected identity:* the ability to develop and represent professional identities effectively in the context of social networks, including social media profiles and personal/professional 'branding'. Building a connected identity is a complex and ongoing process involving sense-making and self-expression through which people selectively organise their experiences into a coherent sense of self and communicate public versions of this sense of self to others.

2. *Making connections:* the ability to develop weak ties (Granovetter, 1973) and extend and expand professional networks, including online and face-to-face networking (de Janasz and Forret, 2008). Making connections focuses on fostering embeddedness into a wide social network, and on developing initial, weak, one-to-many and indirect ties. These ties are important for exposure to new ideas, knowledge, industry and disciplinary trends and career opportunities. When strengthened, they are the foundation for collaboration, learning and ongoing career-enhancing relationships such as mentoring.

3. *Strengthening and maintaining connections:* the ability to strengthen professional connections and develop strong ties through reciprocity, and then maintain these as needed. Strengthening and maintaining connections is central to social connectedness. Embeddedness in social networks and development of weak ties is important for exposure to new ideas, knowledge and various kinds of resources, but strong ties and deeper relationships are required for a significant proportion of other processes within socially based professional, learning and career development and collaborative innovation/problem-solving. For example, strong ties bring new ideas to fruition through integration and refinement; career development is facilitated through strong-tie information and resource sharing, career sponsorship and mentoring processes; and professional learning is facilitated through strong ties in communities of practice and enquiry. While acquiring and growing connections can occur in online or face-to-face modes, or a combination of both, strengthening connections often involves more extended face-to-face contact and interaction.

4. *Working with connections:* the ability to work effectively and profession-ally with collaborators and networks to add value in diverse contexts and for diverse applications. Working with connections involves making the most of connections for purposes such as collaborative innovation and problem-solving, career development and enterprise, and socially-based lifelong learning, as covered briefly in Chapter 1 of this volume.
5. *Social network literacy:* the ability to understand, interpret and evaluate the characteristics and processes of professional networks, and to apply this knowledge and skills for professional purposes. Social network literacy includes the ability to: (1) articulate the roles that social networks play in work and life, and how social networks of different types operate; (2) identify, interpret, analyse and communicate signs and symbols and other data relating to social networks; and (3) to navigate social networks strate-gically and effectively for different purposes.

These connectedness capabilities can be developed through a range of consid-ered pedagogic approaches that typically involve interaction with others and authentic learning activities (see Chapter 6), supported by reflective identity formation learning processes. In turn, these pedagogic approaches are enabled by a range of strategies that foster individual, program, and institutional con-nections with internal and external stakeholders (see Chapter 11). The connect-edness capabilities were initially synthesised from the findings of a series of in-depth interviews with higher education graduates, industry and community representatives, and their validity confirmed by quantitative survey research with higher education students and graduates (Bridgstock, 2019b). There are also three connectedness learning principles that relate specifically to the development of connectedness capabilities. These principles can be used to develop courses and learning experiences to enhance the connectedness capa-bilities of students. They are:

•   Students have the opportunity to develop social connections and relationships.
•   Students develop one or more of the connectedness capabilities, par-ticularly building a connected identity and identifying and growing new connections.
•   Students develop capabilities for career development learning, net-worked learning and/or collaboration for problem-solving or creating new knowledge.

This volume includes three chapters that focus explicitly on the development of connectedness capabilities and the impact of these capabilities on student and graduate outcomes and experiences.

In Chapter 3, Lupton, Oddone and Dreamson use semi-structured interviews with nine students and recent graduates from Queensland University of Technology to explore students' digital literacies and professional digital identities. Mapping students' perceptions of their own digital capabilities according to level of coherence and interaction, the authors distinguish between four professional digital identity clusters: leading, participating, emerging and technical. Each of these identity clusters represents a different combination of confidence, competence and literacy in using digital media. The authors discuss these in relation to students' connectedness capabilities, and the implications for pedagogic practice in higher education.

In Chapter 4, de Villiers Scheepers, McIntyre, Crimmins and English explore the connectedness capabilities of students from a regional Australian university, considering how the use of digital media for professional purposes differs between traditional and non-traditional student populations. Surveying 210 undergraduate students, half of whom had previous full-time work experience, the authors find that students with previous career experience demonstrate a greater awareness and use of social networking for professional purposes than school leavers with no previous employment. Four pedagogical implications are discussed, which identify opportunities for educators to improve students' social media skills and develop their connectedness capabilities.

In Chapter 5, Bridgstock, Jackson, Lloyd and Tofa describe the professional networks and social capital of recent university graduates. Using a survey of over 600 Creative Industries and Business graduates from three Australian universities, the authors find that graduates' professional networks and connectedness capabilities remain underdeveloped, even up to five years after course completion. In particular, social networking literacy, networking/ acquiring new connections, and using networks for career development are all identified as key capability sets that require further development, with the chapter identifying both general and specific opportunities for augmenting and strengthening students' social capital while they are at university.

REFERENCES

Barnett, R. (2006). Graduate attributes in an age of uncertainty. In P. Hager and S. Holland (eds), *Graduate Attributes, Learning and Employability* (pp. 49–65). Dordrecht: Springer.

Barrie, S. C. (2006). Understanding what we mean by the generic attributes of graduates. *Higher Education, 51*(2), 215–241.

Becker, S. A., Cummins, M., Davis, A., Freeman, A., Hall, C. G. and Ananthanarayanan, V. (2017). *NMC Horizon Report: 2017 Higher Education Edition.* Austin, Texas: The New Media Consortium.

Bell, R. (2016). Unpacking the link between entrepreneurialism and employ-ability: An assessment of the relationship between entrepreneurial attitudes and likelihood of graduate employment in a professional field. *Education + Training*, *58*(1), 2–17.

Bridgstock, R. (2009). The graduate attributes we've overlooked: Enhancing graduate employability through career management skills. *Higher Education Research and Development*, *28*(1), 31–44.

Bridgstock, R. (2019a). Graduate Employability 2.0: Education for work in a networked world. In J. Higgs, G. Crisp and W. Letts (eds), *Education for Employability: The Employability Agenda*. Rotterdam: Sense-Brill Publishers.

Bridgstock, R. (2019b). *Graduate Employability 2.0: Enhancing the Connectedness of Learners, Teachers and Higher Education Institutions. Final Report of the National Senior Teaching Fellowship*. Canberra: Department of Education and Training.

Cranmer, S. (2006). Enhancing graduate employability: Best intentions and mixed outcomes. *Studies in Higher Education*, *31*(2), 169–184.

de Janasz, S. C. and Forret, M. L. (2008). Learning the art of networking: A critical skill for enhancing social capital and career success. *Journal of Management Education*, *32*(5), 629–650.

Duncan, G. J. and Dunifon, R. (2012). 'Soft-skills' and long-run labor market success. *Research in Labor Economics*, *35*, 313–339.

Field, J. (2009). Learning transitions in the adult life course: Agency, identity and social capital. In B. Merrill (ed.), *Learning to Change? The Role of Identity and Learning Careers in Adult Education* (pp. 17–32). Frankfurt: Peter Lang.

Forret, M. L. and Dougherty, T. W. (2001). Correlates of networking behav-ior for managerial and professional employees. *Group and Organization Management*, *26*(3), 283–311.

Granovetter, M. (1973). The strength of weak ties. *American Journal of Sociology*, *78*(6), 1360–1380.

Hinchliffe, G. W. and Jolly, A. (2011). Graduate identity and employability. *British Educational Research Journal*, *37*(4), 563–584.

Jackson, D. and Bridgstock, R. (2018). Evidencing student success in the contemporary world-of-work: Renewing our thinking. *Higher Education Research and Development*, *37*(5), 984–998.

Jones, A. (2009). Redisciplining generic attributes: The disciplinary context in focus. *Studies in Higher Education*, *34*(1), 85–100.

Karmel, T. and Carroll, D. (2016). *Has the graduate labour market been swamped? (NILS working paper series No. 228/2016)*. Adelaide, Australia: National Institute of Labour Studies, Flinders University.

Nagarajan, S. and Edwards, J. (2014). Is the graduate attributes approach sufficient to develop work ready graduates? *Journal of Teaching and Learning for Graduate Employability*, 5(1), 12–28.

Oliver, B. and Jorre de St Jorre, T. (2018). Graduate attributes for 2020 and beyond: Recommendations for Australian higher education providers. *Higher Education Research and Development*, 37(4), 821–836.

Rae, D. (2007). Connecting enterprise and graduate employability: Challenges to the higher education culture and curriculum? *Education + Training*, 49(8/9), 605–619.

Shah, M., Grebennikov, L. and Nair, C. S. (2015). A decade of study on employer feedback on the quality of university graduates. *Quality Assurance in Education*, 23(3), 262–278.

Suleman, F. (2016). Employability skills of higher education graduates: Little consensus on a much-discussed subject. *Procedia–Social and Behavioral Sciences*, 228, 169–174.

Tomlinson, M. (2017). Forms of graduate capital and their relationship to graduate employability. *Education + Training*, 59(4), 338–352.

Tymon, A. (2013). The student perspective on employability. *Studies in Higher Education*, 38(6), 841–856.

Yorke, M. (2006). *Employability in Higher Education: What It Is – What It Is Not*. York: The Higher Education Academy.

3. Students' professional digital identities

Mandy Lupton, Kay Oddone and Neal Dreamson

INTRODUCTION

In higher education, educators who value connectedness learning are increasingly looking towards the use of networked social media tools and platforms to support students in developing their connectedness capabilities and building a professional identity (see Chapter 1 in this volume). The affordances of these tools and platforms allow students to create and share digital content such as websites, blogs, video, audio, images, re-mixed media, and curated collections on the open web (i.e. not behind a closed platform). These activities improve engagement through active and collaborative learning (Bennett et al., 2012; Clark, 2010), where evidence of learning can be shared, not only with other members of the class but beyond the walls of the classroom and learning management system (Gray et al., 2010). This ability to share to the outside world enables students to express their digital identities by communicating and showcasing them to professional networks, external mentors, experts and employers (Schroeder, Minocha and Schneidert, 2010; Waycott et al., 2013).

Creating and sharing content via social media necessarily results in individuals developing a range of digital identities. One aspect of a digital identity involves the digital traces, trail, or 'footprints' that enable algorithms to identify us, track us, and personalise our use of the web (Buchanan, 2015). This includes information necessary to establish proof of identity when conducting online business transactions such as purchasing, banking and travel (Wladawsky-Berger, 2016). Another form of digital identity is the way in which we construct particular identities for particular purposes – our multi-identity in social networks such as Facebook, Twitter, Instagram, LinkedIn – as represented by *the self* (a social being) we project to others (Buckingham, 2008). Finally, our confidence and fluency in understanding and utilising social technologies (i.e. digital literacy) is another form of digital identity (Hinrichsen and Coombs, 2014).

In university contexts, the construction of digital identities through creating and sharing digital content would include elements of the student's emerging professional and disciplinary identities. These identities may be influenced by the ways in which students see professional roles, values, ethics, workplace and disciplinary knowledge, culture and practices, and self-image (Trede, Macklin and Bridges, 2012; Trede and McEwen, 2012). Building a connected professional identity would involve "developing an outward-facing (published) professional online presence and social media strategy that is congruent with the norms of the profession/s of interest" (Bridgstock, 2016).

CONSTRUCTING A DIGITAL IDENTITY THROUGH CREATING AND SHARING DIGITAL CONTENT

There is a growing body of research that investigates the experiences of students and educators in creating digital content for assessment tasks. This approach leverages a Web 2.0 philosophy, where students actively create content, and where social networks are used to interact, collaborate and share. For instance, the type of content featured in previous research has included portfolios, blogs, wikis, image creation, and concept mapping (Bennett et al., 2012; Ching and Hsu, 2011).

The most prominent body of work concerns ePortolios: a digital tool that can be used either to showcase one's work, or as a vehicle for reflective learning. The former usage of ePortfolios can contribute to personal branding for employment purposes, while the latter can support learners in building their self-identity and developing an awareness of professional and disciplinary practices (Bennett and Robertson, 2015; Bennett et al., 2016). ePortfolio platforms range from rigid corporatised templates to open web platforms such as Weebly (Blackley, Bennet and Sheffield, 2017) and Wordpress (Reingold and Stommel, 2016). Using an open web platform provides students with more control and agency, allowing them more freedom in expressing their personal digital identity and arguably enabling them to better understand issues relating to privacy and ownership of data (Watters, 2015). It also allows sharing of the portfolio to peers, employers and industry mentors.

Another body of work examines student blogging in higher education. Blogging publicly on the open web engages students with the conventions and affordances of new media (Waycott et al., 2010; Waycott et al., 2013) where the readership is broader than that of a traditional assessment item (Freeman and Brett, 2012). For instance, Clark (2010, p. 34) explains, "blogs [are] one of the highest stakes (although graded as low stakes) forms of writing that my students do; in a single click, they become authors with the responsibility for what they have written". This potential wider readership exposes issues of digital identity, including students' concerns that they have something legitimate to say, and the development of their "authorial online voice" (Waycott et al., 2013, p. 87).

CONSTRUCTING A DIGITAL IDENTITY THROUGH DEVELOPING AND APPLYING DIGITAL LITERACIES

A range of digital literacies are needed by students to create, share and host their digital content. Digital literacies comprise the range of skills, capabilities, attributes, practices and knowledge that allow digital content creation, participation and citizenship in a networked society. These include: basic functional and operational skills needed to navigate online spaces and networks; digital citizenship practices and protocols; ethical use of information; online privacy and cybersafety; critical evaluation of media and information; consumption, creation, curation and sharing of content; participation in networked communities; and development, expression and management of a range of digital identities across platforms (Alexander, Adams Becker and Cummins, 2016; Hinrichsen and Coombs, 2014; JISC, 2014; Wheeler, 2012). These aspects are also captured in the concept of digital career literacy, which "encompass technical, cultural, social and presentational abilities which can be developed in the context of a career" (Hooley, 2012, p. 7).

The fluency and comfort that students have with digital tools, social media and social networking necessarily influences their digital identities. However, the link between digital literacy and digital identity has rarely been explicitly explored. One exception is a study that emphasised the technical aspect of digital literacies in relation to ePortfolios, where a polished website was seen as an expression of professionalism (Blair and Monske, 2009). More commonly, particular aspects of digital literacies are discussed in relation to students' digital identities as constructed via social networking. For instance, Koole and Parchoma (2013) present a conceptual Web of Identity model which incorporates network literacies.

We have found little previous research that explores students' professional digital identities. There is work on students' construction of digital identities through the use of social networking, on use of Web 2.0 for teaching and learning, on digital literacies, and on professional identities, but nothing that we have found that has attempted to bring together these concepts in an empirical study. Thus, the research question underpinning our study was "How do education students and recent graduates construct their professional digital identities through producing web-based digital content?"

METHOD

Semi-structured interviews ranging from 30 to 60 minutes were conducted with nine students/recent graduates from a faculty of education at a large Australian metropolitan university. The participants were recruited via emails to students in the Bachelor of Education and Master of Education and via a Facebook group for Master of Education (Teacher-Librarianship) students and alumni. We chose these groups because as teachers in these programs we knew that students were required to create web-based content as assessment for some subjects in their degree. Of those who volunteered to participate, two participants were enrolled in a Bachelor of Education, three participants were enrolled in a Master of Education, three participants had recently graduated from a Master of Education, and one participant had completed a Master of Education (Knowledge Networks and Digital Innovation) in addition to her Master of Education (Teacher-Librarianship). The participants ranged in age from 19 to 52.

In the interview, participants were asked questions relating to how their content reflected them as a person, who they shared it with, the response (if any) of the people with whom they shared, whether they shared with an employer or potential employer, the knowledge and skills they developed through creating and sharing their content, and their conception of their personal and professional identity through creating their content. It should be noted that we did not collect assignment task sheets or marking criteria and we did not analyse the formal requirements or context of these assignment tasks. Our focus was on the way that participants perceived their professional digital identity through completing the assignment tasks rather than on the tasks themselves. Table 3.1 presents the participants using pseudonyms, along with a descriptive title, vignette summary, study program, and list of digital content discussed in the interview.

The participants reported undertaking a wide range of subjects where they were required to create web-based content. Six of the participants were currently studying or had completed the Master of Education (Teacher-Librarianship) which had a heavy emphasis on digital literacies. These students had created multiple blogs and websites. Within these platforms they had embedded further digital content such as curated collections (using tools such as Pinterest and Scoopit), infographics, mind maps, images, videos, and animations. This content was available on the open web (i.e. not hidden inside a learning management system or other protected environment). Furthermore, seven of the participants were required to create a web-based portfolio using freely available web tools such as Google Sites, Wordpress and Wix, however, these were invite-only or password protected, with the lecturer/marker being the only audience. The purpose of the portfolios was for critical reflection on their development as professionals.

The interviews were transcribed verbatim, and an inductive thematic analysis undertaken following the process outlined by Braun and Clarke (2006). The process began with close reading of the interview transcripts, followed by the generation of initial codes that emerged from each interview. Once each transcript had been analysed, patterns and commonalities were identified in the emergent codes across the interviews. This process required the codes to be collated into possible themes, with the relevant data from each interview gathered according to these themes to ensure alignment remained between the themes and the raw data. The themes were further refined, and interpretations of the data were consolidated (Boyatzis, 1998). This process left us with four overarching themes that described the participants' experiences of digital identity development: interaction, coherence, professional digital identity, and connectedness.

A second level of analysis was conducted using the descriptors of technical, emerging, participatory and leading. These terms were drawn from Baker-Doyle's (2017) transformative teacher development framework. The interpretation of these terms shares some alignment with features of the framework but is also informed by the findings of this study (we discuss this later in the chapter). The experience of the participants was analysed using the descriptors and mapped onto a quadrant framework that combines the themes with the descriptors (Figure 3.1).

FINDINGS

The results of our analysis revealed that participants appeared to be at different stages of developing their professional digital identities (see Table 3.1 and Figure 3.1). These digital identities seemed to be dependent upon the participant's confidence and competence with conducting online interactions, and in the way that they applied digital literacy in different contexts. Those participants with the most limited professional identity also appeared to express the greatest amount of disparity between their student identity and what their professional online presence and activity would be like at some point in the future. This is despite the fact that all but two of the participants were already practicing teachers, and therefore would be considered professionals within their fields. This disparity reduced in those with a stronger professional digital identity.

Table 3.1   Description of study participants

	Name and descriptor	Content	Demographics	Vignette
	Amanda "Building the skills"	Portfolio Blog Website Infographic	MEd student Practicing teacher	Focus on technical skills Future focus for the application of technical skills Skill development closely linked to formal studies
	Boris "Under construct-ion"	Webpage Portfolio	BEd student	Plans for professional identity future focused Current online activities limited to personal interactions and closed to public viewing
	Claudine "Compart-mentalised facets"	Portfolio Website Mindmap Curated collection Video Blog	MEd TL student Practicing teacher	Sees little reason to develop artefacts beyond formal studies Online activities compartmentalised and not seen as contributing to professional digital identity Does not equate current employment with professional digital identity Considers professional digital identity as yet to be formulated
	Dan "The stage is set"	Portfolio Blog x 2 Curated collection Mindmap	MEd TL graduate Practicing teacher	Differentiates between personal and professional sharing and interaction Feels greater confidence revealing professional rather than personal digital identity Plans for increased communication of professional digital identity through online interactions
	Eric "Behind the scenes connector"	Facebook group Curated collection	BEd student	Uses digital literacy skills to create connections between self, others and curated digital content Views technology as a bridge connecting different aspects of personal and professional identity Less concerned with how digital identity is perceived, and more with how his actions might connect others to solve problems
	Frankie "Branching out"	Portfolio Blog x 4 Curated collection x 2 Online quiz Website Animation Video	MEd TL graduate Practicing teacher	Considered herself to have quite high digital literacy skills and had anonymous and personal digital interactions Formal study has raised capabilities to create and publish professional digital content Took small steps to communicate professional digital identity by sharing professional content in local context

Name and descriptor	Content	Demographics	Vignette
Gabrielle "Getting the blend right"	Blog x 2 Curated collection Animated video Images	MEd student Practicing teacher	Considered professional digital identity to be at the novice level Used professional digital content to communicate professional capabilities and creative personality Getting the blend between personal and professional to portray an authentic professional digital identity is important
Helen "Expanding connections"	Portfolio Blog x 2 Website Curated collection Video	MEd TL graduate Practicing teacher	Continued to build digital artefacts beyond formal study Aware of the professional image she has and wants to create Observing professional digital identity of others encouraged her continued development Professional interactions have led to professional opportunities and increased confidence Expanding connections provided a sense of self within the larger profession
Izzie "The established digital profess-ional"	Portfolio Blog x 3 Curated collection	MEd TL graduate MEd Knowledge Networks and Innovation graduate Practicing teacher	Saw digital identity as representative of her ongoing learning journey Maintained separation between personal and professional presence but believed professional digital identity reveals personal attributions such as drive and passion for learning Professional digital identity has played role in securing new employment and invitations to present at conferences Actively cultivated digital identity and used digital literacy skills to create and promote presence Saw the development of professional digital identity as a way to contribute to the profession and receive feedback from others within the profession Continued to build digital artefacts beyond formal study Active Twitter presence

Interaction

Interaction relates to the extent to which the participant connected or interacted with others for professional purposes through digital networks. Interaction may be in the form of sharing stories of practice, publishing content partici-pants had created or redistributing professional information. Those with low interaction worked in isolation and had limited digital interactions. Those with high interaction regularly engaged with others through digital networks.

Amanda's professional digital interaction appeared to be limited to that required by her formal studies. Boris said that his online communications were only with friends and family and indicated that his lack of work experience limited his contributions to online professional discussions. Dan regarded his professional interactions as low, however he observed that it depended upon what he was sharing, and through which platform. He explained that sharing his personal professional opinion in online discussion was quite challenging: "you put it (your opinion) on the web, you're putting it out to the world … you're taking a risk". This contrasted with his relative ease when interacting through a professional platform such as LinkedIn, where Dan said "I find that easier because it's not personal. It's just purely professional and you're just sharing ideas and interesting articles, things like that. I find that very, very easy to do".

Frankie, who talked about cautiously branching out into greater professional interactions online, displayed a growing sense of confidence. For instance, she commented that when publishing her blog, she made it public but not searchable, and after maintaining anonymous accounts on various social media platforms, she created a separate Twitter account that she referred to as her professional account, which was listed under her own name. She also said that she had proudly shared digital content she had produced with colleagues, senior managers and potential employers. These steps seemed to be building her levels of professional interactivity, and confidence in her online professional identity.

Helen described quite high levels of professional interactivity and was working on expanding her connections with others. After creating a range of digital content during formal study, Helen continued to build a professional digital identity through blogging. Observing how others interacted and published content through professional networks influenced Helen's desire to continue building her professional digital identity through increasing her interactivity. She observed that "if I want to get out there and make connections and be known by people then that's what I need to do … actually get online and share stuff or respond to stuff".

Coherence

Coherence describes the way that participants understood their digital literacy, how they transferred it to different contexts and how they applied this understanding to their current professional position. Low levels of coherence were evident when participants viewed digital literacy through the narrow lens of technical skills. These skills were viewed in isolation and may not be transferred to different contexts. For example, Amanda described her digital literacy skills in terms of which digital platforms she interacted with, rather than seeing them as more generic capacities which may be transferred across different tools. Claudine also demonstrated lower levels of coherence. She worked on her partner's business website, sought uncensored current affairs reports through Twitter and created digital content for her formal studies, yet said she created little to share online to grow her professional digital identity, as "I don't think I have the time or any real reason to develop anything at the moment". Her digital literacies appeared highly compartmentalised and were not transferred to her professional digital identity.

Higher levels of coherence were demonstrated when digital literacy skills were seen as an integrated set of capacities that may be used flexibly in different ways to meet different goals. This resulted in coherence between practice and the professional digital identity being portrayed publicly. Participants with higher levels of coherence used tools naturally to access and share digital content as a part of their practice and considered their digital literacy as a part of their professional digital identity.

Eric displayed higher levels of coherence, as he used his digital literacy skills to create connections between himself, other individuals and curated digital content. He curated content as needed, and was open to learning new skills, with a focus on creating solutions to his own and others' problems. Izzie also demonstrated high levels of coherence. This was evident not only in her wide range of digital literacies, including curating, constructing digital content, and developing digital network connections but also through her assertion that "the biggest digital literacy skill that evolved over time is my ability … to be discerning and purposeful in what I do online". Izzie's awareness of her capacities and how she might use them strategically and purposefully connected her practice and her digital professional identity.

The Professional Digital Identity Quadrant Map

Participants have been placed on a professional digital identity quadrant (Figure 3.1) that indicates their level of coherence and interaction with a description of their digital literacy as leading, emerging, participatory and technical.

The four descriptors for the quadrants of the model are drawn from the terms developed by Baker-Doyle (2017, p. 33) in her transformative teacher developmental framework, with the quadrant being our creation. While the descriptors were not used to describe transformative teachers in this research, there is congruence to be found in the evolution from technical, through emerging and participatory to leader in the development of a professional digital identity.

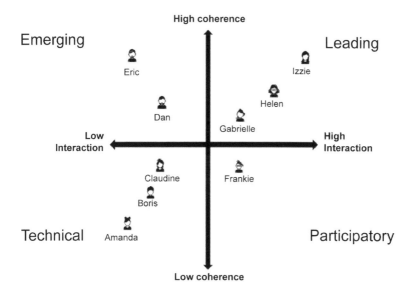

Figure 3.1   Professional digital identity quadrant map

Within the context of our research, the term technical is used to describe those participants who perceived technology primarily as a non-social tool which is used to complete a particular task (Baker-Doyle, 2017). A technical approach to digital literacy is one where skills are seen in isolation and where understanding of one tool or platform is not transferred beyond the context in which it is learnt. Technical is used to mean a narrow and specific understanding of connected digital technologies.

As the individual becomes more competent and confident using digital tools and platforms, they may move into the emerging quadrant. The term emerging is used where participants were expanding and applying their digital literacy skills to carry out professional tasks and to achieve a variety of professional goals. Like those in the technical quadrant, the emerging participants were yet to communicate or interact widely with others using digital means. They continued to develop their digital professional identity in relative isolation. This contrasts with the emerging category in Baker-Doyle's (2017) research, which describes individuals who view connected technologies as primarily a social tool for use in their personal life.

The participatory quadrant in our research describes those who used digital tools to interact and communicate with others but not for the purposes of developing a professional digital identity. The term participatory emphasises higher levels of interactivity and openness to communicating with others using digital technology. Similarly to Baker-Doyle's description (2017), those in the participatory quadrant were becoming more aware of the social complexity of connected digital technologies and the influence this may have on their professional digital identity.

The use of the term leading indicates the high levels of proficiency in digital literacy of those participants in this quadrant. These participants modelled a professional digital identity to others. They developed this identity strategically to enhance their online presence. They interacted fluently through digital tools using high levels of digital literacy. This allowed for greater collaboration and opportunities to share their work with others, in a similar way to those leaders within the transformative teacher developmental framework (Baker-Doyle, 2017).

Leading: high coherence, high interaction

Those participants with high coherence and high interaction were classified as leaders. They described higher levels of digital literacy, which they felt confident in applying in different ways to create solutions. They interacted with other professionals through dialogue, distributing information and resources, and sharing content that they had created. They were aware of their professional online presence and worked strategically towards developing an authentic representation of their professional digital identity.

Izzie, Helen, and Gabrielle fell within this quadrant. Izzie represented an established digital professional. She actively cultivated her professional digital identity, using her digital literacy skills to create and promote her presence. She found this activity to be affirming and rewarding. Helen also highly valued the process of creating a professional digital identity. The potential for almost anybody to view content that she shared online influenced what she published, as she was "really aware of what image I want to create". Helen said that her expanding connections gave her a sense that although she held a singular role within her workplace, she was not alone within her profession. Gabrielle commented that publishing online created an opportunity for others to see "a really good example of the kind of work that I've done in the past but also of my creativity and my personality". She had started to consider how she might use her digital literacy skills to develop a professional digital identity that portrayed a blend of her professional capabilities and her own creative personality.

Participating: high interaction, low coherence

Those with high interaction but low coherence may engage with others through digital networks, but not for purposes aligned with their professional identity. These individuals had a participatory approach to developing their digital identity, but this had yet to be applied to their professional identity online.

Participants within this quadrant described using anonymous accounts or avatars to protect their professional identity when they interacted online. They chose to do so to keep their personal and professional identities separate, or because they felt a lack of confidence in sharing their professional opinions publicly.

Frankie was the only participant whose digital identity could be described as participatory. She was confident with creating web-based content and comfortable with using her web-based university assignments for job applications and interviews, however, as a practicing teacher she felt it important for her professional persona to be anonymous, in particular her Twitter presence. She said, "you can get yourself in a bit of trouble when you're in this sort of position if you make it too public".

Emerging: high coherence, low interaction

Participants who had high coherence, but low interaction had a well-developed alignment between their activities online and their professional identity, but their interactions with others were less public and their professional digital networks were less well developed. Their identity may not have been well communicated.

Dan and Eric both demonstrated an emerging professional digital identity. Dan said he hoped to develop a professional digital identity that would align with his offline professional ideals. He described readying himself to develop a professional digital identity and had begun establishing his presence using social media platforms including LinkedIn. Eric presented a different approach. He worked behind the scenes in using his digital literacy capabilities to create solutions and make connections to information, without necessarily desiring the development of a large digital network. Eric said that he "isn't in it for the fame" and that he believed his actions were an expression of his creativity and his contribution to the greater good. Eric's professional digital identity appeared to be informed by his capacity to create solutions to his own and other's problems, rather than as a professional showcase to promote his capabilities.

Technical: low coherence, low interaction

Low coherence and low interaction describes those participants with a technical level of ability. They may have possessed elements of digital literacy, but these remained unrelated to their current professional identity, and these participants did not engage in a great deal of interaction through professional digital networks. Participants who demonstrated a technical approach to their professional digital identity saw its development as something that would be done once particular levels of digital literacy were attained, or a certain professional goal (such as employment in a specific role) was achieved.

Amanda, Boris and Claudine were all situated in this quadrant. Amanda considered that she was still building the skills required to create a professional digital identity. Her responses to how she might implement digital capacities she was developing during her formal studies were all future focused, despite the fact that she worked in a professional role. Boris had initiated a digital presence; however, it was in the very early stages of construction. His range of digital literacy capabilities had yet to be applied to professional interactions or sharing. Claudine had slightly higher levels of interaction and coherence, yet still saw her digital literacy capabilities as compartmentalised facets, which she did not appear to transfer across contexts. Despite working in a professional role while completing formal study, she had a future focus for her professional digital identity, saying, "I've got all these ideas and plans, I suppose, for once I'm done with the study or once I get a library position".

DIGITAL PROFESSIONAL IDENTITY AND CONNECTEDNESS CAPABILITIES

The experiences of the participants as mapped to the quadrant reveal a number of characteristics that contribute to a stronger or weaker professional digital identity. Despite seven of the nine participants being practicing teachers, they still expressed a digital identity that was heavily influenced by their sense of self as a student. Only Gabrielle, Helen and Izzie were situated within the leading quadrant, with high levels of interaction and coherence combined with well-developed digital literacies. These findings have implications for educators who aim for their students to develop connectedness capabilities as part of a professional digital identity. Thus, in the next section, we discuss the experience of the participants in relation to the connectedness capabilities identified in the Connectedness Learning Approach (see Chapter 1 in this volume): developing social network literacy, building a connected identity, growing connections, strengthening and maintaining connections and working with connections.

Developing Social Network Literacy

Social network literacy involves being able to make meaningful use of social networks for professional purposes, both online and offline. An understanding of fundamental network concepts including connectivity, interactions and interdependence, as well as the ability to work effectively with connections through social networks are features of high levels of social network literacy (see Chapter 1 in this volume; Postholm, 2012).

Most of the participants were required as part of their subjects to use social network platforms such as closed G+ Communities and Facebook to interact and share content with their teachers and peers. However, they were not required to actively share their content outside the class, for instance on platforms such as Twitter and LinkedIn. All participants were developing social network literacy, although they were at different stages of this development.

For Amanda, Boris and Claudine, their lack of interaction with others beyond the requirements of their formal coursework indicated that they were in the early stages of developing social network literacy. They had not initiated the creation of connections beyond their formal study for professional purposes, although Boris had made tentative steps towards this with his LinkedIn profile. Although they may have developed some of the skills needed to work effectively with connections, they had not done so for professional purposes. Their social network literacy remained within the student experience. The only participant to have a well-developed social network literacy was Izzie, who had developed a strong Twitter presence in her work as a teacher-librarian.

Building a Connected Identity

Building a connected identity involves constructing a professional presence online and having a purposeful strategy to develop this presence on professional networks (Bridgstock, 2016). Having recognised the need for a professional presence online, Dan was ready to begin creating a professional digital identity. He, along with Frankie, demonstrated a hesitant acceptance that part of this process involved initiating and growing connections with others for professional purposes. They had a different approach to connectedness than Eric, who demonstrated some competence in working with connections, but appeared to have no strong inclination towards formulating these connections into a connected, cohesive professional identity. Dan and Frankie had moved beyond the immediate student experience to begin transferring their understandings to the context of a professional digital identity, although they were at the early stages of this process.

In developing her connected identity, Gabrielle spoke about the need to negotiate boundaries between one's personal and private interests and personae (Veletsianos, 2013; Veletsianos and Kimmons, 2012). Identifying the boundaries between personal and professional appeared to grow in importance as participants' interactions and digital presence increased. Helen and Izzie also expressed a desire to keep some separation between personal and professional interactions, although Izzie, who had the most well-developed digital professional identity commented that at times there was crossover, or elements of context collapse (Marwick and boyd, 2011). Conveying aspects of personality through a professional digital identity created a sense of authenticity which was valued (Baker-Doyle, 2017). However, all participants, including those who possessed relatively high levels of social network literacy, expressed a wariness of letting too much personal information seep into their professional presence.

Growing Connections

Growing connections involves embedding oneself in professional networks and developing weak ties and reciprocity, including the sharing of content to the network (Bridgstock, 2016). Gabrielle and Helen demonstrated an increasing awareness of the ways in which their digital literacies may be drawn together to grow their connections. As they learned more about maintaining their privacy and managing their identity, they became more confident in sharing content that they had created in channels beyond their student experience. To grow connections, there must be active interaction and contribution to the network (Baker-Doyle, 2017; Nussbaum-Beach and Hall, 2012). As their professional digital identities grew through their connections, Gabrielle and Helen also talked about the ways in which they intended to present themselves professionally online.

Strengthening, Maintaining and Working with Connections

Strengthening, maintaining and working with connections was a capability that only Izzie appeared to demonstrate. While Helen said that she created and disseminated new knowledge through her blog, she indicated that she considered herself at the early stages of this journey, and therefore many of her connections were still within the initial circles she frequented online. Izzie had a much more widely established digital presence, having been invited to deliver keynotes at conferences and run professional development as a result of her online reputation. She used her knowledge and understanding of social networks to broadcast herself to a wider audience and remained active through several social software platforms to maintain her connections and professional digital identity.

LIMITATIONS

One of the limitations of this study was the small group of participants with varying study experience and experience of professional practice. Also, the level of experience of developing web-based content varied widely depending on how far the participant had progressed through their degree. For instance, Frankie (who had recently graduated) described creating four blogs and a portfolio incorporating embedded media for five separate courses in her Master's degree whereas Amanda (who had only completed two courses) had created one website and one portfolio. This range results in our study lacking the cohesion of an alternative approach such as an in-depth case study within one subject or program context. It would not necessarily be possible to generalise the experience of these participants to other contexts. We can, however, make some recommendations for practice based on our findings and on our experience of teaching classes where we have required students to create and share web-based content for assessment.

RECOMMENDATIONS FOR PRACTICE

The findings demonstrate that although the majority of participants were already practicing professionals, the requirement to create web content as part of their study rarely contributed to their professional digital identity. Instead, their identity remained future oriented (Jensen and Jetten, 2016), something to be developed once their studies (whether undergraduate or postgraduate) had been completed. This was compounded by the fact that although some of the participants were already practicing teachers, their vision of their future selves related to a new role that they would move into as teacher-librarians rather than applying what they had learned to their current teaching role. As such, the participants mainly regarded the content they created as assignment content, rather than professional content. This is consistent with the trend we have noticed in our classes where students tend to name their websites/blogs with their student ID numbers and/or the name of the course they are studying, rather than with a more creative name or title.

Only three of the participants demonstrated higher levels of professional digital interaction and coherence between their professional practice and their digital identities. In light of these findings, we make some recommendations to inform curriculum and pedagogy so that students may experience greater connectedness between their identities as a student and as a professional. Such connectedness would allow students to develop the professional digital networks needed to enhance their ongoing professional learning and career development in the digital age (Bridgstock, 2019b; Chapter 1 in this volume).

A CONNECTEDNESS CAPABILITIES APPROACH

A connectedness capabilities approach to curriculum and pedagogy drives the development of learning opportunities that are informed by open learning networks and resources (Chapter 1 in this volume). When teachers and students use social media and other digital tools to create, engage with and share their learning, there is potential for new learning pathways to be constructed and connections beyond the student cohort to be enacted. These opportunities may enhance the student's development of a professional digital identity, as they are able to see their learning within a scope that exists beyond the formal student experience.

Designing and leveraging openly networked, production centred and interest driven learning is central to connected learning (Ito et al., 2014). However, the affordances of connected learning may not be fully exploited if students lack particular digital literacies. These literacies go beyond functional digital skills, and reflect the connectedness capabilities identified by Bridgstock's Connectedness Learning Approach (Chapter 1 in this volume).

As was made evident through this research, students may engage with and even create digital content, but this may not automatically connect their student and professional digital identities. Students who do not know how to initiate and maintain digital network connections, who cannot actively manage their digital identity or who lack the capacity to broadcast their identity across multiple platforms may find it challenging to interact as professionals in open digital networks. Therefore, we suggest building scaffolds into the pedagogical design that may assist students to create an authentic professional identity through connected learning opportunities.

One strategy we use to encourage students to develop a professional identity in our Master's courses is to include assessment standards which award students higher grades if their blog reads as a 'professional conversation', where the audience is their colleagues and their employer. For instance, an excerpt from the standard for a high distinction in one of our courses states:

> Your blog goes beyond that of an assignment piece. It contributes to the professional conversation on inquiry learning curriculum design. Your professional teacher identity is clearly articulated. If someone found your blog in a Google search they would be interested to read it and comment. You can proudly use this blog as an example of your professional digital footprint with colleagues.

In this subject, we encourage our students to use a metaphor or theme as the unifying feature of their blogs and websites rather than the name of the subject. We suggest they write the 'About me' section of their blog/website introducing themselves (using their name or a pseudonym) as emerging professionals or practitioners, depending on their context and experience. However, as several of the participants had undertaken this subject, it is clear from our findings that these strategies do not go far enough.

Developing web-based content will not develop students' connectedness capabilities unless it is practiced within a wider framework of professional connections (Bridgstock, 2019a, 2019b). Teaching and learning activities to encourage professional connections might initially include structured opportunities to network with professionals (e.g. Tweetchats, live webcasts, web conferences), and analysis of online professional learning communities that operate on platforms such as Twitter, LinkedIn and Facebook. As an outcome of this research, we have developed an assignment task which requires our Master's students to explicitly develop a professional learning network (PLN) in their field where they must identify and follow relevant professional Twitter hashtags, follow industry/disciplinary experts on Twitter, become a member of professional online groups and create and share content to their PLN.

CONCLUSION

Shifting students from a student identity to a professional digital identity involves explicit development of digital literacies and professional learning networks (Bridgstock, 2019b). This is not without its risks, as students need to be able to develop their 'voice' (Waycott et al., 2013) in a safe environment, before gaining the skills and courage to enact their professional identity. However, doing so provides rich learning opportunities and rewards beyond the confines of the university and allows students to become agents of their professional identity.

REFERENCES

Alexander, B., Adams Becker, S. and Cummins, M. (2016). *Digital Literacy: An NMC Horizon Project Strategic Brief*. Austin, Texas: The New Media Consortium.

Baker-Doyle, K. (2017). *Transformative Teachers: Teacher Leadership and Learning in a Connected World*. Cambridge, MA: Harvard Education Press.

Bennett, D. and Robertson, R. (2015). Preparing students for diverse careers: Developing career literacy with final-year writing students. *Journal of University Teaching and Learning Practice, 12*(3), 1–16.

Bennett, D., Rowley, J., Dunbar-Hall, P., Hitchcock, M. and Blom, D. (2016). Electronic portfolios and learner identity: An ePortfolio case study in music and writing. *Journal of Further and Higher Education, 40*(1), 107–124.

Bennett, S., Bishop, A., Dalgarno, B., Waycott, J. and Kennedy, G. (2012). Implementing Web 2.0 technologies in higher education: A collective case study. *Computers and Education, 59*, 524–534.

Blackley, S., Bennet, D. and Sheffield, R. (2017). Purpose-built, web-based professional portfolios: Reflective, developmental and showcase. *Australian Journal of Teacher Education, 42*(6), 91–106.

Blair, K. L. and Monske, E. A. (2009). Developing digital literacies and professional identities: The benefits of ePortfolios in graduate education. *Journal of Literacy and Technology, 10*(1), 40–68.

Boyatzis, R. E. (1998). *Transforming Qualitative Information: Thematic Analysis and Code Development*. Thousand Oaks, CA: Sage Publications.

Braun, V. and Clarke, V. (2006). Using thematic analysis in psychology. *Qualitative Research in Psychology*, *3*(2), 77–101.

Bridgstock, R. (2016). Connectedness learning model. Connectedness capabilities. Retrieved 22 January 2019 from http://www.graduateemployability2-0.com/model/connectedness-capabilities/.

Bridgstock, R. (2019a). Employability and career development learning through social media: Exploring the potential of LinkedIn. In J. Higgs, D. Horsfall, S. Cork and A. Jones (eds), *Challenging Future Practice Possibilities*. Rotterdam: Sense-Brill Publishers.

Bridgstock, R. (2019b). Graduate Employability 2.0: Education for work in a networked world. In J. Higgs, G. Crisp and W. Letts (eds), *Education for Employability: The Employability Agenda*. Rotterdam: Sense-Brill Publishers.

Buchanan, R. (2015). Digital footprint: Not everyone is equal and why unis need to teach managing DF as a 21st century skill. Retrieved 22 January 2019, from http://www.aare.edu.au/blog/?p=1291.

Buckingham, D. (2008). Introducing identity. In B. David (ed.), *Youth, Identity, and Digital Media* (pp. 1–22). Cambridge, MA: The MIT Press

Ching, Y. H. and Hsu, Y. C. (2011). Design-grounded assessment: A framework and a case study of Web 2.0 practices in higher education. *Australasian Journal of Educational Technology*, *27*(5), 781–797.

Clark, J. E. (2010). The digital imperative: Making the case for a 21st-century pedagogy. *Computers and Composition*, *27*, 27–35.

Freeman, W. and Brett, C. (2012). Prompting authentic blogging practice in an online graduate course. *Computers and Education*, *59*, 1032–1041.

Gray, K., Thompson, C., Sheard, J., Clerehan, R. and Hamilton, M. (2010). Students as Web 2.0 authors: Implications for assessment design and conduct. *Australasian Journal of Educational Technology*, *26*(1), 105–122.

Hinrichsen, J. and Coombs, A. (2014). The five resources of critical digital literacy: A framework for curriculum integration. *Research in Learning Technology*, *21*, 1–16.

Hooley, T. (2012). How the internet changed career: Framing the relationship between career development and online technologies. *Journal of the National Institute for Career Education and Counselling*, (29), 3–12.

Ito, M., Gutierrez, K., Livingstone, S., Penuel, B., Rhodes, J., Salen, K. … Watkins, S. C. (2014). Connected learning: An agenda for research and design. Retrieved 22 January 2019 from http://dmlhub.net/publications/connected-learning-agenda-for-research-and-design/.

Jensen, D. and Jetten, J. (2016). The importance of developing students' academic and professional identities in higher education. *Journal of College Student Development*, *57*(8), 1027–1042.

JISC. (2014). Developing digital literacies. Retrieved 22 January 2019 from https://www.jisc.ac.uk/guides/developing-digital-literacies.

Koole, M. and Parchoma, G. (2013). The web of identity: A model of digital identity formation in networked learning environments. In S. Warburton and S. Hatzipanagos (eds), *Digital Identity and Social Media* (pp. 14–28). Hershey, PA: IGI Global.

Marwick, A. and boyd, d. (2011). I tweet honestly, I tweet passionately: Twitter users, context collapse, and the imagined audience. *New Media and Society*, *13*(1), 114–133.

Nussbaum-Beach, S. and Hall, L. (2012). *The Connected Educator: Learning and Leading in a Digital Age*. Bloomington, IN: Solution Tree Press.

Postholm, M. (2012). Teachers' professional development: A theoretical review. *Educational Research*, *54*(4), 405–429.

Reingold, J. and Stommel, J. (2016). A brief history of domain of one's own, part 1. Retrieved 30 April 2018 from http://umwdtlt.com/a-brief-history-of-domain- of -ones-own-part-1/.

Schroeder, A., Minocha, S. and Schneidert, C. (2010). The strengths, weaknesses, opportunities and threats of using social software in higher and further education teaching and learning. *Journal of Computer Assisted Learning*, *26*, 159–174.

Trede, F., Macklin, R. and Bridges, D. (2012). Professional identity development: A review of the higher education literature. *Studies in Higher Education*, *37*(3), 365–384.

Trede, F. and McEwen, C. (2012). Developing a critical professional identity. In J. Higgs, R. Barnett, S. Billet, M. Hutchings and F. Trede (eds), *Practice-based Education* (pp. 27–40). Rotterdam: Sense Publishers.

Veletsianos, G. (2013). Open practices and identity: Evidence from researchers and educators' social media participation. *British Journal of Educational Technology*, *44*(4), 639–651.

Veletsianos, G. and Kimmons, R. (2012). Assumptions and challenges of open scholarship. *The International Review of Open and Distance Learning*, *13*(4), 166–189.

Watters, A. (2015). The web we need to give students. Retrieved 30 April 2018 from https://brightthemag.com/the-web-we-need-to-give-students-311d97713713.

Waycott, J., Gray, K., Clerehan, R., Hamilton, M., Richardson, J., Sheard, J. and Thompson, C. (2010). Implications for academic integrity of using Web 2.0 for teaching, learning and assessment in higher education. *International Journal for Educational Integrity*, *6*(2), 8–18.

Waycott, J., Sheard, J., Thompson, C. and Clerehan, R. (2013). Making students' work visible on the social web: A blessing or a curse? *Computers and Education*, *68*, 86–95.

Wheeler, S. (2012). Digital literacies for engagement in emerging online cultures. *eLearn Centre Research Paper Series*, *5*, 14–25.

Wladawsky-Berger, I. (2016). Digital identity: The key to privacy and security in the digital world. Retrieved 20 June 2018 from http://ide.mit.edu/news-blog/blog/ digital-identity-key-privacy-and-security-digital-world.

4. Connectedness capabilities of non-traditional students: pedagogical implications[1]

Margarietha J. de Villiers Scheepers, Joanna McIntyre, Gail Crimmins and Peter English

INTRODUCTION

Work environments are increasingly uncertain (Jackson, 2015), resulting in a discontinuous, fragmented career context. These conditions have led to a new work order where job security is rare and employees are expected to show their value by continuously learning new skills to remain marketable (Gerli, Bonesso and Pizzi, 2015). The traditional career path of permanent full-time employment and advancement with a single employer has been replaced by career paradigms which emphasise interorganisational mobility and flexibility, calling for a boundaryless and/or protean career orientation (Briscoe et al., 2012; Gerli, Bonesso and Pizzi, 2015). These changes require individuals to be increasingly self-directed in their careers.

Within this career context, tertiary institutions need to prepare graduates with not only discipline-specific and transferable skills and knowledge, but also career management competencies, including their capacity to build and maintain connections (Bridgstock, 2009). This means graduates should have the ability to self-manage their careers by not only developing their human capital, but also their social capital and professional networks (de Villiers Scheepers et al., 2018; Hess, 2017). Complicating the issue is that many universities today teach diverse, non-traditional student cohorts (Schuetze and Slowey, 2002). Non-traditional students are heterogeneous in terms of previous education, social and family background, gender, age, life-situation, motivation to study and occupational profiles compared to traditional school-leavers (Schuetze and Slowey, 2002). These students are typically unfamiliar with university expectations, and their social capital, and career expectations differ from the traditional school-leaver (Burke et al., 2016). These changes in career models, the changing needs of non-traditional students, and opportunities to develop professional career connections through social networking platforms provide pedagogical challenges for educators, particularly in the social media space.

The growth of online social networking platforms provides opportunities for students to build their professional networks while studying and exploit these connections for career management (Benson, Morgan and Filippaios, 2014). Platforms such as LinkedIn dominate the professional networking sector with over 467 million registered members (Kemp, 2018). Twitter focuses on online news, with more than 328 million monthly active users, whereas Facebook is known for social connection, boasting more than 60 million active users (Aslam, 2018). The popularity of these platforms, both for professional and social purposes, encourages individuals to communicate and share professional and social interests. As such, it represents a resource for non-traditional students to cultivate connections, shape their digital identity, and project a professional persona. However, despite the potential of these platforms, few students and educators utilise these platforms (Bridgstock, 2016), or appear to understand their benefits.

In this chapter we explore the connectedness capabilities of non-traditional students at a regional university and provide guidelines to help students, and educators, build, maintain and make use of their social networks. The chapter proceeds by first offering an overview of the changing nature of careers, the relevance of social media platforms, and the development of career social capital. Second, it examines the competencies needed for increased career mobility and the pedagogical implications thereof. Third, we discuss the context of our study (non-traditional students within a regional university) before, fourth, presenting empirical data and considering the implications for pedagogy.

NEW CAREER PARADIGMS: BOUNDARYLESS AND PORTFOLIO CAREERS

The unpredictable workplace ecosystem that defines the modern economy has resulted in new career paradigms becoming increasingly associated with mobility and flexibility. The traditional career model, comprising a stable path of progression, upward and linear in trajectory, usually within a single organisation (Lochab and Mor, 2013; Verbruggen, 2012), has changed to one where employees are increasingly mobile and required to be more self-reliant when developing their career paths. Despite these changes, most formal education systems still follow a nineteenth century model, delivering employable professionals and specialised vocationalists to national economies regardless of the rapidly changing demand for skills in globalised labour markets (Chan et al., 2012). Thus, universities need to adapt to these contemporary career models and encourage traditional and non-traditional student populations to take a more active role in their career journeys (Chan et al., 2012).

A self-managed approach to career management helps individuals to be adaptive within an uncertain labour market. Boundaryless and protean career attitudes are distinct but complementary concepts which are valuable in identifying and analysing diverse career paradigms (Briscoe and Hall, 2006). The boundaryless career emphasises opportunities for workers who are physically and psychologically mobile, independent from the boundaries and hierarchies of organisations (Sullivan and Arthur, 2006), and possessing marketable and transferable skills, as well as the ability to continuously update their knowledge and networks (Arthur and Rousseau, 1996; Lochab and Mor, 2013). Comparably, the protean career refers to a self-determination mindset, where career goals are driven by personal values and psychological success, rather than external cues like promotions and pay rises (Briscoe and Hall, 2006). The protean career reflects an individual's freedom, self-direction, and choices based on personal values, rather than organisationally imposed norms (Briscoe and Hall, 2006).

Although these concepts have been critiqued (Lochab and Mor, 2013), they are useful in highlighting not only the nature of work that graduates will experience, but also the opportunities for agency and diversity within their future careers. This new career paradigm is particularly relevant for business, sport and exercise science, communication, and creative industry students. Many business graduates experience boundaryless careers, initially seeking employment in small firms, before transitioning to self-employment at around the age of 35 (Global Entrepreneurship Monitor, 2017). Similarly, many sports graduates initially find work in fitness, leisure, or teaching, before later moving into sports coaching, sales, management or sports coordination roles (Minten and Forsyth, 2014). In the creative and communication fields, boundaryless and/or protean careers often take the form of portfolio careers; that is, "packages of work arrangements for the plying and selling of an individual's skills in a variety of contexts" (Mallon, 1999, p. 358). For example, studies of the independent film industry suggested that project-based employment offered a viable career path, yet success in such a career required workers to develop their professional networks and cultivate personal connections (Tams and Arthur, 2010). Within a world where social media is integral to building relationships socially and professionally, graduates must be adept at maintaining and managing their personal and professional networks.

SOCIAL MEDIA CAREER COMPETENCIES

Using social media professionally for career purposes does not come naturally to most students; in fact Benson and Morgan (2016) found that students were mostly ignorant of the professional implications of their social media use. While some universities offer social media courses, this is generally within niche programs, such as public relations, broadcasting or marketing (Sutherland and Ho, 2017), or as a pedagogical tool for students to engage with disciplinary content (Raineri, Fudge and Hall, 2015). Universities have been criticised for responding too slowly to the changing career requirements that the digital work environment demands (King, 2015; Schech et al., 2017). While employers require graduates to have professional social media skills, the ability to use social media for career management is also essential (Benson, Morgan and Filippaios, 2014; Sutherland and Ho, 2017). Graduate recruiters often use platforms such as LinkedIn, Facebook and Twitter to screen applicants, with many positions also being advertised through these platforms (McDonald and Thompson, 2016). Increasingly, digital professional networking requires that graduates possess the career competencies to build employability connections online (Shah, 2010).

Career competency can be defined on the basis of three interdependent competencies: knowing-why, knowing-how and knowing-whom (DeFillippi and Arthur, 1996). Knowing-why competencies refer to an individual's motivation, identity, and ability to make sense of their career, whereby a coherent sense of self is less reliant on identification with one organisation, but rather on varied job experiences (Eby, Butts and Lockwood, 2003). Knowing-how competencies reflect career-relevant skills, knowledge and experience that are broad, flexible and transferable across organisations (DeFillippi and Arthur, 1994). In digital boundaryless careers this means individuals search for and promote job redesign in fast-changing firms to accommodate their distinctive talents and future aspirations. Knowing-whom competencies denote an individual's internal and external networks, reputation, and mentoring relationships (Sullivan and Arthur, 2006). An extensive, socially-connected network is beneficial to access new contacts, job opportunities and entrepreneurial opportunities. The interdependence of these three competencies highlights that expertise in one competency alone is unlikely to sustain a successful career (Sullivan and Arthur, 2006). Further, contemporary career mindsets require that graduates possess not only personal drive and the continued ability to update their knowledge and skills, but also social media career competencies.

Foundational to the knowing-whom competency is social capital and its functioning in online contexts. Social capital refers to the sum of the relationships and networks that support students in using their human capital to access labour market opportunities (Phua, Jin and Kim, 2017). Social capital is key to individuals' access to employment opportunities, supporting them in achieving indicators of external success (such as promotions and salary) as well as personal career satisfaction and fulfilment (Richardson, Jogulu and Rentschler, 2017; Tomlinson, 2017). Two forms of social capital have been distinguished:

strong ties consist of close, personal relationships which offer bonding social capital, and weak ties reflect casual contacts, providing bridging social capital (Putnam, 2000). Social networking platforms provide a way for individuals to maintain relationships with strong ties but also offer opportunities to accumulate and strengthen weak ties (Phua, Jin and Kim, 2017). In order to enhance their employability, students should have the ability to use social networking platforms as a means of developing and leveraging their networks and ties (de Janasz and Forret, 2008).

The social media career competencies and social capital needed for employability require universities to attend not only to students' knowing-how competencies, but also their knowing-whom and knowing-why competencies. To help them accrue social capital and foster their connectedness capabilities for a successful boundaryless career, it is therefore essential to understand students' knowledge and use of social media, in both professional and non-professional capacities.

NON-TRADITIONAL STUDENTS' SOCIAL MEDIA CAREER COMPETENCIES

Given the widening participation agenda in higher education globally, many universities today teach a diverse, non-traditional student population (Schuetze and Slowey, 2002). Non-traditional students differ from traditional school leavers, as they may be older, come from working class backgrounds, comprise ethnic minority or immigrant populations, have previous work experience and/or vocational training, or be located in regional or remote locations (Schuetze and Slowey, 2002). Higher education pedagogies are typically designed for traditional school-leavers, however, non-traditional students may be unaccustomed to the expectations embedded within such approaches (Marr and Wilcox, 2015). Unless universities acknowledge this mismatch and adapt pedagogies to the changing student population they serve, they risk failing to educate and develop these cohorts (Marr and Wilcox, 2015).

Daddow (2016) advocates that educators should view the knowledge and experience of non-traditional students as assets for learning and incorporate these into the curriculum. For social media career competencies, non-traditional students may already be experienced in using social networking platforms, for professional or social reasons, and as such, students' existing knowledge, experience and networks represent a potential resource through which to cultivate and grow their professional connections via social media. Despite the career connection potential of social networking platforms, at present it appears that few universities are making use of students' existing capabilities, or tailoring their pedagogies to address this (Bridgstock, 2016; Sutherland and Ho, 2017). Furthermore, questions remain as to the extent of students existing competencies, with a notable lack of empirical research specifically focussing on non-traditional students' social media career competencies.

It is therefore crucial for universities to embed social media career competencies into their programs, given the new career paradigms and opportunities social media networks offer to grow students' professional connections. Yet understanding students' current connectedness capabilities represents the starting point, as pedagogies need to be adapted accordingly there-after. Thus, we present a case study of the University of the Sunshine Coast as a regional university serving non-traditional students and explore students' social media career competencies, before proposing appropriate pedagogies to develop and enhance social media career competencies.

CASE STUDY: UNIVERSITY OF THE SUNSHINE COAST (USC)

The University of the Sunshine Coast (USC) is one of Australia's fastest growing public universities, opening its first campus in 1996 with 524 students, expanding to more than 14,000 students in 2018. USC's catchment area ranges from Brisbane to Hervey Bay, a stretch of 300 km on Australia's east coast. USC is considered a regional university within Australia, with most of its campuses located in geographical areas with limited numbers of large employers, and most of the population around its larger campuses being self-employed, working for small firms, non-profit organisations, or as public-sector employees. As a third of Australia's population lives outside capital cities, universities in regional areas are critical in stimulating the local economy and servicing the region. While student enrolment has increased in metropolitan and regional areas in recent years, the basic inequality in education participation prevails, despite the demand driven-system (Shoemaker, 2017). For instance, in 2016 the proportion of people aged 25 to 34 years with a bachelor's degree or higher in cities was 42 per cent, compared to 19 per cent in regional Australia (Australian Broadcasting Corporation, 2017). Though the proportion of low socio-economic status students attending university has increased in recent years, the proportion of regional students has not significantly changed (McAloon, 2017). Furthermore, the data reveals that students at regional universities are more likely to identify as mature age and low socio-economic status compared to cities, and regional universities are more reliant on government funding, as reflected in the USC case.

At USC the student population is characterised by a large percentage of non-traditional students, with 61 per cent female students, and 49 per cent of students older than 21 years (University of the Sunshine Coast, 2017). Graduate employment after graduation is a challenge, with 62 per cent of students securing employment upon graduation, compared to the national average of 71 per cent. However, within five years of graduation this situation normalises and 86 per cent of graduates' secure employment, comparable to the national average (University of the Sunshine Coast, 2017). The initial underemployment could be due to the social disadvantage non-traditional students experience. Sociology of education discourses argue that student learning does not occur in a vacuum and students enter tertiary education as part of social and cultural groups that inhabit social norms and expectations. These norms shape students' aspirations, informing their learning behaviours which are adapted to fit what seems preferable and achievable (Gale and Parker, 2015). This phenomenon known as adaptive preference explains that people's preferences are shaped by available possibilities, customs, prior experiences and a social and cultural gamut of conditions (Doughney, 2007). Thus, tertiary students cannot prefer or pursue an option if they do not know about it, or they believe it is not available to them, or 'people like them'. This perspective acknowledges how structural conditions can restrict the employability of non-traditional students and highlights the need to examine connectedness capabilities in greater detail.

Taking a career competency perspective acknowledges knowing-how, knowing-whom, and knowing-why competencies. By implication, educators should utilise pedagogies designed to enhance student career aspirations and seek to influence the adaptive preferences of non-traditional students (Doughney, 2007). To ensure pedagogies are adapted to develop students' social media career competencies, a survey was conducted to examine USC students' current social media use.

METHOD

This study employed a descriptive research design, using survey data, collected during September 2017. This chapter forms part of a larger research project where students' social network connectedness capabilities are ascertained and developed through a cycle of action research. The results presented in this chapter focus on the social media usage of non-traditional undergraduate students, considering students' familiarity, confidence and competency in using social media for professional and non-professional purposes. Online questionnaires were distributed to all undergraduate students at USC in three disciplines: Business, Communication and Creative Industries, and Sport and Exercise Science, as these students face an uncertain labour market. Undergraduate students in these courses were invited to participate through email and learning management system announcements, to ensure both users and non-users of social media were targeted. The survey was open for four weeks during which 212 responses were collected, of which 210 were useable.

The majority of students in the sample (n=210) are domestic (85.5 per cent), full-time (84 per cent), female students (71 per cent), of which 60 per cent identified as mature-aged students. Respondents in the sample vary from first-year (29.4 per cent), second-year (34.1 per cent) to those in the final years (36.5 per cent) of their degrees. This is comparable to the USC student population, of which the majority are female (61 per cent), and 60 per cent are older than 21 years of age (University of the Sunshine Coast, 2017). While the international student cohort in the sample is not large (17 per cent), more than 26 per cent of domestic students indicate they were not born in Australia. More than a third of students (38.2 per cent) are the first in their families to attend university. As most of the 210 respondents were older than 21, many had work experience, with 47 per cent indicating they had worked in a full-time position before enrolling in studies, while a similar proportion (46.4 per cent) worked part-time. Only 6.6 per cent had never been employed. The prevalence of work experience indicates that the sample represents a heterogeneous non-traditional student population.

Measures

To assess respondents' current online proficiency, they were asked to describe the currency of their online professional profile using a three-point scale, with 1 representing an updated profile, 2 representing a dated profile and 3 representing no profile. Current social media habits for professional and non-professional purposes were assessed by asking respondents how frequently they used a range of social media networks. Networking self-efficacy was assessed using a four-point scale which asked participants how confident they felt networking at a professional event, creating an effective LinkedIn profile, using social media to build a professional identity and using social media to connect professionally. Responses ranged from 1 indicating no confidence to 4 denoting a high level of confidence. Finally, participants completed an open-ended question which asked how they aimed to develop their professional network while at university. This item was answered by 40 per cent of respondents and was intended to give further insight into the quantitative responses.

Analysis

We conducted a descriptive analysis of respondents' social media proficiency and use (n=210), followed by one-way analysis of variance (ANOVA) to assess differences between students based on their work experience. Students were compared in terms of those with work experience, those with part-time work experience and those with no work experience. Analysis was performed using IBM SPSS Statistics 24 with additional thematic analysis conducted on the open-ended survey question to identify emerging themes.

RESULTS

Social Media Competency, Proficiency and Use

Respondents were asked to indicate if they had a professional profile online, either through LinkedIn, their own blog, or an online e-portfolio, and if they considered this profile to be up to date. LinkedIn was the most used platform for compiling a professional profile, with 57 per cent of students having a LinkedIn profile, however only 25.2 per cent kept this profile up to date. Over two-fifths of all students did not have a LinkedIn Profile (43 per cent). Only 16 per cent of students had their own blog, and 11 per cent said it was not updated. Few students reported using online portfolios (11 per cent).

Respondents were also asked to indicate the frequency with which they used social media platforms for professional purposes. The three social media platforms used most often by students for professional purposes were Facebook (41.4 per cent), Instagram (22 per cent) and LinkedIn (17.3 per cent). In terms of the social media used for non-professional purposes, 91 per cent of all students used Facebook to keep up to date with friends, news and entertainment, however, less than one tenth of respondents used LinkedIn (9 per cent) for non-professional purposes. The photo and video sharing social network, Instagram, was regularly used by students (63.5 per cent), showing its growth in popularity compared to platforms such as Twitter (19.3 per cent), Pinterest (22 per cent), Google+ (19 per cent) and Flickr (1.6 per cent), which were rarely used.

Students' self-efficacy in using networking and social media for career purposes is shown in Table 4.1. Self-efficacy was assessed on a four-point scale with 1 indicating little confidence and 4 indicating a high level of confidence. An additional response option of 'not relevant' was included in case participants felt that a particular career competency was irrelevant or unrelated to their discipline.

When the categories of reasonably confident and very confident were combined, it showed that 58.8 per cent of students rated themselves as confident in networking at industry events. This proportion is comparable to those who were confident in creating LinkedIn profiles (56.0 per cent), using social media to build an online professional identity (62.1 per cent), and connecting professionally (66.8 per cent). In contrast, close to two-fifths of all students reported being either not confident or not very confident when asked about networking at industry events (39.7 per cent) or creating an effective LinkedIn profile (40.5 per cent). Similarly, almost a third of students reported low confidence in building a professional social media identity (34.3 per cent) and connecting professionally through social media (30.1 per cent). Fourth-year students were

Table 4.1   *Self-efficacy of respondents in using networking and social media for career purposes*

	Not confident	Not very confident	Reasonably confident	Very confident	Not relevant
Network at an industry event (n=199)	15 (7.5%)	64 (32.2%)	87 (43.7%)	30 (15.1%)	3 (1.5%)
Create an effective LinkedIn profile (n=200)	27 (13.5%)	54 (27.0%)	64 (32.0%)	48 (24.0%)	7 (3.5%)
Use social media to build online professional identity (n=198)	21 (10.6%)	47 (23.7%)	81 (40.9%)	42 (21.2%)	7 (3.5%)
Use social media to connect professionally (n=199)	18 (9.0%)	42 (21.1%)	87 (43.7%)	46 (23.1%)	6 (3.0%)

more confident than first-year students when networking at industry events (p<0.05; F=4.405), however no further differences were found by year of study or previous work experience in relation to these measures. The lack of confidence shown by one-third of the whole sample, linked with the limited variation by age or previous employment, suggests that higher education pedagogies should address these career competencies within discipline degree programs, focusing on developing students' knowing-how, knowing-whom and knowing-why competencies.

Comparison of Work Experience and Social Media Use

One-way analysis of variance enabled us to assess differences in social media use between undergraduate students based on their previous work experience. Comparisons were made between three groups: students with full-time work experience, students with part-time work experience and those with no work experience. Results of the ANOVA and Tukey HSD post-hoc tests revealed that students with work experience were more likely to have an up to date LinkedIn profile (F=4.559; p<0.05), and used LinkedIn for professional purposes more often than those with only part-time or no prior work experience (F=5.273, p<0.01) (see Table 4.2). Students with work experience enrol in university with existing professional connections and therefore may be more likely to use LinkedIn as a way of keeping up to date with industry news and influential career connections compared to those who only work part-time, and perceive their jobs as temporary.

When considering which social media platforms were used for non-professional purposes, significant differences were found in the use of Facebook and Instagram when comparing students with different levels of

Table 4.2   *Mean comparisons of work experience and social networking platform use*

	No work experience (N=14)	Part-time experience (N=98)	Full-time/Career experience (N=99)	Significance
Social Media Use M(sd)*				
Facebook	4.62 (1.61)	5.57 (0.99)	5.27 (1.47)	F=3.719; p=0.033
Instagram	3.15 (2.44)	4.48 (2.04)	3.62 (2.18)	F=4.922; p=0.008
LinkedIn	1.15 (0.38)	1.26 (0.87)	1.78 (1.42)	F=5.273; p=0.006

Note: * Means range from 1–6; higher scores indicate greater usage.

work experience. Students with part-time work experience had the highest frequency of using Facebook for non-professional purposes, compared to students with no work experience (F=3.719; p<0.05). Similarly, students with part-time work experience used Instagram more frequently than other groups (F=4.922; p<0.05).

The open-ended survey question asked participants how they aimed to develop their professional networks while studying. Responses to this item were categorised into four themes: students' confidence about their professional capabilities and career aspirations; students' uncertainty regarding how network connections could be beneficial to them; students' reflections on their own career competencies: and, the benefits of experiential learning and work experience to connectedness learning.

Developing professional capabilities and career aspirations is closely linked to students' networking self-efficacy, however, there were some notable differences between younger (under 21 years) and mature-aged students in their confidence towards using professional capabilities. In responding to the open-ended questions, some mature-aged students indicated that they perceived themselves to be less proficient in using social media professionally than younger students. For example, one final-year mature-aged student with previous work experience suggested that they felt nervous about entering professional employment because they lacked confidence networking with others: "*That's probably why I am afraid of getting out there. I'd love to participate in workshops that would help students create those professionals' links and profiles online.*" Similarly, another mature aged student suggested that activities which focused on "*effectively us[ing] social media platforms and networking sites would be beneficial to many, especially mature-aged students*".

In terms of the benefits of networking for career purposes, some students displayed a single-minded determination to continue developing their knowing-how competency, regardless of work experience, however, those with part-time work experience tended to show a greater awareness of its benefits, both in face-to-face and online contexts. For example, one third-year student who was undertaking part-time work experience in a physiotherapy clinic stated that while they did not yet know how to get the most from the health professionals in the practice, these connections had at least enabled them to get "*a foot in the door*".

When students reflected on their career competencies, they generally valued practical experiential learning, regardless of previous work experience, especially when studying to embrace a different career. As one third-year, mature-aged student with part-time work experience explained: "*My best courses at uni are the ones which are practical. In one course we started a business, we worked together to get something going in 54 hours. This changed my mindset. I realised you can't do it all, you need other people with complementary skills.*" Students in their first and second year of study were generally more uncertain about their professional capabilities and may have limited career aspirations as they are still in a career preparation phase, and thus more reflective than action orientated.

Several students, particularly those in the third year or with prior work experience, also reflected on the benefits of experiential learning in strengthening their connections and career competencies. As one third-year student explained: "*Getting practical and starting a business during the semester made me realise you can think big and you can take that big idea and make it a little smaller and still get the most of what you want and then build it up. This also helps build contacts with mentors outside of uni.*" Furthermore, another school-leaver student described their second-year internship as being "*the best – it helped me land that first entry-level position in journalism*".

DISCUSSION

The results of this study reveal insights into the social connectedness capabilities of USC students through their usage of social media platforms for both professional and non-professional purposes, and, in doing so, outline several key pedagogical implications for educators. A key finding of the survey was that few students utilised social media platforms for professional purposes. Of the seven social media platforms, students used Facebook most often, followed by LinkedIn and Instagram, however, less than 40 per cent used these social media platforms for professional purposes. This finding supports Bridgstock's (2016) research that few students utilise social media for career purposes, highlighting the need for greater awareness and education of the benefits of social media for career connectedness. It also reflects that academics are not fully utilising social media as a tool to support graduate employability within their curricula.

The findings also suggest that non-traditional student populations embrace these new career paradigms to some extent, often studying to transition to careers, by acquiring marketable skills and updating their knowledge and professional networks (Arthur and Rousseau, 1996). Students with previous career experience often possess some social media competencies and have existing professional network connections and competencies, even if not directly relevant to their field of study. These connections include both strong and weak ties, which can be leveraged for their new career, or existing skills which can be used to develop new professional connections. Using LinkedIn as a social media platform can aid in developing further professional social capital, through contacts and professional identity development. In this way, students with work experience are more likely to utilise LinkedIn profession-ally, shaping their identity through their interactions. Their knowing-how and knowing-whom competencies present an unutilised resource for educators.

The survey findings reveal the importance of acknowledging the resources and skills non-traditional students bring, both those with career and part-time work experience. When designing the curriculum, educators should acknowl-edge the different stages students may be at in their professional lives. The patterns of social media use, competencies and confidence identified through the survey highlight the varying proficiencies students bring to – and develop at – university. For example, while more than half have professional profiles on LinkedIn, only a quarter of respondents kept this information up to date. These differences are evident when comparing students with prior career experience, who were more frequent users of LinkedIn and were more likely to have up-to-date profiles compared to those who had only part-time or no previous work experience.

Students with part-time career experience tended to use social media more for non-professional purposes. Despite the potential of developing weak tie professional connections through part-time employment, students working in such roles seemed to view their employment as transitory and tended to focus on social online interactions rather than professional interactions. Facebook and Instagram were the most often utilised social media spaces for these non-professional interactions. In contrast, there was low usage of LinkedIn. This indicates that students with part-time work experience may compart-mentalise their social, professional and future lives, and suggests that their self-concept is closer to that of a student than as a career professional. This approach means they are yet to see the benefits of connectedness competencies for career management. It also highlights potential opportunities for curricu-lum enrichment in relation to both the knowing-how and knowing-why career competencies, particularly early in a degree program, which may support students in making themselves more employable (see Schech et al., 2017).

The qualitative responses to how students develop their professional networks while studying add further support to these findings. Students who were in the earlier stages of their degree tended to express uncertainty about how to develop their professional networks. This was expressed in relation to both developing career capabilities and realising the value and potential benefits of professional networks. As students progressed through their degrees and increased their career connections, they were increasingly able to articulate the value of the knowing-whom competency.

Whilst it may not be surprising that non-traditional students with work experience show greater awareness of the benefits of social media for professional purposes, and are more likely to have a LinkedIn profile, these concepts have not yet fully penetrated HE curriculum pedagogical design. For instance, most universities do not possess well-developed mechanisms for eliciting students' previous work experience. It is rare that soft skills gained through work experience are recognised as prior learning; few institutions employ any formal 'recognition of prior learning' (RPL) process. There is limited focus within curricula to show how students with career experience, even when it is unrelated to their current degree, can leverage their soft or technical skills in pursuing a new career.

Pedagogical Implications

The pedagogical implications of these findings suggest that educators should look towards embedding social media career competencies into the curriculum. This can be achieved by focusing on four approaches. First, it is not enough for educators to simply cultivate knowing-how competencies related to professional social media use. Often non-traditional students should be supported in developing their career aspirations and adaptive preferences for their future careers. If students believe a particular career is out of reach, they may not give it serious consideration, therefore educators should seek to influence these aspirations and develop their self-efficacy. In certain degree programs, such as Business and Communication, there may be a stronger focus on developing a professional social media presence, however these competencies are relevant for all graduates and should be cultivated. The survey revealed that while students utilise LinkedIn professionally, a limited number of students keep their profiles up to date. This suggests a gap between the career competencies of knowing-how (DeFillippi and Arthur, 1996) social media platforms can assist graduate employability, but not necessarily understanding the knowing-why, which can restrict the knowing-whom capability. In other words, students may not understand that employers and collaborators will use LinkedIn to identify the currency of someone's work or career profile. As such, their social connectedness can be limited, preventing the development of social capital and reducing employability.

Second, peer learning is a powerful approach when teaching diverse groups. Educators can design learning activities where students examine and analyse their peers' professional identity through their social media profile. Group activities could also be designed which bring together students with diverse work experience to collaborate and share their knowledge and skills. The analysis and reflective discussion that such opportunities would generate can increase students' awareness of the potential of social media to develop career connections, highlighting avenues through which they can develop and articulate their professional identity.

Third, a personalised bricolage learning activity can be used, where students can self-assess career capabilities and network connections, by reflecting on three questions: "Who am I?", "What do I know?" and "Whom do I know?" The first, "Who am I?" asks students to consider their own strengths, traits, tastes, abilities, passion and interests; in other words, their identity and preferences. "What do I know?" relates to personal knowledge, skills, education and experiences, acknowledging both formal training and education, and knowledge gained through hobbies, and interests. Finally, "Whom do I know?" represents existing social and professional relationships and networks, acknowledging that each individual already forms part of several networks (Barnes and de Villiers Scheepers, 2018). These three questions align with DeFillippi and Arthur's (1994) career competencies by providing a starting point for students to find their own unique capabilities and resources they bring, including how these can be appreciated, developed and leveraged for career purposes through social media connectedness.

Finally, educators can encourage non-traditional students to strengthen, maintain and leverage their professional connections and develop bridging capital of weak ties through work integrated learning activities and volunteering. These learning activities enable students to develop their professional relationships and career capabilities and can often open up further networking opportunities. While the survey findings show that students in the final years of their degrees are more likely to have updated LinkedIn profiles, educators can use a scaffolded approach to curriculum development which aims to raise students' awareness of the importance of professional connections at a foundational level. Intermediate learning opportunities can be designed to develop students' self-efficacy and build relationships beneficial to their career goals. Capstones can then be used to strengthen the bridging social capital through industry projects and involvement. This holistic programmatic approach should be monitored and adapted to ensure it meets the needs of the ever-changing world of work.

CONCLUSION

The purpose of this chapter was to provide an insight into how non-traditional university students use social media platforms for career connections. The changing nature of careers emphasised that graduates are likely to be engaged in flexible, boundaryless and protean employment (see Briscoe and Hall, 2006). This highlights the importance of developing the competencies required for career mobility, which centre on knowing-why, knowing-how, and knowing-whom (DeFillippi and Arthur, 1996). Utilising a sample of 210 students, we identified patterns of social media use within a non-traditional student population. The findings provide opportunities for educators to improve student connectedness using social media to benefit them in future career management. This includes assisting students in developing confidence using social media for professional purposes, developing a broader portfolio of social media spaces, and keeping their professional profiles up to date. The findings also highlight the value of embedding professional social media use for students with limited or no work experience. Students with limited or no previous employment were likely to use Facebook for non-professional purposes only. Therefore, a realignment is required through tertiary education which outlines the benefits of different platforms in preparing well connected graduates who have strong ties to their fields and will subsequently have a greater chance of finding suitable employment after graduating.

Based on the findings, four pedagogical implications were outlined to assist students and educators with developing connectedness capabilities. First, educators should move beyond the knowing-why competencies to explain in greater depth the relevance of knowing-how and knowing-whom career competencies. The aim of this approach is that students would develop greater social capital. Second, peer learning presents as an effective means for teaching in groups with larger non-traditional cohorts. Third, self-assessment of career capabilities and network connections is a valuable learning activity to enhance student 'knowing why' and 'knowing whom' capabilities. Finally, it is important for educators to support students to expand their professional connections and self-efficacy through curriculum development and various work integrated learning projects. Taking these steps can help to prepare students across disciplines for flexible careers by increasing their professional connections and social capital.

NOTE

1. This research was supported by an USC Commissioned Learning and Teaching grant, focused on developing a networked approach to lifelong graduate employability, adhering to ethical standards (USC A/17/983). The authors wish to thank

Dr Inez Mahony for the research assistance provided and Dr Mark Sayers for assisting in the data collection process.

REFERENCES

Arthur, M. B. and Rousseau, D. M. (1996). *The Boundaryless Career: A New Employment Principle for a New Organizational Era*. New York, NY: Oxford University Press.

Aslam, S. (2018). Twitter by the numbers: Stats, demographics and fun facts. Retrieved 4 April 2018 from https://www.omnicoreagency.com/twitter-statistics/.

Australian Broadcasting Corporation. (2017). University education figures. Retrieved 9 September 2017 from http://www.abc.net.au/news/2017-09-18/university-education-figures/8882700.

Barnes, R. and de Villiers Scheepers, M. J. (2018). Tackling uncertainty for journalism graduates: A model for teaching experiential entrepreneurship. *Journalism Practice*, *12*(1), 94–114.

Benson, V. and Morgan, S. (2016). Social university challenge: Constructing pragmatic graduate competencies for social networking. *British Journal of Educational Technology*, *47*(3), 465–473.

Benson, V., Morgan, S. and Filippaios, F. (2014). Social career management: Social media and employability skills gap. *Computers in Human Behavior*, *30*, 519–525.

Bridgstock, R. (2009). The graduate attributes we've overlooked: Enhancing graduate employability through career management skills. *Higher Education Research and Development*, *28*(1), 31–44.

Bridgstock, R. (2016). Educating for digital futures: What the learning strategies of digital media professionals can teach higher education. *Innovations in Education and Teaching International*, *53*(3), 306–315.

Briscoe, J. P. and Hall, D. T. (2006). The interplay of boundaryless and protean careers: Combinations and implications. *Journal of Vocational Behavior*, *69*(1), 4–18.

Briscoe, J. P., Henagan, S. C., Burton, J. P. and Murphy, W. M. (2012). Coping with an insecure employment environment: The differing roles of protean and boundaryless career orientations. *Journal of Vocational Behavior*, *80*(2), 308–316.

Burke, P. J., Bennett, A., Burgess, C., Gray, K. and Southgate, E. (2016). *Capability, Belonging and Equity in Higher Education: Developing Inclusive Approaches*. Newcastle, NSW: Centre of Excellence for Equity in Higher Education, The University of Newcastle.

Chan, K. Y., Moon-ho, R. H., Chernyshenko, O. S., Bedford, O., Uy, M. A., Gomulya, D. … Phan, W. M. J. (2012). Entrepreneurship, professionalism, leadership: A framework and measure for understanding boundaryless careers. *Journal of Vocational Behavior*, *81*(1), 73–88.

Daddow, A. (2016). Curricula and pedagogic potentials when educating diverse students in higher education: Students' Funds of Knowledge as a bridge to disciplinary learning. *Teaching in Higher Education*, *21*(7), 741–758.

de Janasz, S. C. and Forret, M. L. (2008). Learning the art of networking: A critical skill for enhancing social capital and career success. *Journal of Management Education*, *32*(5), 629–650.

de Villiers Scheepers, M. J., Barnes, R., Clements, M. and Stubbs, A. J. (2018). Preparing future-ready graduates through experiential entrepreneurship. *Education+ Training*, *60*(4), 303–317.

DeFillippi, R. J. and Arthur, M. B. (1994). The boundaryless career: A competency-based perspective. *Journal of Organizational Behavior*, *15*(4), 307–324.

DeFillippi, R. J. and Arthur, M. B. (1996). Boundaryless contexts and careers: A competency-based perspective. In M. B. Arthur and D. M. Rousseau (eds), *The Boundaryless Career: A New Employment Principle for a New Organizational Era* (pp. 116–131). New York, NY: Oxford University Press.

Doughney, J. (2007). Women and leadership in corporate Australia: Questions of preference and 'Adaptive Preference'. *Advancing Women in Leadership*, *23*, 1–10.

Eby, L. T., Butts, M. and Lockwood, A. (2003). Predictors of success in the era of the boundaryless career. *Journal of Organizational Behavior*, *24*(6), 689–708.

Gale, T. and Parker, S. (2015). Calculating student aspiration: Bourdieu, spatiality and the politics of recognition. *Cambridge Journal of Education*, *45*(1), 81–96.

Gerli, F., Bonesso, S. and Pizzi, C. (2015). Boundaryless career and career success: The impact of emotional and social competencies. *Frontiers in Psychology*, *6*(1304), 1–17.

Global Entrepreneurship Monitor. (2017). GEM Australia 2016/17 national report. Retrieved 4 February 2018 from http://www.gemconsortium.org/report.

Hess, E. D. (2017). Surviving the digital age: Four corporate transformations. Retrieved 4 April 2018 from https://ideas.darden.virginia.edu/2017/04/surviving-the-digital-age-4-corporate-transformations.

Jackson, D. (2015). Employability skill development in work-integrated learning: Barriers and best practice. *Studies in Higher Education*, *40*(2), 350–367.

Kemp, S. (2018). 11 new people join social media every second (and other impressive stats). Retrieved 5 March 2018 from https://blog.hootsuite.com/11-people-join-social-every-second/.

King, M. D. (2015). Why higher ed and business need to work together. *Harvard Business Review*, Retrieved 20 February 2018 from https://hbr.org/2015/07/why-higher-ed-and-business-need-to-work-together.

Lochab, A. and Mor, K. (2013). Career boundaries in a 'boundaryless' world. *Global Journal of Management and Business Studies*, *3*(2), 119–124.

Mallon, M. (1999). Going 'portfolio': Making sense of changing careers. *Career Development International*, *4*(7), 358–370.

Marr, J. and Wilcox, S. (2015). Self-efficacy and social support mediate the relationship between internal health locus of control and health behaviors in college students. *American Journal of Health Education*, *46*(3), 122–131.

McAloon, C. (2017). Higher education reforms: Fears for future regional universities and student opportunities. *ABC News*. Retrieved 22 November 2017 from http://www.abc.net.au/news/2017-09-18/regional-universities-oppose-higher-education-changes/8949416.

McDonald, P. and Thompson, P. (2016). Social media(tion) and the reshaping of public/private boundaries in employment relations. *International Journal of Management Reviews*, *18*(1), 69–84.

Minten, S. and Forsyth, J. (2014). The careers of sports graduates: Implications for employability strategies in higher education sports courses. *Journal of Hospitality, Leisure, Sport and Tourism Education*, *15*, 94–102.

Phua, J., Jin, S. V. and Kim, J. J. (2017). Uses and gratifications of social networking sites for bridging and bonding social capital: A comparison of Facebook, Twitter, Instagram, and Snapchat. *Computers in Human Behavior*, *72*, 115–122.

Putnam, R. D. (2000). *Bowling Alone: The Collapse and Revival of American Community*. New York, NY: Simon and Schuster.

Raineri, E., Fudge, T. and Hall, L. (2015). Are universities unsocial with social media? In M. Wadha and A. Harper (eds), *Technology, Innovation and Enterprise Transformation* (pp. 164–179). Hershey, PA: Business Science Reference.

Richardson, J., Jogulu, U. and Rentschler, R. (2017). Passion or people? Social capital and career sustainability in arts management. *Personnel Review*, *46*(8), 1835–1851.

Schech, S., Kelton, M., Carati, C. and Kingsmill, V. (2017). Simulating the global workplace for graduate employability. *Higher Education Research and Development*, *36*(7), 1476–1489.

Schuetze, H. G. and Slowey, M. (2002). Participation and exclusion: A comparative analysis of non-traditional students and lifelong learners in higher education. *Higher Education*, *44*(3–4), 309–327.

Shah, R. (2010). *Social Networking for Business (Bonus Content Edition): Choosing the Right Tools and Resources to Fit Your Needs*. Upper Saddle River, NJ: Pearson Prentice Hall.

Shoemaker, A. (2017). A new approach to regional higher education is essential to our economic future. *The Conversation*. Retrieved 23 January 2018 from https://theconversation.com/a-new-approach-to-regional-higher-education-is-essential-to-our-economic-future-88537.

Sullivan, S. E. and Arthur, M. B. (2006). The evolution of the boundaryless career concept: Examining physical and psychological mobility. *Journal of Vocational Behavior*, *69*(1), 19–29.

Sutherland, K. and Ho, S. (2017). Undergraduate perceptions of social media proficiency and graduate employability: A pilot study. *Higher Education, Skills and Work-Based Learning*, *7*(3), 261–274.

Tams, S. and Arthur, M. B. (2010). New directions for boundaryless careers: Agency and interdependence in a changing world. *Journal of Organizational Behavior*, *31*(5), 629–646.

Tomlinson, M. (2017). Forms of graduate capital and their relationship to graduate employability. *Education+Training*, *59*(4), 338–352.

University of the Sunshine Coast. (2017). *Student Statistical Summary*. USC Systems Information Analysis Unit.

Verbruggen, M. (2012). Psychological mobility and career success in the 'new' career climate. *Journal of Vocational Behavior*, *81*(2), 289–297.

5. Social connectedness and graduate employability: exploring the professional networks of graduates from business and creative industries

Ruth Bridgstock, Denise Jackson, Kate Lloyd and Matalena Tofa

INTRODUCTION

'It's not what you know, it's who you know', or so the saying goes. The idea that social connections are important to career success, and can actually be more important than individual knowledge and capabilities, is a common one. It is also an idea that is supported empirically by a raft of studies that demonstrate the relationships between social capital, wages and employment outcomes (Mortensen and Vishwanath, 1994), entrepreneurial success (Ramos-Rodríguez et al., 2010), and career progression (Anderson-Gough, Grey and Robson, 2006), among others. While the notion is often associated with the unfair advantage that class and background can confer over less well connected but more capable individuals, this isn't necessarily the case: through networking behaviour, people from all kinds of backgrounds can obtain career benefit from social connectedness (Wolff and Moser, 2009).

It would appear that networking, if done well, doesn't just yield career benefits for the networker. Developing and maintaining reciprocal relationships with others *for mutual benefit* particularly seems to help us find and secure employment opportunities, obtain access to information and resources, and receive guidance, sponsorship, and support. By contrast, highly instrumental and self-interested 'taking' networking behaviour has been demonstrated to be less effective, and can shrink social networks over time (Gjemmestad and Nasta, 2016).

As a core aspect of the career development repertoire of professionals across all fields, effective networking is underpinned by a range of capabilities that need to be learned, at least in part, through practice (de Janasz and

Forret, 2008). In the twenty-first century, networking has moved online, and professionals now connect via social media, which requires the acquisition of a somewhat different but overlapping set of capabilities to analogue networking (Bridgstock, 2019a).

Given the current near-universal interest in graduate career outcomes among students, parents, industry, the government and universities themselves, one might expect that networking would be a common feature of professional practice curricula. However, in a higher education context that has always focused upon the development of individual disciplinary and (more recently) transferable skills and knowledge, the inclusion of networking in programs is relatively infrequent (Bridgstock, 2017). The outcomes of preliminary survey-based research in the United States and Australia (Benson, Morgan and Filippaios, 2014; Bridgstock, 2019b) indicate that for many students, learning to connect with others professionally online and offline could represent a significant learning opportunity for their employability. The study described in this chapter goes further to describe the professional networks of graduates across three universities and from two very different fields of study. It characterises the extent of their networking capabilities, and identifies learning opportunities through degree programs that will strengthen student employability and career success.

SOCIAL CONNECTEDNESS, NETWORKING AND CAREERS

The majority of research that engages with the effects of social connectedness on career development is concerned with career advancement, including indicators such as job acquisition, promotions, and salary levels. Granovetter (1995) reported that between 40 and 50 per cent of all jobs were acquired through social contacts; in some fields such as the arts, this figure is certainly much higher. Career-orientated social media platforms such as LinkedIn have increased both the reach and impact of social connections. For example, one survey of 3,000 workers found that 85 per cent of them had obtained their most recent roles at least in part through social contacts (Adler, 2016). Members of LinkedIn strongly believe that it can advance their careers, by promoting access to employment opportunities and job acquisition, and facilitating networking (Florenthal, 2015).

The relationship between social connectedness and career advancement has been described in terms of network structures, where 'weak ties' (that is, relationships that are less emotionally intense, with infrequent interaction, and are restricted to one relationship type), may be more likely to provide information about new job opportunities, because weak ties often form bridges between clusters of otherwise unconnected social networks. On the other hand, 'strong ties' (that is, relationships involving more frequent interactions, higher emotional intensity and investment of time and energy) are associated with greater sharing of information and resources, sponsorship and mentoring (Seibert, Kraimer and Liden, 2001), which can help people acquire roles and advance their careers. Studies have demonstrated the utility of weak ties (that is, for improved employment outcomes) (Sharabi and Simonovich, 2017; Zenou, 2013). However, further information on the relationship between weak ties through online networks and graduate employment outcomes is needed; for example, using Facebook network data and graduate outcomes, Mayer (2012) was not able to conclusively demonstrate an association between the use of weak ties and graduate employment. Recent critiques also point out that "assuming a simple dichotomy between the roles of different types of ties" is problematic (Maher and Cawley, 2015, p. 2336), that networks and ties can simultaneously have multiple purposes, not all of which relate to economic motives, and that weak ties can convert to strong ties, or vice versa, over time (Antcliff, Saundry and Stuart, 2016).

Social connectedness does influence career development in other ways than job acquisition and career advancement. For instance, Bridgstock (2019b) discusses socially-based informal learning, which forms the majority of professional enculturation and other knowledge acquisition in workplaces (Eraut, 2004; Webster-Wright, 2009). People who can build and use relationships effectively to learn in an ongoing way are more likely to have up-to-date and relevant skills and knowledge. They are therefore more likely to gain and maintain employment and be successful in professional contexts.

Eraut (2004) notes that in workplaces, while some codified knowledge can be found in textual form, far more uncodified knowledge (often tacit or procedural) is acquired informally. For instance, workplace learning occurs through participation in social activities such as team working. Working alongside others allows people to observe and listen to others at work, which permits transfer of knowledge and expertise, and learning of new practices and perspectives. Working with clients permits learning about the client and their needs. Even if the person is working on a task by themselves, they will receive feedback from others. Informal social learning processes include expert modelling, mentoring, explicit instruction, advice and feedback (Lave and Wenger, 1991).

People also learn professionally through communities and networks beyond the workplace. Balkundi and Kilduff (2005) note that beneath and beyond most formal professional structures and relationships lie a sea of informal ties, which form the basis for important learning. Face-to-face informal professional learning can take the form of a community of practice (Wenger, 1999), involving active relationship building, practice-based interaction, and engagement between individuals with similar interests.

As job roles in the knowledge society continue to change because of digital influences such as automation and increased computer processing power, digital social connections play an important part in helping people learn new capabilities and keep up to date. These connections are not limited to intra-organisational contexts, or face-to-face interactions. Online modes of social informal learning are less likely to employ a community of practice model, but rather a distributed learning network of professionals and other interested people (Albors, Ramos and Hervas, 2008), in which professionals may not even know the people with whom they were interacting, or know them only slightly (that is, weak ties and indirect ties). These networks can be used to obtain 'just in time' quick-turnaround information and skills via social networking sites, obtaining information quickly and then sharing it. This form of social learning is generally much less time and energy intensive than a community of practice model. The other ways that digital networks are often used for learning can be more active, but still rely on weak or indirect ties. These are collective intelligence, and crowdsourced approaches to learning (Leimeister, 2010), one example of which is posting a question to an online industry forum and receiving answers from colleagues all over the world. The power of socially networked learning is such that some theorists have started to suggest that knowledge and capability should not be thought of just in terms of the individual, but instead the individual plus the network to which they have access (Siemens, 2005; Swart and Kinnie, 2014).

It can be seen from the preceding discussion that social connectedness is crucially important for the employability and career success of most people, in terms of their job acquisition, career advancement, and professional learning. People benefit in their careers in different ways from wide networks and strong ties. Wide networks, including online networks, involve people that we don't know well and that can facilitate access to new information and different perspectives. Strong ties such as mentors and close colleagues can provide advice, feedback, resources, support, and facilitation of career opportunities.

It can take some years and several job roles for these professional networks to reach maturity as the individual's career identity and expertise develops. In fact, career identity is shaped through the development of, and exposure to, social networks, which in turn evolve over time (Ibarra and Deshpande, 2007). The relationship between career identity and social network is reciprocal. Social networks shape aspiring members and confer social identity through normative processes. People adapt to new career possibilities through different job and career-related experiences by experimenting with provisional selves. As they pursue chosen identities, they alter their networks and forge new relationships. Thus, it takes time and experience to develop professional social networks, and a career identity. Through these experiences over time, people also develop connectedness capabilities – those needed to grow, navigate and make the most of social networks (both digital and analogue) for professional purposes (Bridgstock, 2019b).

THE PROFESSIONAL NETWORKS AND CONNECTEDNESS CAPABILITIES OF GRADUATES

For many (although not all) graduates from undergraduate programs, the completion of a degree represents an opportunity to pursue new career identities and roles. For school leavers this may be their first career identity, although they may have work experience in non 'career' roles. Mature-aged students will often have previous career identities and networks, and they will therefore also possess some connectedness capabilities, albeit relating to different contexts and roles (see de Villiers Scheepers et al. in Chapter 4 of this volume). Given the importance of professional networks to manifold aspects of career development and success, one might expect that both connectedness capabilities and the professional networks themselves would be included among the learning and teaching priorities that higher education programs seek to address. Jackson (2016) highlights the importance of interaction with the external environment in developing what she terms pre-professional identity, a key aspect of graduate employability. Adopting Wenger's (2006) notion of a landscape of practice, she asserts higher education institutions must facilitate student engagement with relevant communities, including employers, professional associations, clubs and societies, to develop student understanding of and connection with the norms, beliefs and values of their intended profession.

Indeed, for many years constituent elements of connectedness capabilities have commonly been found in university transferable skill/attribute lists around the world, including digital literacies, written and oral communication and team work (Donleavy, 2012). More recently, universities have started to take more holistic approaches to fostering employability beyond transferable skill development. There is also evidence of a growing recognition of the need for connectedness in recent university statements around students' career and leadership readiness and industry engagement (O'Leary, 2017). The category of 'Experience and Networks' is now included in the latest version of the UK Higher Education Academy's (2015) Framework For Embedding Employability in Higher Education, indicating increased sectoral awareness of the need to expose students to professional life. The rise in work integrated learning (WIL) in university employability strategies, catalysed by the National Strategy for WIL (see Universities Australia et al., 2015), evidences the increasing focus on industry engagement. WIL, a form of experiential learning also known as work-based learning or cooperative education, engages students with industry and community partners on authentic learning activities as a formal component of their degree studies. It is considered a valuable opportunity for students to establish and grow their networks, professional enculturation and professional identity development (see Jackson, 2016). An institution-wide evaluation conducted with 1,135 final year undergraduates across 34 WIL units found that one of the most important goals for students when undertaking a WIL unit was enhancing their professional networks (Nay and Corrigan, 2018). Further, the value of WIL in providing professional networking opportunities through industry and community engagement was also highlighted by the low proportion of students (46 per cent) who felt confident using their professional networks to seek work at the beginning of the WIL unit, despite most being in their final year of studies.

Despite the burgeoning interest in connectedness in sector and university publications, studies of the professional networks of students and graduates and the connectedness capabilities that they possess are fairly thin on the ground. The research that does exist indicates that graduates who use their social networks to gain employment tend to have better job acquisition outcomes than those who do not (Jackson, 2014), and may be more likely to acquire jobs that are linked to their degrees and offer good career prospects (Franzen and Hangartner, 2006). Further, in their study of undergraduate Business students, Batistic and Tymon (2017) demonstrated that active industry networking behaviour by students is predictive of enhanced access to career resources and higher perceived employability. Nay and Corrigan (2018) also found that students felt significantly more confident using their professional networks to seek work at the end of a WIL opportunity. However, the professional networks and connectedness capabilities of students and recent graduates can be underdeveloped, and this can be a barrier to their career development and employability.

Bridgstock (2019c) conducted surveys of final year undergraduates across all fields in two Australian universities, and found that more than nine in ten wanted more information about how to network professionally to maximise their career opportunities. The majority of students reported that they had met one employer in their field/s of professional interest (typically through a work integrated learning opportunity), however, nearly one-third said that they had met zero employers. Qualitative follow-ups with a sub-set of the students who had indicated that they knew zero employers revealed that while nearly all had encountered employers through guest lectures, careers fairs or other industry events, some had often not taken the opportunity to speak to the employers or otherwise connected with them individually. Some students were not aware that their teachers at university were industry active and therefore could be included in the category of employers they had met. Others were interpreting 'in their field/s of interest' very narrowly to mean an employer in the specific sub-field that they wanted to enter (such as a user experience design firm vs broader digital design agencies containing user experience design teams).

These findings could all be taken to indicate that many of the students in Bridgstock's study were not yet thinking of the career development possibilities associated with professional networks.

Bridgstock's (2019c) study also suggested that students' professional networks and networking online could be strengthened: while 82 per cent of the final year undergraduates logged in to Facebook every day, only 12 per cent used LinkedIn regularly. Despite acknowledging that networking was important to job acquisition, more than eight in ten recent university graduates surveyed in the study only applied for jobs using direct application methods (e.g. responding to advertisements on job platforms. Social media for professional and career development represents a significant opportunity in university students' career and employability development (Lancaster, 2016). According to one study, merely eight per cent of student members of LinkedIn engage in frequent self-promotion using the platform (Bohnert and Ross, 2010). Repeatedly, it has been demonstrated that informal use of social media by students for personal and social purposes does not translate into confidence or awareness of using these applications for work and career (Benson, Morgan and Filippaios, 2014; Hinrichsen and Coombs, 2014; Pozzi, 2015).

METHOD

The present study used an online self-report survey to provide a comprehensive description of graduates' social network characteristics, their social capital (access to resources, opportunities, sponsorship and support for career purposes), and their connectedness capabilities. Graduates from courses relating to Business (fields of study such as marketing, human resource management, management, economics and finance, innovation and entrepreneurship) and Creative Industries (fields of study from the arts, media and design) were surveyed. The aim was to explore capabilities and networks across diverse fields; that is, from Business where graduates are more likely to pursue 'traditional' careers as employees, and Creative Industries where short-term and part-time contracts and self-employment are very common.

Participants

The sample comprised 620 graduates from Business and Creative Industries undergraduate programs (Business n=338, Creative Industries n=235, double degree n=47) from three metropolitan universities located in different States of Australia (University 1 n=335, University 2 n=128, University 3 n=157). The graduates had completed their courses either one to two years previously (n=296), or four to five years previously (n=324). Their email addresses were retrieved from the universities' official Alumni contact databases. An

Table 5.1   *Demographic profile of participants*

	Graduates 1–2 years after course completion			
	University 1 (n=159)	University 2 (n=67)	University 3 (n=70)	Overall (n=296)
Modal age group (%)	18–24 (60.75%)	18–24 (54.00%)	25–34 (52.57%)	18–24 (58.74%)
% full-time	81.48%	90.20%	79.55%	83.25%
% international	6.48%	38.00%	16.28%	16.42%
% school leaver	67.27%	86.27%	43.18%	66.82%
% first in family	31.78%	32.25%	38.10%	34.50%
% male	29.63%	33.33%	27.27%	30.05%
% Business course	42.76%	71.64%	54.29%	52.03%
% joint Business and CI courses	*6.35%*	*5.97%*	*8.57%*	*8.79%*
	Graduates 4–5 years after course completion			
	University 1 (n=176)	University 2 (n=61)	University 3 (n=87)	Overall (n=324)
Modal age group	25–34 (57.60%)	25–34 (52.63%)	25–34 (43.86%)	25–34 (51.72%)
% full-time	79.23%	79.23%	80.70%	81.42%
% international	6.25%	41.67%	14.93%	13.84%
% school leaver	76.15%	89.74%	42.11%	66.91%
% first in family	33.33%	41.03%	43.86%	35.40%
% male	31.58%	29.13%	31.58%	30.68%
% Business course	48.46%	77.04%	58.62%	56.79%
% joint Business and CI courses	*10.23%*	*3.28%*	*11.49%*	*6.48%*

invitation email and two reminders were sent to all eligible graduates across the period the survey was open from September 2017 to February 2018, and a prize draw for twelve retail store gift cards of $100 or $150 was offered as an incentive. The demographic profile of the participants is shown in Table 5.1. Some differences were observed between the demographic profiles of the universities: University 3 had a greater proportion of non-school leavers participants, and had a higher proportion of 25–34-year-old participants in the 1–2 year graduate range. University 2 had a higher proportion of Business graduate participants than the other two universities, and University 1 had a higher proportion of Creative Industries graduates. These differences are reflective of the balance of the program offerings of the universities.

Measures and Analysis

Social network characteristics. The characteristics of the graduates' social networks were described using a nine-item scale, containing subscales relating to: friends and family and social support; close colleagues (bonding ties); and wider professional networks (bridging ties). These items were adapted from Pinho (2013), and Williams (2006), and were measured using a 1–5 scale ranging from 'strongly disagree' to 'strongly agree'. All items were positively worded.

Social capital. Social capital was measured by a 12-item scale comprising four subscales corresponding to Seibert, Kraimer and Liden's (2001) dimensions of social capital: access to information and opportunities; access to resources; sponsorship; and social support. The chief modification to the scale was to focus on career more broadly rather than intra-organisational and specific-job related factors. All items were positively worded.

Connectedness capabilities. Participants self-rated their connectedness capabilities on a 21-item scale. A total of seven subscales were included, relating to the categories of social network capabilities proposed in Bridgstock's Fellowship (see Bridgstock, 2019c) and piloted in a survey of undergraduate students (social network literacy; constructing a connected professional identity; social network development; social network strengthening and maintenance; working with connections: professional learning; working with connections: career development; working with connections: problem solving). All items were positively worded.

Descriptive statistics for each subscale of social network characteristics, social capital, and connectedness capabilities scales are presented in Table 5.2. For nearly all of the variables included in the survey, the data obtained violated assumptions of normality, so analysis was conducted using non-parametric tests, including Mann-Whitney U tests for comparisons of two independent groups, Kruskall-Wallis tests for comparisons for three or more independent groups, and Wilcoxon signed-ranks test for repeated measures. Both medians and means/standard deviations are reported where relevant in order to provide maximum descriptive information about the data. Where multiple tests of group difference were conducted, a Bonferroni correction was applied to maintain the familywise error rate.

RESULTS

The significant by-group differences across social network characteristics, social capital, and connectedness capabilities are presented textually in the following sections.

Table 5.2   Average ratings for social network characteristics, social capital and connectedness capabilities

	Business graduates (n=338)			Creative industries graduates (n=235)			All graduates (n=620)[a]		
	Mean	SD	Median	Mean	SD	Median	Mean	SD	Median
Social network characteristics subscales									
Close colleagues	3.89	.83	4.00	3.62	.88	3.80	3.80	.86	3.17
Wider networks	3.20	.80	3.17	3.21	.89	3.33	3.21	.83	3.17
Family and friends	4.14	.65	4.17	4.10	.66	4.00	4.14	.66	4.67
Social capital subscales									
Access to information and opportunities	3.42	.86	3.67	3.24	.93	3.33	3.36	.89	3.50
Access to resources	3.54	.75	3.67	3.49	.77	3.67	3.53	.75	3.67
Access to sponsorship	3.43	.90	3.42	3.49	.91	3.67	3.48	.91	3.67
Access to social support	3.54	.84	3.67	3.38	.90	3.33	3.48	.87	3.67
Connectedness capabilities subscales									
Social network literacy	3.29	.99	3.33	3.34	1.04	3.67	3.34	1.01	3.67
Constructing a connected professional identity	3.80	.83	4.00	3.76	.94	4.00	3.80	.86	4.00
Social network development	3.32	.91	3.33	3.35	.98	3.67	3.36	3.67	.94
Social network strengthening and maintenance	3.49	.88	3.67	3.54	.94	4.00	3.54	3.67	.92
Working with connections: professional learning	3.60	.85	4.00	3.74	.83	4.00	3.68	4.00	.84
Working with connections: career development	3.31	.86	3.50	3.26	.95	3.50	3.31	3.50	.90
Working with connections: problem solving	3.92	.76	4.00	3.89	.85	4.00	3.93	4.00	.80

Note: [a] Please note that the overall N includes 47 additional double degree Business/Creative Industries students.

Social Network Characteristics

Overall, the graduates agreed that they possessed enough friend and family ties, and that these were of good quality (mean=4.14, SD=.66, median=4.67). The exception to this was international graduates, who reported significantly lower *friends and family* subscale scores than domestic graduates (U=14,230.500, p<.001). Overall, participants were somewhat less confident about the extent and adequacy of their networks of close colleagues (mean=3.80, SD=.86, median=4.00), and even less confident about their wider networks (mean=3.21, SD=83, median=3.17) ($x^2(2)$=440.542, p<.001) than their friends and family networks. In terms of their close colleague networks, participants tended to agree that they had close colleagues with whom they collaborated well (mean=4.05, SD=.90, median=4.00), but some questioned whether they had enough close colleagues (mean=3.42, SD=1.13, median=4.00). Some did not have one or more career mentors that they could trust (mean=3.50, SD=1.14, median=4.00). With respect to their wider networks, some graduates were not certain whether their professional network was large enough for career development purposes (mean=2.95, SD=1.09, median=3.00), particularly their online professional contacts network (mean=2.95, SD=1.08, median=3.00).

On average, Creative Industries and Business graduates assigned similar ratings to the items relating to the *friends and family* and *wider networks* scales ($x^2(2)$=.30, n.s. and $x^2(2)$=4.03, n.s. respectively), but Creative Industries graduates were less likely to agree that their close professional networks were extensive enough or that they interacted with close colleagues regularly enough. Significantly fewer Creative Industries graduates reported having close colleagues they could trust ($x^2(2)$=19.02, p<.001).

Differences were also found by length of time after graduation. While 1–2 year and 4–5 year graduates were equally likely to agree that they had enough good quality close friends and family ties, 1–2 year graduates were on average significantly less likely than 4–5 year graduates to agree that their close colleague networks were sufficient (U=42,214.500, p<.01). The difference between 1–2 and 4–5 year graduates for *wider networks* was even greater (U=39,242.000, p<.0001), with 4–5 year graduates far more likely to indicate that they had large enough professional networks (U=40,676.000, p<.003), that these networks contained the right kinds of people for their career development (U=40,677.000, p<.002), and that they maintained an extensive network of contacts online (U=38,956.000, p<.0001).

Social Capital

On average, the four subscales of the social capital scale obtained similar ratings, at between 'neutral' and 'agree' (*access to information and opportuni-*

ties mean=3.36, SD=88, median=.88; *access to resources* mean=3.48, SD=86, median=3.67; *sponsorship and mentoring* mean=3.54, SD=.75, median=3.67; *social support* mean=3.48, SD=91, median=3.67). International graduates had significantly lower levels of agreement than domestic graduates to three of the scales: *access to support* (U=14122.500, p<.004), *access to resources* (U=14,437.000, p<.001), and a*ccess to sponsorship and mentoring* (U=14,180.500, p<.003). There was no difference between international and domestic graduates on the *access to information and opportunities* subscale (U=12,401.000, n.s.). More recent graduates indicated lower levels of social capital than 4–5 year graduates across *access to information and opportunities* (U=33,023.000, p<.002), *access to resources* (U=33481.000, p<.006), and *access to social support* (U=33,342.00, p<.004), but not *sponsorship and mentoring* when a Bonferroni correction was applied. Two items that differentiated 1–2 year and 4–5 year graduates were 'I know who to ask about career opportunities' (U=32,688.000, p<.002), and 'I have enough social support for my career development' (U=32,164.000, p<.001). No significant differences in social capital were found by field of study, school leaver status, or first in family status.

Connectedness Capabilities

Of the seven connectedness capabilities subscales, graduates were most confident about their capabilities in *constructing a connected professional identity* (mean=3.80, SD=1.02, median=3.67), and *working with connections: problem solving* (mean=3.93, SD=.80, median=4.00). They were least confident about *working with connections: career development* (mean=3.31, SD=.90, median=3.50), their levels of *social network literacy* (mean=3.34, SD=3.67, median=1.02), and *social network strengthening and maintenance* (mean=3.36, SD=.94, median=3.67). The individual items that obtained the lowest confidence ratings were 'draw upon your professional contacts to find or create work' (mean=3.16, SD=3.00, median=1.19), 'make new contacts online using social media' (mean=3.22, SD=1.15, median=3.00), and 'develop your career by meeting new people at an event' (mean=3.23, SD=1.16, median=4.00).

Graduates who were over the age of 35, and those who had entered university as mature students, were less confident about their capabilities in networking for career development purposes (age $x^2(4)$ 15.941, p<.003; school leavers U=16,030.000, p<.001), and their ability to construct a connected professional identity (age $x^2(4)$=13.503, p<.009; school leavers U=17,143.000, p<.01). This finding was tied to the specific capabilities required to use online social networks and social media to create a connected identity (age $x^2(4)$=16.716, p<.002; school leavers U=16,867, p<.009), and 'making new professional contacts online' (age $x^2(4)=14.725$, p<.005; school leavers U=16,195.000, p<.002). Older graduates lacked confidence in their ability to 'identify opportunities for professional networking' (age $x^2(4)=16.675$, p<.002), while non-school leaver graduates were less confident to 'network effectively at a face to face event' (U=16,354.000, p<.005) and 'use social media to find, obtain or create work' (U=16,356.000, p<.005).

Strong differences in connectedness capabilities were found for international students in comparison with domestic students, this time relating to low confidence in two of the *working with connections* subscales: their capability to learn from social networks (U=15,050.000, p<.0001), and being able to solve problems with others (U=14,264.000, p<.001). Business graduates were also less confident of their *working with connections: professional learning* capabilities than Creative Industries graduates ($x^2(2)=9.474$, p<.009). More specifically, Business students were less confident of their capabilities relating to items 'keeping abreast of developments in your field through social media' ($x^2(2)=10.954$, p<.004), and 'find and take advantage of social opportunities to learn professionally, such as workshops or informal get-togethers' ($x^2(2)=10.513$, p<.005). There was only one difference in the connectedness capability subscales between recent and less recent graduates, once the Bonferroni correction was applied – that of *working with connections: problem solving*, in which 1–2 year graduates were significantly less confident of their capabilities in this area than 4–5 year graduates (U=27,986.000, p<.009).

DISCUSSION

The survey findings indicate that graduates up to five years after course completion believe that they don't have enough professional contacts. At 1–2 years after course completion, graduates report that both close professional ties and wider networks need development. By 4–5 years after course completion, the quality and quantity of close professional ties is better, presumably in part because of more experience in professional workplaces over time. This perception of inadequate professional networks raises concerns given their importance for accessing the hidden job market (Hansen, 2013).

Social network literacy, networking and acquiring new connections, and using networks for career development are identified in the analysis as key capability sets for development, including being able to articulate how social networks are important to a career, developing new contacts, either online or face to face, and drawing upon professional contacts to help with career development. This emphasises the need for higher education providers to engage students in career development learning that targets connectedness. Specifically, this engagement should include how students can effectively develop and maintain networks, how they should be used for career development purposes, and – in particular – provide students with access to relevant networks during their university years. The latter may be achieved, for example, through on- and off-campus networking events in conjunction with employers, industry bodies and professional associations. There is particular underconfidence among graduates about social media and online networking, emphasising the importance of formally introducing students to valuable platforms, such as LinkedIn, and how to use them effectively.

Graduates moving into Creative Industries particularly appear to feel that their close colleague networks are inadequate. This may be reflective of the relatively higher likelihood of self-employment (than organisationally-based careers) in creative industries, and the greater importance of networks for work allocation (Antcliff, Saundry and Stuart, 2016). Educators in this discipline area may consider introducing industry mentoring interventions that may develop trusting relationships proven useful for career counselling, advice and support purposes (for example Adler and Stringer, 2018). Conversely, Business graduates may be less confident engaging in professional learning via networks, for instance through social media or through workshops, and informal get-togethers. Again, this highlights the value of targeted interventions which may involve industry members facilitating both face-to-face and virtual sessions for developing dimensions of student employability or discipline-specific skills and knowledge.

Older students and non-school-leavers, such as those who have come to university to retrain and follow a different career path, would benefit from additional learning opportunities and support to develop their professional identities and professional networks, and to make the most of social media for career development. This may be achieved through WIL where students engage with industry through authentic learning and assessment activities such as internships or practicums, or less immersive experiences such as industry-based projects, consultancies or field work. WIL is increasingly acknowledged as a valuable platform for professional identity development, through exposing students to the reality of the work setting and professional ideology, and providing access to networks (Jackson, 2017).

The findings with respect to international graduates indicate that they are a distinctive group with particular support and development needs. It can be inferred that some international students feel isolated, with insufficient family and friend networks. The international graduates report much lower levels of social capital (particularly access to support, resources and mentoring) than domestic graduates. Quite separate from the finding that all students would benefit from learning experiences targeted at developing and using social networks for career development, international graduates can also be concerned that they don't have the workplace capabilities required to work with connections to solve problems, and to engage in professional learning via their social networks. Further, international students have relatively weak access to professional networks given they find it more difficult to secure WIL opportunities as they are less favoured by local employers due to perceived inadequacies in English language skills and concerns with cultural immersion (Gribble et al., 2014).

As expected, findings confirm that more recent graduates perceive their networks, social capital and connectedness as less adequate than those graduates who have been immersed in professional life for a longer period. This, and the relatively weak ratings in areas previously outlined, highlight a clear need for targeted career development learning interventions in higher education to improve graduating students' social connectedness and thus their employability. Evidence suggests that career development learning may be more effective if embedded into the curriculum, more specifically assessment, to maximise student outcomes (Bridgstock, 2009; Jorre de St Jorre and Oliver, 2018).

CONCLUSION

The research described in this chapter characterises the professional networks and social capital of recent Australian higher education graduates from Creative Industries and Business disciplines, and identifies opportunities for augmentation and strengthening of students' social capital while they are at university, particularly those who are likely to be less well connected, such as first in family and international students. The study clearly illuminates a need for higher education to better engage students with effective ways to network professionally, particularly through online means, and provide them with access to relevant and meaningful networks. Higher education educators need to carefully consider how they can engage the broader student body to enhance their social connectedness, as well as develop targeted interventions for certain student groups.

A limitation of the study is its reliance on self-report data which some consider unreliable for gauging learning and development (see for example Sitzmann et al., 2010) and concern for common method variance, given data were gathered using one survey instrument at one particular time point (Podsakoff et al., 2003). The latter, however, is somewhat alleviated by the multi-institutional and transdisciplinary research design, drawing on more than one sample of graduates. In relation to directions for future research, extending the study to other disciplines may add further insight. Complementing the survey findings with qualitative data, gathered via focus groups or semi-structured interviews with graduates, may enrich our understanding beyond the status of graduates' social connectedness as to why and how certain groups are better connected than others, and the challenges faced in the process of networking and connecting with others.

REFERENCES

Adler, L. (2016). New survey reveals 85% of all jobs are filled via networking. Retrieved 2 January 2018 from https://www.linkedin.com/pulse/new-survey-reveals-85-all-jobs-filled-via-networking-lou-adler/.

Adler, R. and Stringer, C. (2018). Practitioner mentoring of undergraduate accounting students: Helping prepare students to become accounting professionals. *Accounting and Finance*, 58(4), 939–963.

Albors, J., Ramos, J. C. and Hervas, J. L. (2008). New learning network paradigms: Communities of objectives, crowdsourcing, wikis and open source. *International Journal of Information Management*, 28(3), 194–202.

Anderson-Gough, F., Grey, C. and Robson, K. (2006). Professionals, networking and the networked professional. In R. Greenwood and R. Suddaby (eds), *Professional Service Firms (Research in the Sociology of Organizations, Volume 24)* (pp. 231–256). Greenwich, CT: JAI Press.

Antcliff, V., Saundry, R. and Stuart, M. (2016). Networks and social capital in the UK television industry: The weakness of weak ties. *Human Relations*, 60(2), 371–393.

Balkundi, P. and Kilduff, M. (2005). The ties that lead: A social network approach to leadership. *The Leadership Quarterly*, 16(6), 941–961.

Batistic, S. and Tymon, A. (2017). Networking behaviour, graduate employability: A social capital perspective. *Education+ Training*, 59(4), 374–388.

Benson, V., Morgan, S. and Filippaios, F. (2014). Social career management: Social media and employability skills gap. *Computers in Human Behavior*, 30, 519–525.

Bohnert, D. and Ross, W. H. (2010). The influence of social networking web sites on the evaluation of job candidates. *Cyberpsychology, Behavior, and Social Networking*, 13(3), 341–347.

Bridgstock, R. (2009). The graduate attributes we've overlooked: Enhancing graduate employability through career management skills. *Higher Education Research and Development*, 28(1), 31–44.

Bridgstock, R. (2017). The university and the knowledge network: A new educational model for 21st century learning and employability. In M. Tomlinson (ed.), *Graduate Employability in Context: Research, Theory and Debate*. London: Palgrave Macmillan.

Bridgstock, R. (2019a). Educational practices for employability and career development learning through social media: Exploring the potential of LinkedIn. In J. Higgs, D. Horsfall, S. Cork and A. Jones (eds),

Challenging Future Practice Possibilities. Rotterdam: Sense-Brill Publishers.

Bridgstock, R. (2019b). Graduate Employability 2.0: Education for work in a networked world. In J. Higgs, G. Crisp and W. Letts (eds), *Education for Employability: The Employability Agenda* (pp. 268–282). Rotterdam: Sense-Brill Publishers.

Bridgstock, R. (2019c). *Graduate Employability 2.0: Enhancing the Connectedness of Learners, Teachers and Higher Education Institutions. Final Report of the National Senior Teaching Fellowship.* Canberra: Department of Education and Training.

de Janasz, S. C. and Forret, M. L. (2008). Learning the art of networking: A critical skill for enhancing social capital and career success. *Journal of Management Education, 32*(5), 629–650.

Donleavy, G. (2012). Proclaimed graduate attributes of Australian universities: Patterns, problems and prospects. *Quality Assurance in Education, 20*(4), 341–356.

Eraut, M. (2004). Informal learning in the workplace. *Studies in Continuing Education, 26*(2), 247–273.

Florenthal, B. (2015). Applying uses and gratifications theory to students' LinkedIn usage. *Young Consumers, 16*(1), 17–35.

Franzen, A. and Hangartner, D. (2006). Social networks and labour market outcomes: The non-monetary benefits of social capital. *European Sociological Review, 22*(4), 353–368.

Gjemmestad, S. and Nasta, L. E. (2016). Sharing is Caring: Reciprocal Behaviors and Professional Networking. Retrieved 2 January 2018 from https://brage.bibsys.no/xmlui/bitstream/handle/11250/2444114/MSc0612016.pdf?sequence=1.

Granovetter, M. (1995). *Getting a Job: A Study of Contacts and Careers.* Chicago: University of Chicago Press.

Gribble, N., Dender, A., Lawrence, E., Manning, K. and Falkmer, T. (2014). International WIL placements: Their influence on student professional development, personal growth and cultural competence. *Asia Pacific Journal of Cooperative Education, 15*(2), 107–117.

Hansen, K. (2013). *A Foot in the Door: Networking Your Way into the Hidden Job Market.* Cleveland, Ohio: Ten Speed Press.

Higher Education Academy. (2015). Framework for embedding employability in higher education. Retrieved 2 January 2018 from https://www.heacademy.ac.uk/system/files/downloads/embedding-employability-in-he.pdf.

Hinrichsen, J. and Coombs, A. (2014). The five resources of critical digital literacy: A framework for curriculum integration. *Research in Learning Technology, 21*, 1–16.

Ibarra, H. and Deshpande, P. H. (2007). Networks and identities: Reciprocal influences on career processes and outcomes. In H. Gunz and M. Peiperl (eds), *Handbook of Career Studies* (pp. 268–282). Thousand Oaks, CA: Sage.

Jackson, D. (2014). Factors influencing job attainment in recent bachelor graduates: Evidence from Australia. *Higher Education, 68*(1), 135–153.

Jackson, D. (2016). Re-conceptualising graduate employability: The importance of pre-professional identity. *Higher Education Research and Development, 35*(5), 925–939.

Jackson, D. (2017). Developing pre-professional identity in undergraduates through work-integrated learning. *Higher Education, 74*(5), 833–853.

Jorre de St Jorre, T. and Oliver, B. (2018). Want students to engage? Contextualise graduate learning outcomes and assess for employability. *Higher Education Research and Development, 37*(1), 44–57.

Lancaster, T. (2016). Teaching students about online professionalism: Enhancing student employability through social media. In V. Benson and S. Morgan (eds), *Social Media and Networking: Concepts, Methodologies, Tools, and Applications* (pp. 1784–1805). Hershey: IGI Global.

Lave, J. and Wenger, E. (1991). *Situated Learning: Legitimate Peripheral Participation*. Cambridge: Cambridge University Press.

Leimeister, J. M. (2010). Collective intelligence. *Business and Information Systems Engineering, 2*(4), 245–248.

Maher, G. and Cawley, M. (2015). Social networks and labour market access among Brazilian migrants in Ireland. *Journal of Ethnic and Migration Studies, 41*(14), 2336–2356.

Mayer, A. (2012). The structure of social networks and labour market success. *Applied Economics Letters, 19*(13), 1271–1274.

Mortensen, D. T. and Vishwanath, T. (1994). Personal contacts and earnings: It is who you know! *Labour Economics, 1*(2), 187–201.

Nay, C. and Corrigan, L. (2018). *Professional and Community Engagement (PACE): 2017 Evaluation Report*. Sydney: Macquarie University.

O'Leary, S. (2017). Enhancing graduate attributes and employability through initiatives with external partners. *Practice and Evidence of the Scholarship of Teaching and Learning in Higher Education, 12*(3), 505–518.

Pinho, J. C. (2013). The e-SOCAPIT scale: A multi-item instrument for measuring online social capital. *Journal of Research in Interactive Marketing, 7*(3), 216–235.

Podsakoff, P. M., MacKenzie, S. B., Lee, J. Y. and Podsakoff, N. P. (2003). Common method biases in behavioral research: A critical review of the literature and recommended remedies. *Journal of Applied Psychology*, *88*(5), 879–903.

Pozzi, M. (2015). 'Create a Better Online You': Designing online learning resources to develop undergraduate social media skills. *International Journal of Social Media and Interactive Learning Environments*, *3*(4), 305–321.

Ramos-Rodríguez, A.-R., Medina-Garrido, J.-A., Lorenzo-Gómez, J.-D. and Ruiz-Navarro, J. (2010). What you know or who you know? The role of intellectual and social capital in opportunity recognition. *International Small Business Journal*, *28*(6), 566–582.

Seibert, S. E., Kraimer, M. L. and Liden, R. C. (2001). A social capital theory of career success. *Academy of Management Journal*, *44*(2), 219–237.

Sharabi, M. and Simonovich, J. (2017). Weak ties for a weak population: Expanding personal social networks among the unemployed to increase job-seeking success. *Journal of Employment Counseling*, *54*(1), 12–22. doi: 10.1002/joec.12047.

Siemens, G. (2005). Connectivism: A learning theory for the digital age. *International Journal of Instructional Technology and Distance Learning*, *2*(1).

Sitzmann, T., Ely, K., Brown, K. G. and Bauer, K. N. (2010). Self-assessment of knowledge: A cognitive learning or affective measure? *Academy of Management Learning and Education*, *9*(2), 169–191.

Swart, J. and Kinnie, N. (2014). Reconsidering boundaries: Human resource management in a networked world. *Human Resource Management*, *53*(2), 291–310.

Universities Australia, Australian Chamber of Commerce and Industry, Australian Industry Group, Business Council of Australia, and Australian Collaborative Education Network Limited (2015). National strategy on work integrated learning in university education. Retrieved 2 January 2018 from http://acen.edu.au/wp-content/uploads/2015/11/National-WIL-Strategy-in-university-education-032015.pdf?x99824.

Webster-Wright, A. (2009). Reframing professional development through understanding authentic professional learning. *Review of Educational Research*, *79*(2), 702–739.

Wenger, E. (1999). *Communities of Practice: Learning, Meaning and Identity*. Cambridge: Cambridge University Press.

Wenger, E. (2006). Introduction to communities of practice: A brief overview of the concept and its uses. Retrieved 2 January 2018 from http://wenger-trayner.com/introduction-to-communities-of-practice/.

Williams, D. (2006). On and off the 'net: Scales for social capital in an online era. *Journal of Computer-Mediated Communication, 11*(2), 593–628.

Wolff, H.-G. and Moser, K. (2009). Effects of networking on career success: A longitudinal study. *Journal of Applied Psychology, 94*(1), 196–206.

Zenou, Y. (2013). Social interactions and the labor market. *Revue d'économie politique, 123*(3), 307–331.

PART II

Connectedness pedagogies

6. Connectedness pedagogies

Ruth Bridgstock and Neil Tippett

INTRODUCTION

The first section of this volume explored what connectedness capabilities are, characterising the connectedness of higher education students and graduates in different fields, and demonstrating some of the career and broader life outcomes that can result from an individual's ability to forge and then make the most of their social networks. This section starts to consider the role that higher education can play in fostering these capabilities, examining the learning experiences and pedagogic approaches that can support graduates' connectedness, both face-to-face, and via digital platforms including social media.

Pedagogic thinking in higher education has come a long way in the last few years. There is now widespread acknowledgement that students require more nuanced, and qualitatively different, pedagogic strategies in order to develop their capabilities so that they can live and work productively and meaningfully in an increasingly dynamic and complex society. The familiar transmissive lecture-tutorial model that has been the hallmark of many degree programs in higher education since the inception of the industrial age university has come under fire. However, evidence suggests that it is still the dominant approach used within much of the contemporary university, despite the widespread shift to blended and online modes of delivery that might be expected to disrupt it.

In part, this adherence to old models of pedagogy may be because educators now need to teach at scale. We have moved from elite models of higher education where only a select few attend university to massified and 'populist' models where hundreds, if not thousands, of students are enrolled in courses simultaneously. It may also be because the adoption of different pedagogies requires a significant shift in teachers' thinking about how teaching should be conducted, a process which must be supported through the development of new teacher capabilities; a significant challenge when considering the time-poor teaching context. In part, it may also be symptomatic of the teaching spaces and resources (both physical and virtual) provided by universities. Tiered lecture theatres and traditional learning management systems are geared towards promoting transmissive (learning through transmission of information), or at best transactional (learning through interaction with learning material), approaches to teaching.

Despite the persistence of the transmissive model, higher education has recently begun to see the rise of highly connected and networked learning experiences, such as work integrated learning and the adoption of authentic, situated pedagogies, particularly within capstone courses. Industry, community, alumni and student consultation, and in some instances overt collaborative processes, are being employed to develop and deliver a more meaningful curriculum. By offering direct engagement and interaction with industry and community, including via professional events and social media, these pedagogies and practices are moving students beyond the physical and virtual walls of the university, fostering both their connectedness capabilities and their actual connections and networks.

This chapter explores current pedagogic approaches in higher education by considering how they align with graduate employability, and how they could be adapted to better support graduates in developing their connectedness capabilities. Building upon this, the chapter examines how higher education can use connectedness learning to support graduate outcomes, setting out seven principles which can guide pedagogic practice, and outlining seven existing pedagogic strategies that have shown a demonstrated impact in enhancing graduates' connectedness capabilities. Finally, the chapter introduces four empirical studies (covered in Chapters 7–10 of this volume), which explore how connectedness pedagogies have been integrated into higher education learning and teaching in different universities, and the impact they have had on student connectedness and graduate outcomes.

TEACHING FOR CONNECTEDNESS

Until relatively recently, most university students enrolled in conventional degree programs would have been offered few opportunities to form meaningful professional connections outside of their institutions prior to graduation. Any connections formed inside the university, such as with fellow students or teachers, were largely incidental to educational experiences, which focused primarily on developing disciplinary skills and knowledge. The extent and development of students' connectedness capabilities were not a focus of university learning, and, for the most part, were left to chance. As a result, proactive, career-engaged students, and those with prior career experiences, tended to be more capable networkers and thus were advantaged in their careers. School leavers with little or no career experience, and those from diverse backgrounds without access to existing family-based networks, were at a disadvantage.

Traditional university pedagogy is typically classroom-based. There are exceptions to this, particularly for degree programs where 'hands-on' skill development is required (often for professional accreditation), such as health practice, teaching, and the arts. However, for many disciplines, there has traditionally been relatively little explicit and authentic connection to the world or people outside the classroom. Under this pedagogic model, opportunities for students to develop their interpersonal communication, teamwork, and collaborative skills are largely limited to group work involving other students (Rossin and Hyland, 2003). This form of collaborative learning corresponds with the *working with connections* capability of the Connectedness Learning Model, however, such experiences can lack authenticity and are often unpopular among students. Furthermore, being able to work with connections is only one subset of the connectedness capabilities that graduates require in the world of professional work. Tailoring these learning experiences to offer 'real life' industry/community linked problem-based learning tasks, while at the same time ensuring diversity of group members, including diversity of disciplinary background, could provide students with greater opportunities for connectedness learning. Furthermore, such authentic collaboration would also support students in *making* and *strengthening connections*, *building a connected identity*, or becoming *social network literate*, however, these core connectedness capabilities are often overlooked in student group work scenarios, and in higher education learning and teaching more generally.

Universities are only just starting to recognise the important role that social connectedness plays in education, life and work, however, some of the pedagogies that they can use to support it are already in place. The rise of the graduate employability agenda in higher education has led to many universities already embedding connectedness pedagogies within their curricula, as these approaches are also known to foster students' employability skills more broadly. Authentic learning – that is, learning that focuses on real-world, complex problems and their solutions, addressed in real-world ways (Stein, Isaacs and Andrews, 2004) – is a key principle that underlies these pedagogic approaches. Part of the authenticity in this type of learning can be the development and use of social connections for work and career related activities.

Work integrated learning (WIL) is one type of authentic learning. It brings together learning and productive work with theory and practice through the use of learning that is situated within the act of working (Cooper, Orrell and Bowden, 2010). This includes work which is performed in service to the community. WIL has become ubiquitous in higher education, particularly in capstone courses, but also distributed throughout the curriculum and in co-curricular programs (Jackson, 2015). It encompasses a range of pedagogic approaches (Gannaway and Sheppard, 2017), which include:

- *Work Placements/Internships*: Students undertake short- or long-term placements in a relevant place of work (including public sector agencies, professional bodies, industry partners and community organisations).
- *Projects:* These may be commissioned through clients, developed by industry or community partners to meet a specific need or problem, or designed by students themselves as a way of solving problems or creating new knowledge.
- *Entrepreneurship:* Students undertake specific activities that develop their own intellectual property, business or social enterprise in order to address a need or fill an identified gap in the current market.
- *Field observations and study tours:* Opportunities in which students are exposed to a professional working environment or other location outside the university, allowing them to observe the application of theory into practice, and in some instances apply their learning to practice.

WIL can be an effective approach to foster both students' connectedness and their connectedness capabilities in an authentic way (Billett, 2009). Several studies have shown that undertaking WIL with an employer can be a pathway into employment with that employer (Brooks and Youngson, 2016; Jackson and Collings, 2018), in part through the development of a trusting work relationship during the WIL experience. A range of work relationships can be established and developed when the student goes on site to undertake a place-ment or internship, but industry partnered projects and enterprise activities can also be opportunities to foster connectedness.

WIL is not the only way that students can start to develop connections beyond the university. Industry mentoring programs, professional network-ing events, guest lectures and opportunities to interact with industry active teaching staff are all ways to make connections that can then be strengthened through further interaction and collaboration. Co-curricular opportunities such as student leadership roles and volunteering can also grow connections and associated capabilities, as can paid work. Students-as-partners initiatives are one type of student leadership role that can be used to foster *working with connections* capabilities, while at the same time developing other employabil-ity skills (Cook-Sather, Bovill and Felten, 2014). In these initiatives, students work with one another and/or with university-based collaborators to enhance learning and teaching, develop curriculum, and strengthen the broader student experience.

Social media and ePortfolios represent another important set of oppor-tunities to connect students into much wider networks. As Bridgstock and

Tippett discussed in Chapter 1, digital networks can expand the reach of students' learning, career development, and work activities by helping them to form and maintain weak and indirect ties online. LinkedIn is a particularly useful tool in supporting the development of social network literacies and professional branding, providing stellar opportunities to make connections and weak ties. Although strengthening connections and getting to know people well professionally is still primarily the purview of face-to-face interaction, digital networks can nurture students' ability to form, maintain and use social networks (Bridgstock, 2019a). Through using social media and ePortfolios, students also learn how to represent themselves, their capabilities and their work online, and become familiar with using digital tools to find and learn about others (Pozzi, 2015). From this, they can practice building and using their wider digital networks in an authentic way, opening up digital platforms as an important source of formal and informal learning (Ito et al., 2014). While concerns are often raised about the risks to privacy and safety resulting from student learning activity on social media, being able to manage these risks is part of being social network literate and should be included in connectedness curricula (Bridgstock, 2019a).

CONNECTEDNESS PEDAGOGIES

Based on this evidence, the Connectedness Learning Approach outlines seven key pedagogic approaches which represent the differing ways in which universities can foster learners' professional networks and connectedness capabilities. These connectedness pedagogies were initially synthesised from the findings of a series of in-depth interviews with higher education graduates and teachers, along with a review of the literature (Bridgstock, 2019b). The implementation of each pedagogic strategy should be undertaken to maximise the development of learners' connectedness capabilities, bearing in mind that each pedagogic strategy has different strengths, and that for optimal results they be implemented as part of a complementary suite of strategies. The seven connectedness pedagogies are:

1. *Work integrated learning:* learning that occurs at the intersection and engagement of theoretical and practice learning – for-credit learning that incorporates key elements of the workplace, including:
    internships and work placements, practice;
    industry/community-partnered projects;
    collaborative student projects (particularly cross-disciplinary);
    enterprise and entrepreneurship learning, start-ups;
    study tours.

2. *Industry teaching and engagement:* direct industry teaching into programs, including industry guest lectures and seminars, career mentoring programs, face-to-face and online networking events and fora, sessional teaching by industry-active staff and informational interviewing programs.
3. *Alumni teaching and engagement:* teaching approaches, as for 'industry teaching and engagement' above, with a specific emphasis on program graduates or broader disciplinary area.
4. *Co-curricular activities:* facilitation, support and recognition (formal or otherwise) for activities undertaken by students outside the formal curriculum, such as volunteering, student leadership roles, community engagement and service learning, and paid work.
5. *Student partnerships:* students work with one another and/or with university-based collaborators to enhance learning and teaching, the broader student experience or other university functions. This includes 'students as partners' initiatives, clubs and societies, university ideas jams and student representation of the program/faculty/university at external events. These collaborations may or may not be included in co-curricular support and recognition schemes.
6. *Social media and ePortfolios:* developing and maintaining a professional online presence, e.g. through ePortfolios, LinkedIn and other social media platforms. Through individual development of social media profiles and ePortfolios, students can evidence formal and informal learning and capability development and provide artefacts in support of this.
7. *Connected learning:* online and face-to-face learning through open, industry authentic collaborative and social mechanisms and networks (e.g. blogs, Twitter). Connected learning is learning that occurs through communities of enquiry and practice, and also distributed via online and offline networks. Connected Learning is often based in inquiry, problem-solving, creativity, communication and collaboration.

Underlining the implementation of these strategies, the Connectedness Learning Approach also sets out seven key connectedness learning principles which guide higher education learning and teaching in effectively supporting students' connectedness capabilities. These principles are:

- The learning is authentic and occurs in real professional contexts, involving professional activities and interactions with professionals. This could involve the use of open, industry-authentic tools and technologies.
- Students co-design a learning experience that is meaningful for them.
- Industry/community partners provide input into designing a learning experience that is meaningful for them.

- Partners are carefully selected for alignment with student and program needs and will benefit from/find value in the partnership themselves.
- Appropriate just-in-time resources and learning activities are provided to help students connect with networks effectively.
- The program is tailored to partner, learning context and specific student needs.
- Students maintain the connections they have made and continue to benefit from them, including having ongoing engagement with the program (e.g. as alumni).

This volume includes four chapters that focus on connectedness pedagogies, their implementation, and the outcomes of this across three universities.

Chapter 7 evaluates an attempt to integrate connectedness learning into a third-year careers and employability course within one Australian university. Using LinkedIn as a pedagogical tool to support career identity development and connections with professional networks, Brown et al. report that students were able to recognise the value that connectedness could offer for future employment. Using digital social networks to connect with others, reflect on employability strengths and weakness, and establish career goals were all identified as positive outcomes of the program. The authors outline a series of recommendations for both educators and careers and employability specialists through which connectedness learning can be embedded within courses to support graduate employability.

In Chapter 8, Radoll et al. explore the cultural interface in connectedness learning by considering Indigenous and non-Indigenous approaches to knowing, learning and connecting. Connectedness, with people, places and things, is a core component of Aboriginal and Torres Strait Islander culture and pedagogy. Applying Yunkaporta's (2009) 8 Ways of Learning within three undergraduate subjects, this chapter explores ways in which contemporary modes of university learning might be beneficially adjusted by blending with Indigenous ways of learning and connecting. Drawing parallels between the Connectedness Learning Approach and Indigenous and non-Indigenous pedagogy, the authors discuss how the outcomes of this pilot project could be further applied in developing a genuine cultural interface for connectedness learning that could be adopted across the higher education sector.

In Chapter 9, Goodwin et al. consider how connectedness learning can be applied through the use of capstones: final-year units which aim to consolidate students' learning and orient them towards future work or study. Discussing the redesign and re-imagining of a selection of final-year capstone units in the Bachelor of Arts program at the University of Melbourne, the authors describe five principles for creating an authentic, connected capstone experience. The chapter explores the challenges and insights encountered throughout the redesign process, and provides advice and practical recommendations to support educators and learning designers in changing their own capstone programs to offer students an authentic, connected learning experience.

In the final case study within this section, Chapter 10 documents a university-wide initiative to transform curriculum, pedagogy and assessment practices within the University of Wollongong, with a view to providing students with learning experiences that support the development of twenty-first century employability skills. Focusing specifically on the pedagogical aspects of the model that align with connectedness learning, namely first-year experience, blended learning, ePortfolios, cross-cultural and interdisciplinary learning, and capstones, Bedford and Bell, explore how this model has been implemented across the institution, and provide a preliminary consideration of its impact in supporting students' connectedness capabilities.

REFERENCES

Billett, S. (2009). Realising the educational worth of integrating work experiences in higher education. *Studies in Higher Education, 34*(7), 827–843.

Bridgstock, R. (2019a). Educational practices for employability and career development learning through social media: Exploring the potential of LinkedIn. In J. Higgs, D. Horsfall, S. Cork and A. Jones (eds), *Challenging Future Practice Possibilities*. Rotterdam: Sense-Brill Publishers.

Bridgstock, R. (2019b). *Graduate Employability 2.0: Enhancing the Connectedness of Learners, Teachers and Higher Education Institutions. Final Report of the National Senior Teaching Fellowship*. Canberra: Department of Education and Training.

Brooks, R. and Youngson, P. L. (2016). Undergraduate work placements: An analysis of the effects on career progression. *Studies in Higher Education, 41*(9), 1563–1578.

Cook-Sather, A., Bovill, C. and Felten, P. (2014). *Engaging Students as Partners in Learning and Teaching: A Guide for Faculty*. New York, NY: John Wiley and Sons.

Cooper, L., Orrell, J. and Bowden, M. (2010). *Work Integrated Learning: A Guide To Effective Practice*. London: Routledge.

Gannaway, D. and Sheppard, K. (2017). WIL in liberal arts programs: New approaches. In T. Bowen and M. T. B. Drysdale (eds), *Work-Integrated Learning in the 21st Century: Global Perspectives on the Future* (pp. 51–66). Bingley, UK: Emerald Publishing.

Ito, M., Gutierrez, K., Livingstone, S., Penuel, B., Rhodes, J., Salen, K. … Watkins, S. C. (2014). Connected learning: An agenda for research and design. Retrieved 8 January 2018 from http://dmlhub.net/publications/connected-learning-agenda-for-research-and-design/.

Jackson, D. (2015). Employability skill development in work-integrated learning: Barriers and best practice. *Studies in Higher Education*, *40*(2), 350–367.

Jackson, D. and Collings, D. (2018). The influence of work-integrated learning and paid work during studies on graduate employment and underemployment. *Higher Education*, *76*(3), 403–425.

Pozzi, M. (2015). 'Create a better online you': Designing online learning resources to develop undergraduate social media skills. *International Journal of Social Media and Interactive Learning Environments*, *3*(4), 305–321.

Rossin, D. and Hyland, T. (2003). Group work-based learning within higher education: An integral ingredient for the personal and social development of students. *Mentoring and Tutoring*, *11*(2), 153–162.

Stein, S. J., Isaacs, G. and Andrews, T. (2004). Incorporating authentic learning experiences within a university course. *Studies in Higher Education*, *29*(2), 239–258.

Yunkaporta, T. (2009). *Aboriginal pedagogies at the cultural interface*. Doctor of Education PhD thesis, James Cook University, Townsville, Qld.

7. Connectedness learning in the life sciences: LinkedIn as an assessment task for employability and career exploration

Jason L. Brown, Michael Healy, Louise Lexis and Brianna L. Julien

INTRODUCTION

"You've been doing employability the wrong way" would be the click-bait headline if this chapter were to be published in an online news website. The prevailing approach to promoting graduate employability taken by higher education around the world is focused on the development of *human capital*, that is, work-related skills and knowledge (Clarke, 2017). However, graduate employability frameworks and strategies often overlook significant dispositional and contextual factors that contribute towards a person's employability. To more adequately promote the development of graduate employability, universities need to do more to connect students to their extensive networks of alumni and industry and provide careers and employability learning that helps students learn to explore and express their emerging professional identities (Bridgstock, 2017).

In this chapter we will explore the approach taken within one Australian university to enhance the employability of life science students through embedding into the curriculum a careers and employability learning module that uses social media, specifically LinkedIn, as a pedagogical tool to develop students' career identity and connect them with professional networks.

EMPLOYABILITY

We take the view that employability is a psycho–social construct that enables people to proactively manage career and work related changes (Fugate, Kinicki and Ashforth, 2004). Employability is recognised by many scholars as being more complex than just a set of skills (Clarke, 2017; Fugate and Kinicki, 2008; Fugate, Kinicki and Ashforth, 2004). In the vocational psychology and career development literature, employability is conceptualised to have multiple dimensions: personal dispositions; adaptability; career identity; and human, social (Fugate and Kinicki, 2008; Fugate, Kinicki and Ashforth, 2004), psychological, and cultural capital (Williams et al., 2015). From a sociological perspective employability can be viewed through the lens of possession of skills and knowledge, position within society, and the process of finding and obtaining employment (Holmes, 2013). Connectedness learning is concerned with the social connections that universities can create, providing environments which enable professional learning, career development, and innovation (Chapter 1 in this volume), thus emphasising the social capital dimension of employability (Fugate, Kinicki and Ashworth, 2004).

Career identity, an integral element of employability, guides proactive career behaviour (Bridgstock, 2019; Jackson, 2016) and is evident in individuals' stories about their past, present and future selves (McAdams and Pals, 2006; Meijers and Lengelle, 2012; Savickas, 2012). Career identity is developed through activities directed towards exploration and interaction with the environment and evolves over a lifetime (Meijers, 1998; Praskova, Creed and Hood, 2015). Proactive, or career adaptive behaviours, are actions that individuals take to increase their skills, knowledge, and other attributes that support career development and achievement of career goals (Lent and Brown, 2013).

GRADUATE CAPABILITIES AND CAREER READY CAPABILITIES

La Trobe University (La Trobe) is a multi-campus institution in Australia with a large campus in Melbourne, and smaller campuses located in four major regional cities in the state of Victoria. Established in 1964, La Trobe places particular importance on educating students from diverse backgrounds, and currently has more than 35,000 students enrolled.

Graduate capabilities (La Trobe University, 2018b) are taught and assessed in all bachelor degree programs and include skills consolidated into four key domains: literacies and communication skills; inquiry and analytical skills; personal and professional skills; and discipline-specific knowledge and skills. The Career Ready capability framework (La Trobe University, 2018a), however, was co-designed with employers, staff and students to support the enhancement of student employability. It complements the graduate capabilities, providing students with language that aligns with capabilities used by employers. The framework includes three components: students' purpose and career management (career identity); eight Career Ready capabilities; and four personal attributes (see Table 7.1 for details). The Career Ready capability framework is enacted through the Career Ready Advantage award program, in which students reflect on the learning they have achieved from completing employability related curricular and extracurricular activities.

CONNECTEDNESS PEDAGOGY: SOCIAL MEDIA

Social media has been recognised for several years as a means of enabling career development through increasing digital career literacies and collaborating online with professional networks (Longridge, Hooley and Staunton, 2013). However, university students often have an unsophisticated understanding of how to use social networking sites for career development purposes (see Lupton, Oddone and Dreamson in Chapter 3 and de Villiers Scheepers et al. in Chapter 4 of this volume) and limit their use to job searching (Benson, Morgan and Filippaios, 2014), creating an online profile, and connecting with existing networks (Gerard, 2012). Students have demonstrated limited awareness of the value of social networking sites for the development of career competencies and professional identity (Starcic et al., 2017), and tend not to engage in more mature forms of networking such as cultivating strong networks, sharing information, engaging in dialogue, or collaborating with connections (Gerard, 2012).

LinkedIn is a global social networking site that allows users to set up a professional profile and connect with other professionals, present an online résumé, find employment opportunities, and connect with co-workers or classmates (Florenthal, 2015). LinkedIn globally has 546 million users, including over 9 million users in Australia (LinkedIn, 2018). LinkedIn has particular value for higher education students and graduates as they explore their career options, establish their professional identity, and build their networks online (Hooley, Bright and Winter, 2016; LinkedIn, n.d.).

Bridgstock (2019) argues that although LinkedIn provides numerous affordances to higher education students as a career development tool, many students are unaware of the full range of benefits that can be attained, such as developing their connectedness capabilities, career self-management skills, professional communication skills, digital literacies, and digital citizenship. Starcic et al. (2017) found that only 24 per cent of the engineering students that they surveyed had LinkedIn accounts, although all of them had Facebook accounts. This lack of engagement with LinkedIn may be particularly acute in non-business related fields: only 11 per cent of Australian final-year students in health profession courses reported using LinkedIn (Usher et al., 2014). LinkedIn has been used as the basis for assessable learning activities in university curricula in an effort to increase student engagement with it (Gerard, 2012; McCorkle and McCorkle, 2012). This chapter is a new case study of such an assessment task.

CASE-STUDY CONTEXT: A LIFE-SCIENCES CURRICULUM IN NEED OF EMBEDDED CONNECTEDNESS LEARNING

The Bachelor of Health Sciences course at La Trobe is a non-vocational three-year degree with over 1,000 students. The degree is a pathway to at least 30 distinct professions (Lexis and Julien, 2018), predominantly in allied health fields. The human physiology and anatomy major (comprised of eight core subjects completed across the second and third year) is popular with Bachelor of Health Sciences students but may also be taken by students in other non-vocational courses such as biomedical science and human nutrition.

In 2010, student feedback indicated that many students who were about to complete the major had little idea of their desired future career path and were unaware of the breadth of career pathways available to them. In response, we designed and delivered employability modules in third year subjects of the major. Although these modules had some success, they were limited to career exploration and self-reflection activities, and were lacking in connectedness pedagogies, such as social media and ePortfolios (see Bridgstock and Tippett, Chapter 6 in this volume). Taking inspiration from the Connectedness Learning Approach, we decided to expand the existing modules using LinkedIn, encouraging students to develop more connected career identities by observing and connecting with established professionals who used the network. Accordingly, this research explores how students perceived the value of the module, particularly the use of LinkedIn, and the impact that this approach had upon students' career identity and connectedness capabilities.

METHOD

Project Design and Delivery

The authors – two life sciences lecturers and two careers and employability educators – collaborated to embed employability modules into two final (third) year core subjects of the human physiology and anatomy major. The module described in this case study was delivered in semester one to 109 students over a 12-week period, using a blended format which included two face-to-face classes (weeks 1 and 11) and a suite of online support materials. The face-to-face classes included guest sessions by careers and employability educators on employability, professional identity, and the use of LinkedIn, and several alumni, who shared their career experiences and employability advice. The online materials included an employability section on the online Learning

Management System which housed a student forum, student module guide, and LinkedIn resources (LinkedIn, n.d.).

Students were assessed through two assignments: (1) an oral presentation on careers and educational pathways worth 10 per cent of the final subject grade, and (2) a LinkedIn profile and an associated employability report, worth 15 per cent of the final subject grade.

Oral presentation on career or educational pathways

In week 12 of the semester, students delivered an individual 3–5 minute oral presentation on their preferred choice of postgraduate study or career path upon completion of their degree. This assessment was designed to facilitate active participation in career exploration – since individuals who engage in career exploration and planning activities have been found to develop clearer career identities (Praskova, Creed and Hood, 2015) – and was also intended to be preparation work for the development of a meaningful LinkedIn profile.

Creation of a LinkedIn profile and associated employability report

In creating a LinkedIn profile, students were tasked to connect with at least three professionals in the field that they wished to enter following graduation. Assessment criteria focused on the quality of the profile's headline statement, professional summary, profile photo, employment experience, education, skills, and expertise. To accompany this, we also provided an employability report template to students, with a suggested word count of 1,000 words. The template, which included headings and instructions for students to respond to several discrete reflection tasks, is described below:

Reflection on building a LinkedIn profile: Students reflected on the experience of creating a LinkedIn profile and connecting with professionals. First, students described how they went about writing their professional profile and how they felt about the experience. Second, students summarised the career stories of two of their professional connections and described what they saw in their profiles that was helpful in some way; for example, the path their connection took to their current employment, the kind of material they share on their LinkedIn timeline, or what the person describes as their key professional skills.

Employability strengths and weaknesses: Students reviewed La Trobe's graduate capabilities and the Career Ready capability framework, then reflected on their employability strengths and weaknesses. We instructed students to provide evidence from university, work, or volunteering activities to support their claims. Students were also encouraged to consider the LinkedIn profiles of professionals in their desired field that they had connected with.

Goal setting: We asked students to state three goals based on their self-identified employability weaknesses, explain how each of the goals would contribute to the development of their employability, and then outline one of those goals in detail, using the SMART goal structure (Specific, Measurable, Attainable, Realistic and Time-bound; Conzemius and O'Neill, 2009).

Student Feedback

At the end of the semester, we invited students to complete a paper-based evaluation of the module in which they rated the importance of, and their ability level on, a range of items relating to the module on a five-point Likert scale. The survey comprised numerical items and an open-ended section which allowed students to provide additional comments. Eighty students completed the survey, which is a response rate of 73 per cent. Two authors, life sciences lecturers, conducted descriptive statistical analysis of the quantitative data and conducted inductive or data-driven thematic analysis, using the approach described by Braun and Clarke (2006), on the responses to the open-ended question "Which specific aspects of the employability module have contributed most to your learning?" Frequency of responses within the identified themes are presented quantitatively.

Qualitative Analysis of Student Employability Reports

Two authors, careers and employability educators who were not familiar with the students or involved in the grading of the assignments, conducted a template analysis of 104 anonymised employability reports using NVivo qualitative data analysis computer software. Template analysis "is a form of thematic analysis which emphasizes the use of hierarchical coding" (Brooks et al., 2015, p. 203). A priori themes were used to develop an initial coding template which was applied to a sample of the data, then iteratively revised until the researchers had exhausted all main emerging themes. The coding templates (see Tables 7.1 and 7.2) were developed using items from La Trobe's graduate capabilities (La Trobe University, 2018b) and Career Ready capability framework (La Trobe University, 2018a), the connectedness capabilities from the Connectedness Learning Approach (Chapter 1 in this volume), and a list of career adaptive behaviours (Lent and Brown, 2013). Together, the coding frameworks represent a wide range of skills, attitudes, and behaviours that students were expected to communicate in their LinkedIn profiles, draw on in their reflections, and reflexively self-evaluate themselves against. The coders worked closely on coding decisions and refinements to the template, revised some of the coding to be more consistent and accurate, and concluded the coding when thematic saturation and coding consensus was achieved.

RESULTS

Student Feedback

Overall: Feedback on the employability module showed that students valued it as a learning experience, with 75 per cent agreeing or strongly agreeing that the module was relevant to their career development needs. Seventy-seven per cent agreed or strongly agreed that the skills they learned would be useful in the future. Forty-six per cent of students rated the extent to which they had begun to apply the skills learnt in the employability module in real life as high or very high, with 32 per cent neutral and 22 per cent rating it as low or very low.

Oral presentation: Student feedback on the value of the oral presentation for future study or employment was positive, with 84 per cent of students agreeing or strongly agreeing that the presentation helped them to learn about their study or employment options after graduation and 78 per cent of students rating their confidence in researching a course or job they would like to apply for as high or very high. Responses on the open-ended question showed that 67 per cent of students listed research for, and delivery of, the oral presentation as contributing the most to their learning in this module.

Analysis of the oral presentations revealed that 99 per cent of students wanted to undertake further study, with physiotherapy the most popular course (40 per cent), followed by occupational therapy (16 per cent), dietetics (7 per cent), medicine (5 per cent), and osteopathy (5 per cent). Only one student chose to deliver their oral presentation on a career pathway as opposed to a study pathway.

LinkedIn profile and connecting with professionals: Feedback indicated that although they recognised the value of networking on LinkedIn, students did not rate their ability to use it highly. Sixty-three per cent of students believed it was very or somewhat important to create a LinkedIn profile and 71 per cent of students reported that it was very important or somewhat important to connect with people via LinkedIn. Students' confidence in using LinkedIn was lower than their recognition of its value, with 53 per cent reporting that their ability to use LinkedIn was very high or high. Despite recognising the value of LinkedIn in general, in the open-ended question only 17 per cent of students cited using LinkedIn as contributing the most to their learning and just 3 per cent reported that connecting with professionals in their field contributed the most to their learning.

Employability strengths and weaknesses: Students recognised the importance of reflecting on and describing their employability strengths and weaknesses, with 79 per cent of students considering it to be important or very important. Students also expressed some confidence in doing this, with 48 per cent of students rating their ability to reflect on and describe their employability skills as high or very high and 41 per cent rating it as adequate.

Goal setting: Feedback showed that students recognised the value of goal setting and expressed confidence that they could achieve their goals. Eighty-three per cent of students considered goal setting to be important or very important. Forty-eight per cent of students reported that their ability to set goals was very high or high. Fifty-nine per cent of students rated the likelihood that they would achieve their goals as high or very high and a further 38 per cent rated it as medium.

Qualitative Analysis of Students' Reflections

In this section we explore in depth the results of the qualitative analysis of students' reflections.

LinkedIn profile and connecting with professionals: The first section of the written task was a reflection on the experience of using LinkedIn and connecting with three professionals. Student reflections in this section were coded against the five connectedness capabilities (Chapter 1 in this volume), with multiple codes applied where students' writing alluded to more than one capability. The analysis showed that student reflections mostly referred to three of the five connectedness capabilities: *building a connected identity* (72 per cent of student reflections); *developing a social network literacy* (82 per cent); and *growing connections* (72 per cent). Student reflections included significantly less reference to *strengthening and maintaining connections* (5 per cent) and *working with connections* (11 per cent). Despite being in their final year of an undergraduate degree, most students were only operating at the foundational level of each competency, as evidenced by the statements described below.

For many students, signing up to LinkedIn and creating a profile was a new experience, with 82 per cent of students reflecting on learning about the features, usability, and career management affordances of LinkedIn and therefore indicating engagement with the connectedness capability *developing a social network literacy*. For example, student #04 wrote:

> Being able to self-advertise myself to the wider community is something I didn't think I would be doing until I had finished my degree and [started] job searching. Thus, this early exposure to LinkedIn has fast tracked this process as well as helped me to see what other [allied health clinicians] do and what they have done to get where they are today.

Many student reports demonstrated that the experience contributed to their connectedness capability *building a connected identity* (72 per cent). They found the act of putting their professional identity into words challenging but appreciated the importance of developing this skill. Student #06 wrote:

> Creating a LinkedIn profile to me was like gathering all of your life accomplishments into one space and exposing yourself to the world. The thing I found the most difficult was thinking of a summary in my profile, it made me confront myself. I had some idea of where I wanted to go with my career but actually visualizing the pathway I needed to take was another process altogether.

Students also reported that they used their connections' LinkedIn profiles as exemplars as they developed their own, simultaneously *building a connected identity* and *developing a social network literacy*. They looked to others' profiles for ideas on how to write about themselves and which skills to highlight. Several students described being *inspired* in some way by what they learned, reporting that viewing the work and study histories of professionals in their chosen field made them feel more confident that they could achieve their goals and had encouraged them to be more open to experience, or helped them become comfortable with self-promotion. Student #78 wrote:

> What I found difficult about making my LinkedIn profile was being able to promote myself and talk about what skills I have that I thought were my strengths. At first I was hesitant to write anything down but I found that after viewing a range of people's profiles that it was no longer so daunting. […] I looked at other professionals in the field and saw what they had as their 'best' skills and tried to see if I had any that were similar. This then allowed me to see that I have acquired many useful skills throughout my studying so far, and to realise that promoting myself isn't a scary or daunting thing at all.

Numerous students recognised the opportunity LinkedIn presents in exercising the connectedness capability of *growing connections* (72 per cent). It should be noted that connecting with people was a stated requirement of the assignment, whereas other connectedness capabilities were not explicitly elicited in the assignment prompts. Students reported connecting with people at a range of levels of seniority in the field, from fellow students up to leaders at the highest levels of their profession. Several students described difficulties connecting with people, such as making connection requests and receiving no replies, itself an important element of *social network literacy*. Student #02 described how they learned from this experience:

> I attempted to add individuals who came up as LinkedIn members however [I] wouldn't get any response, until I decided to add a [health professional] who I had a mutual friend with, then once they accepted me, I was able to add and connect with a large number of [health professionals].

The connectedness capabilities *strengthening and maintaining connections* (5 per cent) and *working with connections* (11 per cent) were only evident in a small number of cases. Few students described how they could use LinkedIn to develop existing connections or pursue opportunities for real-world engagement with their connections. This again highlights that the final year undergraduate students in this study were operating at a foundational level, having only begun building their connections as a requirement of this assignment.

Employability strengths and weaknesses: The second part of the assignment was an employability self-evaluation, where students reflected on the strengths and weaknesses of their employability skills. We coded students' evaluations of their employability strengths and weaknesses against all three competency frameworks (see Table 7.1). An additional code was created to reflect the fact that students considered the presence of work experience a strength and the lack of it a weakness in and of itself. Frequencies of the codes are found in Table 7.1.

The Career Ready capability framework and graduate capabilities overlap significantly, so we were unable to analyse students' self-evaluation of discrete competencies with accuracy. However, the reflections do show a broader thematic consistency, in that students cited social and interpersonal competencies as strengths approximately twice as often as they did cognitive or analytical competencies (see Table 7.1). Several students cited the same competency as both a strength and a weakness, demonstrating some depth of reflection and an understanding of the complex and contextual nature of the frameworks.

A perceived lack of relevant work experience was the most frequently cited employability weakness, despite not appearing in the frameworks that students were asked to reflect on. Thirty per cent of students indicated that work experience had strengthened their employability while 60 per cent identified a lack of work experience as an employability weakness. As student #90 reflected:

> A lack of experience in a healthcare environment leaves me unprepared for a new job in this field. [...] I have not participated in any 'placement' and therefore have no valid healthcare environment experience. Overall, without further volunteer work and a background of experience in healthcare, other applicants would likely get a job over me.

Many students described their lack of experience in this way, as a lack of career capital on their résumé, rather than the absence of professional learning experiences which would themselves help develop a range of employability competencies and characteristics.

Although we only asked students to reflect on the two competency frameworks used at La Trobe, we also coded responses in this section against the five connectedness capabilities to see if they emerged through student reflections.

Table 7.1   Coding of reflections on employability strengths and weaknesses (N=104)

Categories	Codes*	Strength	Weakness
Connectedness Capabilities			
	Building a connected identity	5	14
	Growing connections	4	18
	Strengthening and maintaining connections	1	1
	Developing social network literacy	0	2
	Working with connections	0	4
Graduate Capabilities			
	Personal and professional skills	77	24
	Discipline-specific knowledge and skills	49	35
	Literacies and communication skills	42	20
	Inquiry and analytical skills	37	9
Career Ready Capabilities			
Cognitive flexibility	Results orientation	23	11
	Innovative thinking	6	3
	Business and digital acumen	5	7
	Big picture awareness	2	3
Social intelligence	Communicating and influencing	5	1
	Collaboration	34	10
	Personal judgement	12	14
	Cultural awareness	9	7
Personal attributes	Passion	20	5
	Empathy	12	0
	Resilience	10	3
	Curiosity	7	2
Other codes			
	Work experience	31	63
	Other skills	9	8
	Extra-curricular	5	1
	Academic performance	3	3
	Qualification or credential	1	8
	International student	0	1

Note: * Codes are sorted in each category by highest to lowest frequency of strength.

Ten per cent of cases cited connectedness capabilities as a strength and 37 per cent cited connectedness capabilities as a weakness. Two capabilities – *connected identity* and *growing connections* – were the most frequently coded connectedness capabilities, both of which were often seen as potential weaknesses. Student #49 alludes to both capabilities as weaknesses:

> My current employability weaknesses would include my lack of current connections I have made on LinkedIn. Although I have connected with those who have helped shape my own profile and compared education pathways with, I must expand on my current connections which will expose myself to future employers and possibly open more potential job opportunities or volunteering roles.

Employability goal setting: The final section of the assignment was a goal-setting exercise. We coded the employability goal-setting section of the students' reports against connectedness capabilities and career adaptive behaviours (Lent and Brown, 2013) (see Table 7.2), as a reflection of students' intended future action. We added an additional adaptive behaviour, *seeking a credential or qualification*, to reflect many students citing this as a goal.

Most students identified goals focused on developing their employability skills, gaining relevant experience, and seeking credentials or qualifications. In this assignment, students were asked to list their goals after reflecting on their employability weaknesses, which may explain why *developing employability skills* was cited so frequently as a goal.

The other two most frequently cited goals relate to qualities of employability that were not present in the frameworks, but that students felt were important enough to add themselves: career-relevant experience and professional qualifications and credentials. Overall, student goals demonstrated a transactional approach to employability where the primary goal was simply to improve career capital on their résumé, rather than to pursue opportunities for professional learning experiences through which they could develop their employability competencies and characteristics. This may be in part due to the students' ambitions to enter clinical health professions, such as physiotherapy or occupational therapy, in which a specific qualification and accreditation is required.

Despite students recognising the need to develop their employability skills and gain relevant experience, few described an intent to draw on resources in their professional network in pursuit of those goals. For example, student #98 claimed that their goal to get more relevant experience "can be accomplished by emailing numerous [health professionals] and dropping my résumé, asking if I could sit in on sessions or get some work experience. First step is to formulate a template to email [them]." This student is describing a high volume cold-calling approach, rather than reaching out to existing contacts

Table 7.2   Coding of goals relating to connectedness capabilities and career adaptive behaviours (N=104)

Categories	Code	Frequency
Goals related to Connectedness Capabilities		
	Growing connections	30
	Working with connections	12
	Building a Connected Identity	6
	Developing social network literacy	4
	Strengthening and maintaining connections	2
Goals related to Career Adaptive Behaviours		
	Developing employability skills	115
	Acquiring career-relevant experiences	76
	Seek a credential	45
	Exploring career paths	10
	Search for and obtain employment	9
	Engaging with profession	4
	Managing transition from study to employment	3
	Knowledge	2
	Implementing decisions	1

Note: * Codes are sorted in each category by highest to lowest frequency.

or strategically-chosen new connections with more personalised communications, and does not refer to using LinkedIn at all. Student #84 described a similar approach to securing volunteer work, "by phoning up as many clinics as possible and asking if they would be willing to take me on [for work experience]".

Overall, few students described goals employing connectedness capabilities. Among those who did, mention was largely limited to growing the number of connections. Only 1 per cent of students described strengthening existing relationships and only 5 per cent described working with connections. Importantly, those who referred to strengthening relationships or working with connections demonstrated more mature and strategic understandings of careers and employability than those who did not, such as student #23, who described a specific plan to develop their entrepreneurial skills by "arranging a meeting with [business owner] over the holidays so that I can get some ideas about web solutions that may be beneficial to my future business". Similarly, student #29 described a plan to approach specific connections to seek experience relevant to their own research interests: "I have spoken to [researcher] regarding an internship in their lab, studying [disease]. I have a meeting with [researcher] in the coming days and hope to learn and gain experience through this opportunity".

DISCUSSION

This study shows that students valued the employability module overall, and analysis of 104 student employability reports, based on student use of LinkedIn, provides empirical evidence supporting the conceptualisation of five capabilities described in the Connectedness Learning Approach (Chapter 1 in this volume), but also demonstrates the importance of scaffolding connectedness learning from early on in the curriculum.

Our research shows that students valued the employability module, and that some had begun to apply the skills learnt outside the classroom in real-life. Overall, students most valued the oral presentation component of the module, in which they researched and presented on potential educational and career pathways, and 78 per cent of respondents rated their confidence in researching a course or job they would like to apply for as high or very high. This is a positive outcome, as career exploration is both an antecedent and outcome of career decision making self-efficacy (Ireland and Lent, 2018), which develops students' vision of their future work self and their sense of career concern, confidence, control, and curiosity (Guan et al., 2017), and promotes more coherent career identities (Praskova, Creed and Hood, 2015).

Students' positive feedback on the value of networking on LinkedIn, reflecting on their employability strengths and weaknesses, and setting goals clearly demonstrates that students recognise the value and relevance of connectedness pedagogies to their career and employability development. The fact that they were largely operating at the foundational level of connectedness capabilities is not an indication that they did not authentically engage with the module, but rather that they needed more time and support to mature and consolidate their use of connectedness capabilities to develop their professional identities and networks.

Students demonstrated the connectedness capabilities of *developing a connected identity, building social network literacy,* and *growing connections,* albeit that these competencies were limited to the foundational level. The capabilities *strengthening and maintaining connections* and *working with connections* were only evident in a small number of students, and reflects the stage of development of students in this study, rather than a lack of support for the existence of these capabilities.

The students in this study expressed their networked identities as observers of, rather than participants in, their professional communities. Although students valued the career exploration activities in the module, their exploration was largely limited to credentials and pathways into graduate study. As there is much competition for enrolment places in graduate study, it is not surprising that students are reluctant to commit to a professional identity until they are accepted into a vocationally-specific graduate program. However, we did expect that the vocational focus of the Bachelor of Health Sciences as a pathway to a range of careers (Lexis and Julien, 2018) would have resulted in stronger expressions of professional identity, especially in relation to a specific occupation.

Our analysis also showed that students tended to demonstrate a possessional approach to employability (Holmes, 2013) which focused on development of human capital, often to the exclusion of other aspects of dispositional employability. They described career-relevant experiences and qualifications as a kind of currency in a transactional employment market, rather than as learning experiences through which they could develop their career identity, build marketable skills, and find their place in their professional community. Students seldom reflected on dispositional aspects of employability – such as their career identity – as contributing to their employability, nor did many students identify connectedness capabilities as strategic approaches to adopt in pursuing their employability development goals. For many students, membership of a professional community was much more a matter of gaining credentials than developing reciprocal professional relationships.

Application for Practice

This chapter provides evidence that employability modules including social media and connectedness learning are an effective way to develop graduate employability. However, careful consideration needs to be given to timing and scaffolding, with employability curricula ideally embedded across all year levels of a course, as well as the development of collaborative relationships between academic lecturers and careers and employability specialists.

The evidence from this study demonstrated that students' development of connectedness capabilities was at the foundational level. Connectedness capabilities in general, and the use of LinkedIn specifically, clearly require more time, scaffolding, and explicit instruction and assessment to allow students to build their proficiency and cultivate their networks to greater professional maturity, a point made by a number of other researchers (Benson, Morgan and Filippaios, 2014; Gerard, 2012; Starcic et al., 2017). Benson, Morgan and Filippaios (2014) recommend a scaffolded approach that introduces undergraduate students in the first year to develop basic social network literacy. In the second year, they recommend expanding students' understanding of using social networks in employment contexts, especially for obtaining internships and volunteering opportunities, and focusing in their final year on researching organisations and employment opportunities. Therefore, we recommend that students should be introduced to employability modules including social media and connectedness learning at the beginning of their program, with curriculum designed to scaffold the development of connectedness capabilities to a more advanced level by the end of the degree program.

It was evident through the students' goals that their focus was on developing employability skills and gaining career experiences rather than on acquiring connectedness capabilities. Scholars and practitioners developing a similar employability module may need to consider how to change the mindset of students so that they place greater emphasis on making and developing strong connections. Career exploration activities in the curriculum, combined with the early introduction of social media such as LinkedIn, could go some way to achieving this as it gives students more time to consider the range of pathways available to them.

Central to the Connectedness Learning Approach is the need for enabling strategies, such as taking an integrated approach to pedagogies and partnerships; identifying, developing and strengthening key relationship broker roles; using connectedness-enabling digital tools, like LinkedIn; and reducing institutional barriers to connectedness to ensure modules like this can be authentically integrated into the curriculum (Chapter 1 in this volume). At La Trobe, the time was right to introduce and pilot employability modules as the university had stated its intention to support employability through the strategic plan (La Trobe University, 2017) and supported the development of the Career Ready capability framework and Career Ready Advantage. Furthermore, this project was the result of a strong collaborative relationship between life sciences academics and careers and employability educators, based on a shared vision of students' employability and understanding of their needs, which can serve as an exemplar of a collaborative approach to careers and employability learning based on collective learning and transformational leadership (Lodders and Meijers, 2017). Such relationships, which distribute careers and employability expertise and promote professional learning, should be enthusiastically encouraged and supported by all levels of university leadership.

The module described in this chapter is not inherently specific to life sciences and could easily be tailored to the specific needs of other disciplines. For a discipline where there is an obvious path to employment in a defined and regulated profession like medicine, law, or education, the focus might be on developing and working with networks, whereas with a generalist discipline like humanities, science, or psychology, the module might need to focus on students' exploring potential career paths and establishing a career identity.

Finally, it is important to consider ethical and privacy implications in using social media as a pedagogical tool. Students should be introduced to the privacy, security, social etiquette, and accessibility issues surrounding the use of social media in teaching and assessment (Benson, Morgan and Filippaios,

2014; Longridge, Hooley and Staunton, 2013; Rodriguez, 2011). Furthermore, there are legitimate reasons why people choose not to use LinkedIn, such as law enforcement or social work professionals not wanting their personal and professional details to be found online, or people suffering harassment and stalking. Students should be allowed to opt out of creating a LinkedIn profile and offered alternate assessment tasks if they so choose.

CONCLUSION

This research shows that an employability module comprised of research into career and educational pathways, networking on LinkedIn, reflecting on employability strengths and weaknesses, and goal-setting was valued by students. Our analysis of the students' employability reports showed that despite being in their final year of an undergraduate degree, development of their career-identity and connectedness capabilities was at the foundational level. As the students have plans to pursue postgraduate study in a clinical health field, many appear to be not fully committing to a career identity until they are accepted into postgraduate study. Students who are planning to find employment after their undergraduate degree may be more receptive to an employability module focused on developing their career identities and connectedness capabilities. Future research should examine the Connectedness Learning Approach and the use of LinkedIn as a pedagogical tool in the curriculum of different programs and subject areas.

Finally, it is important to note that the students in this module were doing what was asked of them by the prevailing culture of graduate capabilities and employability skills, in which capabilities are listed in subject guides and checked off in learning and assessment tasks. It is not surprising that students demonstrated that they hold a human capital view of employability. To help students more effectively develop the attitudes, behaviours, and capabilities that will allow them to pursue and achieve their career goals, the university leaders who set employability strategies, and the university educators who deliver them, need to evolve their own understandings of and approaches to employability, away from lists of skills and towards authentic connectedness with professional communities.

REFERENCES

Benson, V., Morgan, S. and Filippaios, F. (2014). Social career management: Social media and employability skills gap. *Computers in Human Behavior*, *30*, 519–525.

Braun, V. and Clarke, V. (2006). Using thematic analysis in psychology. *Qualitative Research in Psychology*, *3*(2), 77–101.

Bridgstock, R. (2017). The university and the knowledge network: A new educational model for 21st century learning and employability. In M. Tomlinson (ed.), *Graduate Employability in Context: Research, Theory and Debate* (pp. 339–358). London: Palgrave Macmillan.

Bridgstock, R. (2019). Employability and career development learning through social media: Exploring the potential of LinkedIn. In J. Higgs, D. Horsfall, S. Cork and A. Jones (eds), *Challenging Future Practice Possibilities*. Rotterdam: Sense-Brill Publishers.

Brooks, J., McCluskey, S., Turley, E. and King, N. (2015). The utility of template analysis in qualitative psychology research. *Qualitative Research in Psychology*, *12*(2), 202–222. https://www.ncbi.nlm.nih.gov/pubmed/27499705.

Clarke, M. (2017). Rethinking graduate employability: The role of capital, individual attributes and context. *Studies in Higher Education.* Advance online publication.

Conzemius, A. and O'Neill, J. (2009). *The Power of SMART Goals: Using Goals to Improve Student Learning*. Bloomington, IN: Solution Tree Press.

Florenthal, B. (2015). Applying uses and gratifications theory to students' LinkedIn usage. *Young Consumers*, *16*(1), 17–35.

Fugate, M. and Kinicki, A. J. (2008). A dispositional approach to employability: Development of a measure and test of implications for employee reactions to organizational change. *Journal of Occupational and Organizational Psychology*, *81*(3), 503–527.

Fugate, M., Kinicki, A. J. and Ashforth, B. E. (2004). Employability: A psycho-social construct, its dimensions, and applications. *Journal of Vocational Behavior*, *65*(1), 14–38.

Gerard, J. G. (2012). Linking in with LinkedIn®. *Journal of Management Education*, *36*(6), 866–897.

Guan, Y., Zhuang, M., Cai, Z., Ding, Y., Wang, Y., Huang, Z. and Lai, X. (2017). Modeling dynamics in career construction: Reciprocal relationship between future work self and career exploration. *Journal of Vocational Behavior*, *101*, 21–31.

Holmes, L. (2013). Competing perspectives on graduate employability: possession, position or process? *Studies in Higher Education*, *38*(4), 538–554.

Hooley, T., Bright, J. and Winter, D. (2016). *You're Hired! Job Hunting Online: The Complete Guide*. Bath, UK: Trotman.

Ireland, G. W. and Lent, R. W. (2018). Career exploration and decision-making learning experiences: A test of the career self-management model. *Journal of Vocational Behavior*, *106*, 37–47.

Jackson, D. (2016). Re-conceptualising graduate employability: The importance of pre-professional identity. *Higher Education Research and Development*, *35*(5), 925–939.

La Trobe University. (2017). 2018–2022 Strategic Plan. Retrieved on 1 November 2018 from https://www.latrobe.edu.au/__data/assets/pdf_file/0005/846455/2018-2022-Strategic-Plan.pdf.

La Trobe University. (2018a). Get the career ready advantage. Retrieved on 1 November 2018 from http://www.latrobe.edu.au/students/opportunities/careers/career-ready.

La Trobe University. (2018b). Graduate Capabilities. Retrieved on 9 February 2018 from http://www.latrobe.edu.au/dvca/la-trobe-framework/graduate-capabilities.

Lent, R. W. and Brown, S. D. (2013). Social cognitive model of career self-management: Toward a unifying view of adaptive career behavior across the life span. *Journal of Counseling Psychology*, *60*(4), 557–568.

Lexis, L. and Julien, B. (2018). *Bachelor of Health Sciences Career Pathway Guide*. Melbourne: La Trobe University.

LinkedIn. (2018). About LinkedIn. Retrieved on 13 February 2018 from https://about.linkedin.com/.

LinkedIn. (n.d.). The Student Job Hunting Handbook Series. Retrieved on 15 April 2018 from https://students.linkedin.com/.

Lodders, N. and Meijers, F. (2017). Collective learning, transformational leadership and new forms of careers guidance in universities. *British Journal of Guidance and Counselling*, *45*(5), 532–546.

Longridge, D., Hooley, T. and Staunton, T. (2013). Building online employability: A guide for academic departments. University of Derby. Retrieved on 1 November 2018 from http://hdl.handle.net/10545/294311.

McAdams, D. P. and Pals, J. L. (2006). A new big five: Fundamental principles for an integrative science of personality. *American Psychologist*, *61*(3), 204–217. https://www.ncbi.nlm.nih.gov/pubmed/16594837.

McCorkle, D. E. and McCorkle, Y. L. (2012). Using LinkedIn in the marketing classroom: Exploratory insights and recommendations for teaching social media/networking. *Marketing Education Review*, *22*(2), 157–166.

Meijers, F. (1998). The development of a career identity. *International Journal for the Advancement of Counselling*, *20*(3), 191–207.

Meijers, F. and Lengelle, R. (2012). Narratives at work: The development of career identity. *British Journal of Guidance and Counselling*, *40*(2), 157–176.

Praskova, A., Creed, P. A. and Hood, M. (2015). Career identity and the complex mediating relationships between career preparatory actions and career progress markers. *Journal of Vocational Behavior*, *87*(1), 145–153.

Rodriguez, J. E. (2011). Social media use in higher education: Key areas to consider for educators. *Journal of Online Learning and Teaching*, *7*(4), 539–550.

Savickas, M. L. (2012). Life design: A paradigm for career intervention in the 21st century. *Journal of Counseling and Development, 90*(1), 13–19.

Starcic, A. I., Barrow, M., Zajc, M. and Lebenicnik, M. (2017). Students' attitudes on social network sites and their actual use for career management competences and professional identity development. *International Journal of Emerging Technologies in Learning, 12*(5), 65–81.

Usher, K., Woods, C., Casella, E., Glass, N., Wilson, R., Mayner, L. … Mather, C. (2014). Australian health professions student use of social media. *Collegian, 21*(2), 95–101.

Williams, S., Dodd, L. J., Steele, C. and Randall, R. (2015). A systematic review of current understandings of employability. *Journal of Education and Work, 29*(8), 877–901.

8. Indigenous[1] perspectives on connected and networked learning: towards holistic connectedness pedagogies

Peter Radoll, Peter Copeman, Scott Heyes, Mary Walsh, Sam Byrnand, Brian Egloff with Lance Bartram, Kerani Cameron, Fehin Coffey, Sarah Falusi, Victoria Hales, Robert Liesagang, David Jolley, Catherine Lampe, Natalie Lutan, Joshua Naivalurua, Chilli Platt, Thomas Rigon and Caroline Wallace. Project Elder: Aunty Roslyn Brown, University of Canberra[2]

 STARTING POINTS[3]

In Western higher education systems, knowledge construction has tended to focus not only on specialised professional knowledge, but also on development of students' individual capabilities of critical, creative and analytical thinking, and problem-solving (Rasmussen, Baydala, and Sherman, 2004). More recently, as the present volume attests, the rapid increase in online interaction and communication has created opportunities, if not imperatives, for university students to begin to build connected professional networks while studying, as a strategy for collaborative career development, innovation, problem-solving and socially-based learning (Bridgstock, 2016).

Historically, however, connectedness in learning and work goes much farther back than the emergence of digitally-mediated communication and social media; indeed, much farther even than the formation of professions and professional networks. In particular, connectedness is at the core of Aboriginal and Torres Strait Islander culture, pedagogy and occupation. As Tyson Yunkaporta (2009, p. 1) states, for Indigenous peoples, "there are always connections between all things, places where different elements are no longer separate but mix together and become something else". For Gary Thomas (2015, p. 3), such Indigenous connectedness consists of "those related and relatable states in which individuals, families, cohorts, professions, communities, systems and societies come together", and is "the current in which these relationships flow and then becomes both a practice and value of culture". This also extends to profound connection to country and to the cosmos.

Yunkaporta (2009, p. 1) goes on to assert that, while there is a wide diversity of Indigenous identities and languages in Australia, there are also many ways and values held in common within and across this diversity, including and notably in approaches to learning. He calls for the pursuit of a reconciliation between Indigenous ways of learning and Western best practice pedagogy to achieve mutually beneficial learning "at the cultural interface" (p. 3). If this can be achieved, then according to Dreamson et al. (2017), "Indigenous pedagogical values have the potential to reposition all students as equal co-participants of new relationship building, new pedagogy creation and learning community building, thereby precipitating the ongoing formation of intercultural identity", including in the global connectedness of online learning and digital communication.

Within this context, the University of Canberra (UC) *Aboriginal and Torres Strait Islander Strategic Plan 2017–2021* pledges to move Indigenous education in the university beyond bolted-on approaches such as discreet elective Indigenous subject units or the inclusion of occasional Indigenous case studies and resources among the raft of mainstream ones. A more built-in model is envisaged, whereby Indigenous ways of knowing, learning and connecting are embedded to underpin curriculum design and delivery in all disciplines across the university, on the hypothesis that the learning experience for all UC students, both Indigenous and non-Indigenous, might be thereby holistically enriched. This commitment was taken up by the Deputy Vice-Chancellor (Academic) as a core strand of a university-wide curriculum review launched in 2017.

The first phase of this strand mandated a pilot project in a small number of undergraduate subject units to investigate whether contemporary modes of university learning and connectedness could be beneficially adjusted by blending with Indigenous ways of learning and connecting, and generating recommendations for further action more widely across the university. Four research questions were established:

1. Can learning and connecting in Indigenous studies subject units be enhanced by the integration of Indigenous ways of learning and connecting? If so, how?

2. What common factor(s) cohere and connect the ways of knowing and learning as a holistic unity?
3. Could Indigenous ways of knowing, learning and connecting be beneficially applied more widely in mainstream courses and units across the university? What might be the benefits, and risks?
4. What correlations might exist between Indigenous ways of learning and connecting and progressive contemporary non-Indigenous pedagogic and connectedness approaches, to promote a beneficial cultural interface in university teaching and learning generally?

The choice of subject units for this initial pilot was limited to existing ones that already had an Indigenous focus, on the expectation that the teaching staff and the students enrolled in them would have a degree of sympathetic predisposition towards the project aims. From this limited group, three small-cohort (for manageability) undergraduate subject units were identified:

- Indigenous Politics and the State (Faculty of Business, Government and Law) – Unit 1;[4]
- Indigenous Heritage and Landscapes (Faculty of Arts and Design) – Unit 2;
- Graduation Studio – Landscape Architecture (Faculty of Arts and Design) – Unit 3.

Consistent with Indigenous approaches to knowledge-seeking, the unit teaching staff and the students in these subject units were all invited to participate in the project as co-researchers, at appropriate levels.

 DECONSTRUCTING INDIGENOUS WAYS OF LEARNING

Literature documenting Australian Indigenous ways of knowing, learning and connecting – for example Harris (1984); Robinson and Nichol (1998) – as well as international research in North American Indigenous pedagogies – for example Wheaton (2000); Battiste (2002); Marker (2006) – were reviewed by Yunkaporta (2009) on his research journey to synthesise "intercultural ways of learning that any teacher and learner might approach together as familiar territory from their own cultural standpoints" (p. 46). The framework he thus developed distils *eight ways of learning* common across Aboriginal identities, countries and languages, as a pedagogical framework in which "teaching through Aboriginal processes and protocols, not just Aboriginal content, validates and teaches *through* Aboriginal culture and may enhance the learning for *all* students" (p. 1).

Each of the eight ways is represented by an Indigenous symbol, together with an explanation of its origin and meaning, as follows (adapted from Yunkaporta, 2009, pp. 4–7):

 Story Sharing – the killer boomerang. A story starts with normal life (the handle end) then builds to a climax (the elbow), but at the end (the boomerang tip) when things return to normal, life is never the same.

 Learning Maps – the winding path represents a journey. These can be drawn as a map with points of understanding indicated along the way rather than at the end. Learning journeys never take a straight path but wind, zig-zag or go around.

 Non-verbal Learning – the symbol of the hand represents all knowledge that can be acquired or understood without words, including gestures, inference, expressions, eye movement, kinaesthetic learning, images and revealed knowledge such as dreams, insight, inspiration and reflection.

 Symbols and Images – this symbol represents people sitting at a meeting place yarning. It is a simple image that represents deeper information and understandings. Symbols and images can be used to represent words and concepts, or even learning processes.

 Land Links – this symbol represents a river. All the animals, plants and geographic forms in land and water contain deep knowledge. They also provide metaphors for concepts. Knowledge of local land and place is central to Indigenous ways of knowing.

 Non-linear Processes – the symbol represents circular logic at the centre, and the lines on either side show the interface between opposites. Opposites meet to create something new, with symmetry and balance concepts valued above oppositional thinking. Learning does not go straight from one side to the other. It bends out to the side, bringing in knowledge that might seem to be off topic, but that creates deeper understandings and richer learnings.

 Deconstruct/Reconstruct – The symbol of the Torres Strait Islander drum represents the way knowledge can be learned by back-tracking through the concept and the whole in supported stages, then reproduced independently. The shape shows the balance between independence and support.

 Community Links – the knowledge spiral shows how creation patterns at the local level are repeated at the non-local level throughout the universe. It also shows how non-local information is viewed and used from local standpoints for community benefit, with all learning returned to the community.

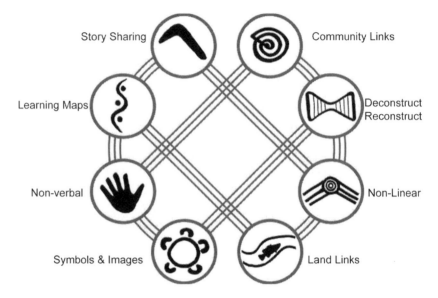

Figure 8.1   Yunkaporta's eight ways of learning

Cardinally, moreover, Yunkaporta's eight ways of learning are represented not as a linear list or progression, but as an elegant cross-linked topological network, as shown in Figure 8.1.

Yunkaporta's framework has considerable standing in the Indigenous education field and with Indigenous communities across Australia, so we decided to adopt it as the model for application in our pilot project.

   OUR WAYS OF KNOWLEDGE-SEEKING

Karen Martin-Booran Mirraboopa (2008) has challenged non-Indigenous researchers "to engage research as an interface where conceptual, cultural and historical spaces come alongside each other based on new relationships to knowledge, to research and to self ... [In this way the power of researcher over researched can be neutralised]. Thus, the Indigenist research interface is no longer a site of resistance, but a site of decolonisation and transformation" (p. 131). To answer this challenge, we chose as our method community-based participatory research (CBPR), in which researchers work with communities to generate knowledge about and solutions to problems the community is facing (Baum, MacDougall, and Smith, 2006). This approach values the knowledge of 'ordinary' people by positioning them not as the object of the research but as participants in the research process, so that the researched also become co-researchers. It encompasses methods such as participatory action research, partnership research and collaborative inquiry, and is widely acknowledged as a technique that is congruent with Indigenous cultural principles of relationality and connectedness (Mooney-Somers and Maher, 2009).

Within the overall CBPR framework, we then adopted Yarning Circles – a ubiquitous Indigenous custom for culturally secure story-sharing, community decision-making and conflict resolution (Kovach, 2010) – as our core data-gathering method. Yarning Circles are not altogether unlike focus groups, except that the distinction between 'researcher' and 'subject' is largely absent (Bessarab and Ng'andu, 2010, p. 47) except in some circumstances where participants who have recognised authority within the group may lead the discussion more overtly (Martin-Booran Mirraboopa, 2008). The conversation also tends to be somewhat unstructured and meandering compared with the pre-set questions and discussion points that normally characterise focus groups. Yarning Circles generally embrace the following protocols (adapted from Queensland Government Department of Education, n.d, p. 2):

- The group forms a complete circle, ensuring that everyone is seated equally and can see all other participants.
- The circle is a safe place where everyone is required to contribute and where all opinions are valid and valued.
- A response may be brief or extended.
- An artefact is passed from participant to participant to signal when it is their turn to speak, until everyone in the circle has had a chance to contribute at least once. Participants are permitted to pass without speaking on second or subsequent turns.
- Participants cannot talk without the artefact, and there can be no conversation across the circle. All must await their turn, even if they want to address something just said.
- When the holder of the artefact is speaking, all must listen attentively and respectfully.
- The yarning concludes when all feel that they have no more to contribute to the topic.

 ## GATHERING OUR DATA IN THE SUBJECT UNIT COMMUNITIES

The selected subject units commenced in Semester 2, 2017, observing their normal curriculum. The research project was not introduced until around mid-semester, so as to allow the participating students to make something of a reflective comparison between the two halves. At the time of introduction, a presentation about the research was made to each unit's cohort community, explaining the nature and intentions of the project and inviting the students'

participation as co-researchers. The students were also at that stage introduced to Yunkaporta's (2009) 8 Aboriginal Ways of Learning and asked to apply that framework as a lens through which to reflect on their activities and experiences in their units for the remainder of the semester. It was also foreshadowed that at the end of the semester, each unit would hold a Yarning Circle to share and capture the results of their reflections. The initial general response of the students to the prospect of participation appeared to be warm interest, tempered by some cautiousness. At that stage none declined to participate, even though that option was offered.

For the remaining classes of the semester, the unit teaching staff continued to follow their normal curriculum activities and tasks, but with some reference to and discussion of connections between each of these and the 8 Ways schema.

 ## SHARING STORIES IN THE YARNING CIRCLES

The Yarning Circles were conducted in the final class session of each subject unit and facilitated by one of the core researchers not involved with the actual unit teaching. In accordance with the Yarning Circle protocols, that facilitator was also a contributor to the conversation, as were the unit teaching staff. With the written consent of all participants the discussion was recorded, so that the artefact for passing around became the recording device itself. To foster some consistency across the three units, pre-determined conversation prompts based on Research Questions 1 to 3 were used at all three sessions (Research Question 4 was not considered in the Yarning Circles), but encouragement was given for broad interpretations and responses rather than sticking to a close interpretation of the questions. The prompts were:

1. Did you have any knowledge of Indigenous ways of knowing, learning and connecting before they were raised in this unit? Was this knowledge *about* these things, or have you actually *applied* them in your learning?
2. Thinking back over this semester, what learning methods have you experienced in this unit that resemble any of the 8 Ways?
3. What's different about these ways of knowing, learning and connecting from other ways you've experienced?
4. Indigenous ways of knowing, learning and connecting are traditionally integrated with each other in a joined-up way. Can we find that kind of connectedness in a contemporary, secular, globalised society? How?
5. Do you think that, in an Indigenous Studies unit, it makes sense to consciously use Indigenous ways of knowing, learning and connecting?
6. Should Indigenous ways of knowing, learning and connecting be embedded in other units and courses with no Indigenous content? What would be the benefits? Any risks?

Attendance at the Yarning Circles was around 50 per cent of the enrolled students in Unit 1 – Indigenous Politics and the State and Unit 2 – Indigenous Heritage and Landscapes units, and 100 per cent of the students in the Unit 3 – Graduation Studio – Landscape Architecture unit, with a total number of seventeen participants across all three sessions. Participation at all sessions was attentive and respectful, and characterised by deep, active listening and thoughtful, perceptive, often courageous responses.

 ## DECONSTRUCTING AND RECONSTRUCTING THE YARNING CIRCLE EXCHANGES

The Yarning Circle sessions were transcribed and submitted to conversational analysis to identify emergent themes and patterns. These are presented below under the heading of each prompt topic. Because of the small total number of participants and, as it turned out, a high level of consensus across the three units, response results are presented and analysed here in combined form rather than separately for each unit. However, areas of divergence among the three cohort's responses are also reported.

Topic 1

Did you have any knowledge of Indigenous ways of knowing, learning and connecting before they were raised in this unit? Was this knowledge about these things, or have you actually applied them in your learning?

Of the student participants, two had previously encountered the 8 Ways model. One was an education student completing an Indigenous Studies major, who had learnt about the 8 Ways in another unit and applied it subsequently in her teaching. Another had experienced it first through learning and then later teaching in a non-mainstream school system, and then later through previous studies at another university. Two others had heard that there were Indigenous ways of knowing and learning, but nothing more explicit and with no prior opportunity to apply them wittingly and purposefully. For example, one student stated that on reflection he realised that in another Indigenous subject unit he had "experienced them but didn't know that there was some framing … or terminology you could put around it". The other had worked in the Kimberley region with young Aboriginal children in a manner that was "open and flexible and moving away from education that's about sitting, listening and … having things written in a certain way" towards approaches that involved "going out on the land and just hanging out and talking and doing".

The remaining students had no prior knowledge of Indigenous ways of knowing and learning – neither Yunkaporta's eight ways nor any other – although they did have some understanding of the importance of connectedness in Indigenous cultures. However, the exposure in this unit had aroused their interest. As one student put it, "It's very interesting for me, the connection that they hold with each other is a lot closer than I would have with a lot of other Europeans ... they're very close-knit, and that's most of what I've learnt."

One participating unit lecturer, revealing his own heritage from an oppressed cultural minority, stated that he found an affinity with Australian Indigenous people when he was previously taught by an Aboriginal woman who, as he put it, "taught me through, song ... through yarning circles ... and got us to take off our shoes and socks and walk on the grass and sit down and chat to each other." More recently, he had also received close guidance from Indigenous mentors on campus. Another lecturer had had more extensive experience of Indigenous ways from an early age, not only with Aboriginal Australians but also with Native Americans and Papua New Guinea highlanders. The third lecturer, with a history of considerable engagement with Aboriginal Australians and Indigenous Canadians – especially Inuit and Métis – had come across the 8 Ways framework previously, and also had familiarity with other similar models.

Topic 2

Thinking back over this semester, what learning methods have you experienced in this unit that resemble any of the 8 Ways?

All of the students agreed that the 8 Ways were embedded implicitly in the approach to teaching and learning taken in their units, although not explicitly until the framework was introduced mid-semester. They could identify:

- story-sharing both by the lecturer and among themselves;
- the use of symbols and images via video and photo imagery;
- learning maps through clear, incremental alignment of learning tasks and assessments through the semester's engagement;
- deconstructing and reconstructing Indigenous-focused socio-political phenomena;
- non-linear, non-verbal self-directed learning;
- community links through guest appearances by Indigenous contributors; and
- non-verbal learning by seeing, deeply listening and doing.

As one participant said: "relating things to personal life and experiences ... builds a connection. I really like that not only are you given things to read ... you can also look at things that are visual ... For me, talking and listening, watching and listening and reading really impacts and embeds what I have to learn."

Participants in all three units expressed appreciation for now having the 8 Ways as an explicit lens and language through which to reflect on and connect up their learning experiences. They also acknowledged the story-sharing and connectedness-building value of their participation in the Yarning Circles.

One area of divergence emerged under this topic, related to the land links element of the 8 Ways. In Units 2 and 3, land links were strongly and clearly embedded in the curriculum, via:

- In Unit 2, a class trip with a local Indigenous ranger to Yankee Hat, an Aboriginal rock art site in the mountains south of Canberra, which all concurred was a highlight of the semester. As one student stated, not only did they get "to see drawings on a rock face, but ... we yarned before the hike started, we were shown the bark falling from the trees, and the shape of an ant's nest, and what all these meant".
- In Unit 3, for which a major assessment requirement for students in this unit involved the authentic task of investigating how the nationally-significant Bundian Way Aboriginal cultural, spiritual and trade route – stretching 350 kilometres from the Snowy mountains to the South Coast region of NSW – could be represented in design installations in a proposed arts precinct for the Moneroo Bubberer Gudu Keeping Place at the Eden Local Aboriginal Land Council's Jigamy Farm near Pambula. Land links were therefore well to the fore in their experiences, but they also acknowledged that all the other ways in Yunkaporta's model had formed part of their semester's learning. One of the students even included the 8 Ways diagram in his final design presentation.

By contrast, students in Unit 1 constructively noted that land links had not really been addressed as a way of learning. The participating lecturer acknowledged this relative shortcoming and undertook to consider amendments in future iterations.

Topic 3

What's different about these ways of knowing, learning and connecting from other ways you've experienced?

The major difference expressed by the students between their learning experiences in these subject units and those in their other units of study can be mainly classed under a heading of a sense of group connectedness, expressed on a range of words and phrases such as "empathy", "respect for everyone", "yarning group work", "bringing humanity back into it", "working together and encouraging everybody", "respect", "relatedness" and "collectivist". An observed spinoff benefit from this was that attendance at classes was higher than for other units, with students "showing up ... because they legitimately want to learn [in] a way that things are shared". Another perceived benefit was that the Indigenous approach to learning "gives people a chance to play to their strengths, but also discover what their strengths are".

Participants were all strongly appreciative of these differences in comparison with more traditional Western models of teaching and learning, which they variously characterised as the "old academic model", "just based solely on information", "very individualised and assumes knowledge and skills", "learning by theory", and being "told what to think".

An additional response from the Unit 3 cohort, derived from the fact that they had developed an ongoing relationship with the Jigamy people over several consecutive years, was to stress the importance of a curriculum that is joined up or connected coherently over an extended timeframe. As one stated, "That sort of learning can't be accommodated in a twelve-week semester. The relationships actually build up over time".

Topic 4

Indigenous ways of knowing, learning and connecting are traditionally integrated with each other in a joined-up way. Can we find that kind of connectedness in a contemporary, secular, globalised society? How?

Participants in all three groups quickly acknowledged that the primary force for Indigenous connectedness resides in a spiritual cosmology of the relationality of all creation. They equally quickly asserted that spirituality in the form of organised religion was generally more of a force for conflict in the world than for connectedness.

The task of arriving at an equivalent force for connectedness for a secular globalised society took more time and exercised them considerably. Nonetheless, their responses ultimately all pointed to the idea that connectedness itself is the binding force. For example, one student suggested that the answer might lie in "getting rid of the things that separate us and focusing on the things that connect us ... the fact that we're human beings and the fact that we're emotional beings". Another proposed that we should "connect with people around us ... with like thoughts or interests or experience, or different ways of learning, and then sharing that and passing it on. So it's maybe not just about learning but not being jealous of that knowledge". Others talked about "finding common ground", being "more collegiate [and] community oriented". One student encapsulated this trajectory as a profound humanism, which can "really help people get that connection with everyone ... regardless of who they are or where they're from and trying to respect them and live your [own] life as if ... the person you're affecting is yourself". A participating lecturer in a different group expressed similar sentiments, declaring that he did not believe "that there is a connection that all seven and a half billion of us on the planet can identify except for the fact that we are human beings. ... Lifting each other up, I think that's something we could strive for as a connection". However, one student also cautioned that the 8 Ways schema itself might be a seductive oversimplification of the complexities of connected learning: "Some of the circles might be bigger than others at certain times of the year, certain phases of our lives ... and some might have stronger connections".

Again because of their practical focus on working within landscapes, the Unit 3 cohort placed additional emphasis on the importance of a shared sense of place in fostering connectedness. As one participant put it, "when you belong in a place you're connected to that place. When you see things cut down or broken you feel hurt. In a sense that's a spiritual connection in some regard. ... There's a huge disconnect within our teaching systems that don't support a sense of belonging".

Under this topic the participants also grappled with the question as to whether the global connectivity of digital media and the Internet could contribute to a sense of secular connectedness. There was a tentative consensus that such platforms could and should make a contribution, but also that they were more of a tool than a solution in themselves; that they were means of communication rather than connectedness. While it was acknowledged that digital tools "might also be liberating for some people who in other ways might feel isolated in their community or in a country where some things are not publicly acceptable" and so feel "some sort of hope or solidarity or freedom ... they otherwise don't get", it was also a matter of concern that they could also be instruments of oppression because digital anonymity allows people to "connect only to kind of disconnect ... to be aggressive". One student suggested that social media, in particular, could be "a real barrier to people enhancing their social skills and emotional intelligence", and hence a barrier to their capacity for connectedness. Another from a different cohort similarly asserted that web and social media "addiction" could adversely affect people's employability in jobs requiring face-to-face interaction. Another student asserted that "in a physical community you don't have that choice to disconnect from people you don't agree with, whereas with the Internet you do", while yet another in a different group observed that most things the class had learnt in the unit were "not learnt from the media, not learnt from the Internet, they were learnt from personal experience and then shared in class". One of the participating lecturers, in some contrast, stated that by using digital "ways of connecting outside the mainstream social media" he personally has found a "level of connectivity that has been ... valuable" to him.

Another participating lecturer introduced a divergent issue under this topic, by asserting that "Indigenous learning is gendered. The men teach the boys and the women teach young women, and they build up groups and organisations that sustain that way of learning. I'm not sure how one would approach it in a university system". One of the students responded by agreeing that "as a male person, it's not respectful to learn the female ways of a particular culture, and how that could be melded into university studies is probably something to seek further advice about from Elders".

Topic 5

Do you think that, in an Indigenous Studies unit, it makes sense to consciously use Indigenous ways of knowing, learning and connecting?

There was a strong and unqualified consensus across participants in all groups that Indigenous ways of knowing, learning and connecting should be explicitly used and taught in other Indigenous units. For example, one declared this matter to be a "no-brainer", while another stated that she had originally expected that there would be "such an intro to Indigenous culture or tradition when [she] first came into the uni".

Topic 6

Should Indigenous ways of knowing, learning and connecting be embedded in other units and courses with no Indigenous content? What would be the benefits? Any risks?

Student participants across all three units were cautiously optimistic about the prospects for extending Indigenous pedagogies to non-Indigenous units, with principal potential benefits identified as the broadening of teaching approaches beyond 'theory lectures' to embrace multiple diverse active and connected ways of learning, making classes safer places for inclusive participation by all students. As one put it, "following these different pathways, these eight pathways through university study, and even through life, would lead to a more rounded person that has the ability to step up and speak or engage or listen and then engage", while another stated that she could generally not "see any risks in applying this way of learning across the whole university, only benefits". Even so, five potential risks were in fact identified:

1. There was concern that some teaching staff might have incompatible approaches to teaching. "Their own cultural background might be quite different and their ways of communicating to students might mean that implementing Indigenous ways of teaching and learning might be quite difficult for them to achieve", which might lead to "the students not grasping the concepts because their teacher doesn't really connect properly with the way that they're teaching".

2. A similar concern, but from the student perspective, was that there might not be "an appetite for some students to learn from the beginning about these kinds of things … until they … have come to terms with who they are as an individual … as a human being. … And if that's the case then there's got to be accommodations for things to fail. Other systems have to accommodate around it".

3. A further risk concerned a possible lack of applicability of the 8 Ways to learning in some specific disciplines such as accounting or mathematics.

4. There was also disquiet expressed about processes of professional accreditation of courses, designed as they are to assure "an equal form of learning across the board, so that as students move through the ranks they can talk to their counterpart in another city … at the same stage of learning … [and] … professional proficiency". The professions might therefore be unwilling to accept more individual distinctiveness in course design.

5. Another anticipated risk was that problems might arise for students with restricted mobility in participating in field trips or excursions.

To address these risks, the student participants suggested that teaching staff would need clear training and guidance in the transition to these different approaches, and that it would also be beneficial if their students were taken into the teacher's "trust network" in the process, with the changes to Indigenous ways of learning introduced in "baby steps … just implement one thing at a time, one thing that's different … one option that takes them outside their comfort zone in terms of the methodology that they're using to teach". They also recommended that strategies and processes for implementation of Indigenous ways of learning and connecting should be developed in consultation with Indigenous communities and Elders, and that professional accreditation bodies should be consulted early and regularly through the processes.

 APPROACHING THE CULTURAL INTERFACE

The responses from participants to the Yarning Circle prompt questions (addressing Research Questions 1–3) were sufficiently positive – notwithstanding the caveats expressed – to give the research team confidence in proceeding to address Research Question 4:

What correlations might exist between Indigenous ways of learning and connecting and progressive contemporary non-Indigenous pedagogic and connectedness approaches, to promote a beneficial cultural interface in university teaching and learning generally?

Table 8.1   Mapping of the 8 Ways with contemporary non-Indigenous pedagogies and connectedness pedagogies

The 8 Ways	Connectedness Learning Approach – Connectedness Pedagogies	Contemporary Non-Indigenous Pedagogies
Story Sharing	Social Media and ePortfolios; Connected Learning	Narrative-based Learning; Story-based Learning; Portfolio Practice; Learning Journals
Learning Maps	Student Partnerships	Learning Plans; Curriculum Co-Design; Students-As-Partners
Non-Verbal	Work Integrated Learning	Learning By Doing; Imitation Method; Concrete Learning; Kinaesthetic Learning
Symbols and Images	Social Media and ePortfolios	Visual Learning; Mind-Mapping; Visual Representation; Arts Across the Curriculum; Learning Through Metaphor; Abstract Learning
Land Links		Place-based Learning; Land-based Learning; Community-based Learning; Field Trips
Non-Linear	Co-curricular Activities; Alumni Teaching and Engagement; Industry Teaching and Engagement	Flexible Learning; Personalised Learning; Self-Directed Learning; Informal Learning; Social Learning
Deconstruct Reconstruct	Connected Learning	Problem-based Learning; Situated Learning; Simulation; Case Studies; Teaching with Analogies
Community Links	Work Integrated Learning; Industry Teaching and Engagement; Alumni Teaching and Engagement	Work Integrated Learning; Authentic Learning; Industry Networking; Experiential Learning; Community-based Learning; Service Learning; Volunteering

To address this question, we undertook a preliminary mapping of the Yunkaporta 8 Ways against:

• contemporary non-Indigenous pedagogies, and
• the seven key pedagogic approaches outlined in the Connectedness Learning Approach.

This mapping is presented in Table 8.1.

This cross-tabulation signifies a promising potential for alignment between the 8 Ways and the Connectedness Learning Approach's key pedagogic approaches, as well as many contemporary non-Indigenous pedagogies. It is noteworthy that there seems to be little or no place in this mapping for the teacher-centred 'factory models' of teaching (Johnson, 2006), such as behaviourism and instructivism, that still persist in contemporary higher education (as indeed was noted by students in the Yarning Circle sessions). It therefore seems possible that the mapping might be taken by university teaching and learning development advocates to imply that engaging with Indigenous ways of learning and connecting is simply a matter of being better, more progressive teachers in contemporary non-Indigenous terms, and to thus reassure those who are apprehensive about transitioning to Indigenous-embedded ways that the challenge may not be as daunting as it might initially appear. In turn, this might engender desirable outcomes in terms of better learning experiences for students, both Indigenous and non-Indigenous. However, to fully actuate the cultural interface, university teaching needs not only to be progressively connected and aligned within itself and across the whole curriculum, but also framed by historical and contemporary Indigenous systems of holistic relationality and connectedness, and their non-Indigenous correlatives.

 NEXT STEPS IN THE JOURNEY

As acknowledged in the Yarning Circles, secular correlatives to the spiritual connectedness of Indigenous communities are difficult even to identify, let alone ingrain in practice. Yet without them, attempts to mobilise a genuine cultural interface model may be reduced to tick-box exercises, and thus ultimately counter-productive. One potentially fruitful line of future investigation articulated in the Yarning Circles may revolve around questions of place. There is already published research that explores the possibility of adapting Indigenous wisdom and insight around connection to a country towards the development of an integrated Indigenous-based global socio-economic-ecological framework (Sangha et al., 2015), with the implication that at one level, 'country' might refer to the whole planet. If so, there will surely have to be a role for digitally-mediated connectedness strategies, developed and deployed to avoid the pitfalls raised in the Yarning Circles. Such questions and ideas will need to be investigated in future stages of the continuing Indigenising the Curriculum Program at UC.

Another question from the Yarning Circles was whether Indigenous ways of learning and connecting are gendered. This is not raised as an issue in Yunkaporta (2009), nor in any of the literature that supported that study, and since publication the 8 Ways have been applied in female, male and mixed learning contexts. However, the fact that Indigenous knowledges and cultural roles are often gendered perhaps implies that the associated pedagogies may also be – at least to some extent – so this will also warrant investigation in subsequent stages of the program. Similarly, whether professional accreditation processes may potentially impede the intent of the overall project will also need to be addressed in future stages; one way of doing this may be to select at least one accredited course for further piloting.

With all these matters in mind, the immediate next stage will be to conduct a somewhat similar exploration, refined from the findings of the present study and addressing the issues arising from it, to test whether embedding Indigenous ways of learning and connecting resonate as positively with students and staff in subject units that do not already have an Indigenous content focus. This would be a logical next step on the journey towards an ultimate consummation of a genuine cultural interface between Indigenous and non-Indigenous pedagogies and topologies that could be adopted across the higher education sector to:

> nurture and graduate ever more Aboriginal and Torres Strait Islander students who will enjoy challenging, rewarding and influential careers; grow awareness and cultural competence in non-Aboriginal and Torres Strait Islander students and the broader community, who will have the knowledge and skills to work with Aboriginal and Torres Strait Islander peoples for a reconciled Australia … and be an independent voice in service of reconciliation. (Calma, 2017)

Such capabilities in all university graduates could contribute towards a more connected, reconciled and culturally enriched society as a whole.

NOTES

1. Unless explicitly stated otherwise, 'Indigenous' in this chapter refers to Australian Aboriginal and Torres Strait Islander people.
2. The authors wish to pay respect and gratitude to the traditional owners of the ancestral lands on which the University of Canberra is built – the Ngunnawal Peoples. As, in this chapter, we share our own knowledge, teaching, learning, and research practices, we also pay respect to Ngunnawal knowledge and traditions. The authors are also grateful for the support and encouragement of the leaders and staff of the University of Canberra's Office of Aboriginal and Torres Strait Islander Leadership Strategy, Ngunnawal Centre, Teaching and Learning unit, and participating faculties.
3. As this chapter deals with the cultural interface between Indigenous and non-Indigenous pedagogies and topologies, the authors have endeavoured to embed this in the naming of the chapter sections, including with visual symbols. The meanings of the symbols are detailed in the second section.
4. For convenience of reference in the data-gathering and in this chapter, the units were numbered according to the sequence of primary data collection.

REFERENCES

Battiste, M. (2002). *Indigenous Knowledge and Pedagogy in First Nations Education: A Literature Review with Recommendations*. National Working Group on Education and the Minister of Indian Affairs. Ottawa, ON: Indian and Northern Affairs.

Baum, F., MacDougall, C., and Smith, D. (2006). Participatory action research. *Journal of Epidemiology and Community Health*, *60*(10), 854–857.

Bessarab, D., and Ng'andu, B. (2010). Yarning about yarning as a legitimate method in Indigenous research. *International Journal of Critical Indigenous Studies*, *3*(1), 37–50.

Bridgstock, R. (2016). Educating for digital futures: What the learning strategies of digital media professionals can teach higher education. *Innovations in Education and Teaching International*, *53*(3), 306–315.

Calma, T. (2017). Message from the Chancellor *University of Canberra Reconciliation Action Plan 2018–2020*. Canberra: University of Canberra.

Dreamson, N., Thomas, G., Lee Hong, A., and Kim, S. (2017). Policies on and practices of cultural inclusivity in learning management systems: Perspectives of Indigenous holistic pedagogies. *Higher Education Research and Development*, *36*(5), 947–961.

Harris, S. (1984). Aboriginal learning styles and formal schooling. *The Australian Journal of Indigenous Education*, *12*(4), 3–23.

Johnson, A. P. (2006). No child left behind: Factory models and business paradigms. *The Clearing House: A Journal of Educational Strategies, Issues and Ideas*, *80*(1), 34–36.

Kovach, M. (2010). Conversational method in Indigenous research. *First Peoples Child and Family Review*, *5*(1), 40–48.

Marker, M. (2006). After the Makah whale hunt: Indigenous knowledge and limits to multicultural discourse. *Urban Education*, *41*(5), 482–505.

Martin-Booran Mirraboopa, K. (2008). *Please Knock Before You Enter: Aboriginal Regulation of Outsiders and the Implications for Researchers*. Teneriffe, Qld: Post Pressed.

Mooney-Somers, J., and Maher, L. (2009). The Indigenous Resiliency Project: A worked example of community-based participatory research. *New South Wales Public Health Bulletin*, *20*(8), 112–118.

Queensland Government Department of Education. (n.d). Supporting learning resource – Yarning Circles, retrieved on 16 January 2019 from https://harlaxtonss.eq.edu.au/Supportandresources/Formsanddocuments/Documents/yarning-circles.pdf.

Rasmussen, C., Baydala, L., and Sherman, J. (2004). Learning patterns and education of Aboriginal children: A review of the literature. *The Canadian Journal of Native Studies, 24*(2), 317–342.

Robinson, J., and Nichol, R. (1998). Building bridges between Aboriginal and Western mathematics: Creating an effective mathematics learning environment. *Education in Rural Australia, 8*(2), 9–17.

Sangha, K. K., Le Brocque, A., Costanza, R., and Cadet-James, Y. (2015). Ecosystems and indigenous well-being: An integrated framework. *Global Ecology and Conservation, 4*, 197–206.

Thomas, G. (2015). Connection and connectedness: Realizing the imperative for Indigenous Education. *International Education Journal: Comparative Perspectives, 14*(2), 1–9.

Wheaton, C. (2000). An Aboriginal pedagogical model: Recovering an Aboriginal pedagogy from the Woodlands Cree. In R. Neil (ed.), *Voice of the Drum: Indigenous Education and Culture* (pp. 151–166). Ottawa, ON: Kingfisher Publications.

Yunkaporta, T. (2009). *Aboriginal pedagogies at the cultural interface.* Doctor of Education PhD thesis, James Cook University, Townsville, Qld.

9. The capstone experience: five principles for a connected curriculum

Mitch Goodwin, Kay Are, Michael 'Maxx' Schmitz, Bryonny Goodwin-Hawkins, Wajeehah Aayeshah and Elizabeth Lakey

POSITIONING THE CAPSTONE EXPERIENCE

As it is presented in the international literature, 'capstone' is the name commonly given to final-year units of study designed, on the one hand, to consolidate learning gained throughout a course of study and, on the other, to orient students towards life beyond tertiary study (Leahy et al., 2017). The existing scholarship suggests three main objectives for capstone experiences: to enable students to synthesise prior learning (e.g. Leahy et al., 2017); to prepare students for professional practice (e.g. Ryan, Tews and Washer, 2012); and to serve quality-assurance purposes, such as evaluating course-level learning outcomes (e.g. Lee and Loton, 2015). Together, these objectives emphasise the *twofold* nature of capstones: at once looking back over a learning path, and ahead to professional practices (Hauhart and Grahe, 2010; McNamara et al., 2015).

A PRACTICAL APPROACH

In this chapter, we contribute to advancing thinking around capstone experiences by drawing on the Connectedness Learning Approach which, we argue, can more closely address the challenges brought to higher education in our particular moment in the twenty-first century.

Our intention is thoroughly practical: below, we synthesise the approach into five principles, then describe how these might be applied to curriculum design in capstone-like units of study. While we provide insights specific to four units at the University of Melbourne – Creative Writing, Anthropology, History, and Media and Communication Studies – we agree with commentators who note that no single model can or should guide capstone curricula (van Acker et al., 2014). In one sense, their ambition and distinctive remit does make for shared challenges in design and practice: incorporating 'non-traditional' elements into curricula has implications for professional development, workload, logistics, and budget that are comparable across most disciplines (e.g. Lee and Loton, 2017). Capstones can also raise generalisable questions about the student experience and the achievement of learning outcomes (e.g. Fernandez, 2006). However, factors such as varying institutional policies (Lee and Loton, 2017), professional accreditation requirements (Rowles et al., 2004) and the wealth of disciplinary diversity in contemporary universities clearly call for capstones that are tailored, not templated.

The need for specificity explains why much existing scholarly work on capstones reports on individual units or considers capstones at a disciplinary level (Haney, 2017; Jarman and Wiley, 2007; Lee and Loton, 2015; Upson-Saia, 2013). In general, the STEM disciplines and business schools have dominated this literature (Jarman and Wiley, 2007; Upson-Saia, 2013; van Acker et al., 2014). The wide applicability of an Arts education as an employability hazard is a well-documented myth (Olejarz, 2017; Shulman, 2017) but Humanities, Arts and Social Sciences (HASS) capstones are, too often, about students becoming *disciplined*, which exacerbates this perception. We would suggest that certain disciplines' high engagement with capstone design and evaluation emerges from their strong awareness of professional connections: Finance and Engineering, for example (Schedin and Hassan, 2014), interface with 'real world' careers in ways that Philosophy and English Literature, traditionally at least, do not. Accordingly, HASS disciplines typically appear in capstone literature through their more professionally-oriented programs, such as Journalism (Cullen, 2017; Haney, 2017). To be sure, many of the capstone's concerns are also found in the growing field of Work Integrated Learning (WIL) (Smith, 2012), where traditional academic learning is integrated into workplace exposure (von Treuer et al., 2010) and on-campus employment-related experiences (Fleischmann, 2015). WIL activities have produced documented evidence of improvement in student capacities including problem solving, team work, communication, information literacy and professionalism (Coll et al., 2009) – all skills recognised for their potential to increase graduate employability (Cleary et al., 2007). WIL is therefore not out of place in units designed to focus students' attentions on the cumulative usefulness of their learning to workplace futures.

We argue, however, that the concentration of capstone literature in professionally-oriented disciplines is responsible for an overly narrow emphasis on WIL, employability and market-responsiveness. This developmental bias has, we suggest, skewed the potential for capstones to address students' progress more holistically. It fails to consider learning as a social activity, which has strong implications for learning outcomes in a liberal arts education

(Matthews, Andrews and Adams, 2011; Williamson and Nodder, 2002), just as the advent of personal learning networks have become an important part of student and civic engagement within the networked commons (Rheingold, 2018). The relative absence of HASS from conversations around capstones is a missed opportunity for the conceptual development of capstones as enablers of socially, culturally and psychologically well-integrated *people*, rather than employees. And it is here, we will argue, that the concept of connectedness can help. Rather than delimit the capstone's scope, 'employability' can revivify the capstone's agenda – *if* we take employability to mean the capacity to '*employ*' one's '*abilities*', as Bridgstock and Tippett suggest we do in their introduction to this volume (see Chapter 1). The Connectedness Learning Approach affirms 'the ability to harness one's skills, knowledge and other attributes' and redirect them to multiple ends and within manifold networks throughout a life. This also acknowledges that learning is only partly derived from exposure to workplaces. It suggests that the more transformative learning perhaps results from students' ability to draw acquired knowledge and skills into *making sense* of the industrial, academic and interpersonal networks students navigate. That is, into constructing networks that are meaningfully interconnected with each other (see Chapter 1 in this volume). Therefore, the underlying metaphor for the capstone experience is not completion but *connection*.

THE MELBOURNE CONTEXT

The Faculty of Arts at the University of Melbourne offers one of the largest Arts programs in Australia. With 45 discipline areas across six schools, each with its own culture and traditions, effecting change across the undergraduate program is a considerable challenge. In mid-2016, the Faculty's Teaching and Learning portfolio established the five-member Curriculum Design Lab (CDL) to assist academics to transition their classes into Arts West, a new $65 million teaching facility designed to foster innovative active-learning strategies and leverage emergent technologies. The CDL and Arts West represented a significant investment in physical and intellectual infrastructure, whose launch rhetorically enabled structural change.

In quick time the CDL's remit evolved to include a more holistic re-evaluation of the BA program. A top-down approach, or a faculty-wide mandate, would be impractical and politically difficult to execute, contingent on buy-in from the various Schools and departments and their various hierarchies. Thus, we sought a gateway into a deeper, more roots-and-branch approach to curriculum (re)design, identifying capstones – an all-but compulsory element of every Melbourne discipline since 2008 (Holdsworth, Watty and Davies, 2009) – as the most adequate avenue to widespread renewal.

FIVE PRINCIPLES FOR CONNECTED CAPSTONES

We built the Arts Capstone Experience Project at the University of Melbourne around five key design principles, all of which correspond to ideals articulated by the Connectedness Learning Approach. We arrived at these principles by means of reflective practice over time rather than in advance as a prescriptive roadmap. Our priorities were also informed by our faculty's strategic emphasis on active learning, critical thinking and leadership, and, more recently, student wellbeing (The University of Melbourne, 2015, 2017).

From the outset, we were aware of the need to formulate a set of guiding design principles in order to strengthen and justify the project's foundation. We also saw that schematisation would later become an important part of enabling unit coordinators to autonomously devise their own curricula. The capstone curriculum invites particularly careful consideration, responsible as it is for orienting students towards pathways on which they often have already embarked without full awareness. Capstone experiences can be the most challenging yet satisfying experiences in a degree because performance is tested not only before teaching staff and peers but also in public spheres, both familiar and newly acquired. Students reaching the capstone are expected to have a solid theoretical grasp of their chosen discipline and, ideally, to be capable of using their learning critically and creatively as they move into new realms (Houghton and Stewart, 2017; Hwang et al., 2017).

Our curriculum design activities had always been research-led, informed by the team's mixed discipline skillset in studio and theory-based instruction as well as ethnographic and creative modes of research and scholarship. We habitually drew on best practice in, among other areas, 'connected learning' (e.g. Ito et al., 2014), 'connective learning' (e.g. Siemens, 2005) and 'autonomous motivation' (Baik and Larcombe, 2016). But, at a time when we were consolidating a project that sought to identify and leverage the specific kinds of connections-for-learning that capstones afford, we were fortuitously introduced to the Connectedness Learning Approach. It spoke to and expanded our interpretation of the capstone's potential utility as a site for *learning from connections* as well as for *learning to connect*. The Approach provided a vocabulary with which to reflect on our own experiences of flows and blockage in capstone development and to refine our program going forward. We here outline how each of our five design principles intersects with Connectedness Learning.

First, in order for a capstone unit to enable students to recognise their connection to networks and, in turn, their networks' interconnectedness, learning activities should strive to be authentic: interaction should occur in real rather than simulated contexts and involve genuine social and professional partners.

Authenticity of experience reportedly emerged as an important element of Connectedness Learning in response to Bridgstock's finding that Australia's tertiary sector was largely failing to capitalise on existing social networks as sources of learning and support, particularly for students transitioning to life beyond their degrees (see Chapter 1 in this volume). The Connectedness Learning Approach theorises five 'connectedness capabilities' as central to students' ability to capitalise on their social networks for career-building purposes. We observed that whereas 'growing connections', 'working with connections' and 'developing social literacy' are skill sets that can arguably be achieved in simulated environments, two of the five capabilities demanded authenticity: 'strengthening and maintaining connections' beyond university study can only be achieved if connections with genuine partners are made and 'building a connected identity' can only be the result of discovering in practice the authentic relevance of these partnerships to students' identities (Bridgstock, 2019b). We saw that the capstone, as the culmination of a course of study, was the appropriate forum for embedding authentic experiences in support of these latter two capabilities.

Second, experiences of connection in a capstone should be reflective, providing avenues for students to reflect on their place within networks, on their existing contribution to networks and on their potential ongoing value to networks. Constructivist theories of learning nominate reflection as a primary vehicle to lifelong learning and the development of learner identity (Bozalek and Zembylas, 2017; Walker, Boud and Keogh, 1985). Thus, in positioning reflection as a principle of capstone development, we were responding to the Approach's emphasis on the development of a connected identity. Furthermore, several of the pedagogies privileged by the Approach also implicitly call on student reflection – such as student co-design of connective experiences, student partnerships and alumni engagement – this, again, echoed our approach, already underway.

Third and fourth, we wanted capstone units to be creative and celebratory. Given that capstones mark the maximal point in the acquisition of a degree's theoretical and technical skills, capstone students are more likely to be able to deploy their cognitive and critical awareness in innovative ways – a milestone to be celebrated. The Connectedness Learning Approach suggested, however, that this milestone would only be celebrated by final-year students to the extent that they saw their new capacity as valued by their networks. This reinforced the need for students' creative expressions of their learning to find authentic audiences and the need for institutional strategies that ensured affirming outcomes for student work.

Finally, and perhaps most obviously, we affirmed as our fifth design principle that capstones should be socially and industrially networked – that core student activity should build and strengthen new networks, identify and maintain existing networks and meaningfully engage with nodes along multiple networks, within the one unit. The value of networks underpins the Connectedness Learning Approach, and here we found support for our wager that insofar as students are able to creatively use their disciplinary skills to contribute to responsive and authentic partnerships, they will come to *value networks as resources* that can support their movement between worlds of work and study.

In what follows, we detail how our nominated five principles have shaped practical decisions made as we attempted to incorporate each of them into our collaborative (re)design of capstone units in Creative Writing, Anthropology, History, and Media and Communication Studies.

1.   THE AUTHENTIC CAPSTONE EXPERIENCE

A curriculum that is cognisant of its discipline's place and function in broader social and cultural spheres should readily draw an authentic connection between students' disciplinary knowledge and its deployment within these spheres. This is particularly important to HASS students who graduate without a specific professional qualification but rather a set of academically oriented skills and fairly rigid situational awareness. This situation informs how students view their own employability; the anxiety of transitioning to full employment – which can be acute in disciplines where there has traditionally been a reduced focus on embedding employability skills – can in part result from a failure to articulate to students how their learning does indeed translate to the workforce (Gannaway, 2016). This is reflected in studies on graduate capabilities that indicate students often interpret learning outcomes as overly generic and not necessarily orientated towards employment, reinforcing the need to design assessment and learning experiences that clearly communicate to students when industry-relevant learning is taking place (Jorre de St Jorre and Oliver, 2018).

Ensuring that students are aware of skills gained and how these contribute to employability is important (Biggs and Tang, 2011); equally so is developing students' confidence in their ability to deploy these skills in different and unforeseeable environments (Bridgstock, 2016). This is readily achieved by making assessment in the capstone an authentic experience in which skills lead to devising an authentic outcome. Accordingly, assignments should:

- emphasise real-world problems and projects;
- assess professional standards of presentation, communication and project execution;
- provide parameters that are discipline-specific and industry-relevant;
- recognise the value of interdisciplinary collaboration.

The challenge is identifying what an authentic output looks like when traditional career pathways, already broad for BA graduates, are rapidly changing and diversifying (Susskind and Susskind, 2015). One tendency has been to resort to guidance for disciplinary concerns, but these are often too inward-looking to serve the connected student. For instance, the legacy Anthropology capstone emphasises a disciplined, rather than authentic, approach to assessment design by insisting students, in groups of three to five, read and report on a contemporary ethnographic monograph. The group's 5,000-word report reviews the monograph, while analysing one theoretical text it draws upon and one earlier ethnographic monograph it cites. While obviously engaged with how anthropological knowledge is produced, the learning is only authentic to academic anthropology – a profession few of the students will enter. It thus offers no practice of non-academic skills, nor does it alert them to the careers their major makes available to them through the application of this knowledge in other contexts.

Similarly, it is not uncommon that History students attest to a lack in work-relevant skills, given that it is unlikely that content knowledge will form the basis of employability for the majority of History graduates. Recommendations we made for the re-design of the History capstone not only clearly articulate the cognitive skills already taught within the discipline but also build digital literacy (Reyna, Hanham and Meier, 2018). This unit's assessment strategy now imparts skills in design, media production, publishing and exhibition, which allows students to apply their cognitive skills to a broad range of authentic scenarios connected to a range of identifiable – and explicitly identified – occupations. As with this unit, capstones might introduce a number of skills sessions to develop the digital literacy skills that will be relevant not only to the production of their capstone project but also to understanding the ways in which disciplinary knowledge can be communicated to different audiences. In the case of History, we have recommended that students be required to participate in a minimum number of extended digital literacy workshops provided by the university library, which focus on the creation of historical content and digital media content more generally. Students thus develop sought-after content-creation skills in a mix of media including audio, video, and web-based text publishing. Because audience modelling and consideration for user experience are among its key components, this task develops fundamental skills associated with authentic content creation, beyond the writing of a research essay which has limited use in a vocational setting outside of academia (Healey et al., 2013).

Incorporating an event to mark the celebratory nature of the capstone experience (see discussion below) also has implications for the authenticity of the connections the unit enables. In both the History and Creative Writing capstones, students work in groups to co-develop an end-of-semester public exhibition and festival respectively. This significantly increases the size and changes the nature of the audience from a wholly academic to a much broader one, reflective of the multiple communities to whom the students' outcomes could have importance. Furthermore, the group-work component reflects common workplace practice and requires students to overcome the frustrations commonly associated with collaboration as they engage with the logistics of event management – industry representatives, guest lists, venue managers, caterers, promotion and budgets – as a team.

2.   THE REFLECTIVE CAPSTONE EXPERIENCE

Effective assessment offers students the opportunity to reflect on their learning and to see the value of the learning experience (Hauhart and Grahe, 2015; Neary et al., 2014). Reflection allows students to uncover and contrive connections between discrete learning experiences (Dewey, 1998), while a comparative media studies approach enables a student to decode those experiences in a digital media environment (Hayles, 2012). Reflection allows learning to become meaningful by means of its invitation to students to select and order experiences on the basis of personal priorities, rather than on the basis of externally contrived rewards and punishment. This is understood to facilitate durable learning because it catalyses students' "knowledge transformation rather than [privileging] knowledge transmission" (Ryan and Ryan, 2013). Given that it allows the conversion of lived experience into episodic representation, reflection is also an important life and workplace skill because the selective assimilation of numerous and disparate experiences is the mechanism by which meaning is derived from lived conditions and events (Walker, Boud and Keogh, 1985).

Connected capstones encourage students to recognise and nurture connections across life, study and work experiences; in other words, to enhance the meaningfulness of these spheres' lived intersections. There are a number of ways different types of reflection can work to this end:

- 'Reflection in action' refers to reflection that occurs whilst the action is still being undertaken with the opportunity to make changes when they can still benefit the current project (Edwards, 2017; Schön, 1983);
- 'Reflection on action' occurs after the completion of an action or project and teaches that even in failure there can be positive outcomes through its critical evaluation.

For example, an approach recommended in the redesign of the History capstone grew from research on reflective journaling (e.g. Moon, 2004). An assessable journal can solidify students' reflections on their disciplinary journey and function as a 'reflection-on-action' record for students as they create an exhibit for the final capstone event, in which to consider how to improve future outcomes. Reflection can also aid in portfolio development, particularly appropriate to disciplines like Media Studies and Creative Writing. A capstone in these fields presents the opportunity to assemble assignments accumulated over a course and critically evaluate them against industry standards. This is not only a test of employability but a map of personal growth, identifying ways in which their disciplinary skill set enables them to contribute to communities beyond academia. Such reflective work teases out the connections that are durable and that can be built upon outside of the academic bubble.

The capstone experience can act as a crucial, demystifying bridge between typical academic achievement – the acquisition of knowledge and the art of critical thinking – and the often insular and dense lexicon of industry. A unit that demands particular standards in assessment, that makes class project work visible outside of the academy, that invites industry expertise to curriculum-design meetings and to provide feedback on assessment, will give students an ear for the discourse of professional practice and a critical, external reference point for reflective self-evaluation. This is important, since reflection encourages students to create their own understanding of the value of their accomplishments to their personal and professional communities. Accordingly, experiential modes as diverse as object-based, inquiry-led, problem-based and collaborative learning, among others, premise learning on building-in opportunities for self-reflexivity (Bozalek and Zembylas, 2017). Note that because deep reflection helps students develop and practice critical thinking, its practice should ideally be incorporated throughout the major and not just in the capstone.

3. THE CREATIVE CAPSTONE EXPERIENCE

Creativity should form a central pillar in the design of a capstone experience; a capstone should not become merely a final opportunity to impart disciplinary knowledge. As Phil Race observes, "Academics often defend the importance of essay-writing skills, but in practice for most learners, these tend to be skills that they are unlikely to need when they leave post-compulsory education" (Race, 2014, p. 101). Essay-based assessments likely linger in many HASS disciplines for two reasons. First, they reflect the more 'traditional' curriculum that most academics themselves experienced in their undergraduate studies. Second, they can indeed work to test disciplinary knowledge, the acquisition of which is privileged in the traditional curriculum over the acquisition of transferable skills. Although there is certainly a place for traditional assessment tasks at research intensive institutions like the University of Melbourne in which further study is quite often an expectation, there are further reasons a capstone experience should be different. In an international context, what constitutes a traditional dissertation in an undergraduate degree is changing from a strictly research-orientated outcome towards an experience – the act of 'doing', the act of 'making' – *informed* by scholarship (Healey et al., 2013).

Creative approaches allow students in a capstone unit to utilise a more sophisticated blend of technologies in the service of communicating their learning to a wider audience (Sharpe and Beetham, 2010). Forms of student expression in a capstone should reach beyond the confines of the traditional assignment, beyond the classroom, beyond the Learning Management System (LMS), to an audience not only of peers but also of friends, family, industries and associated networks. By opening up the possibilities of how students communicate their learning, we encourage them to take ownership of their learning and to bring existing skills, experiences and competencies – aspects of individuals acquired through connections beyond the university – to enrich their discipline. Creativity, which requires that students recognise alternate possibilities and take considered risks, encourages attributes such as flexibility, intelligence and lateral thinking (Craft, 2005). The shared experience of working on a creative output furthermore exposes students to each other's ideas and demonstrates that received instruction can result in multiple effective learning outcomes.

Although there are numerous ways in which creativity can be embedded in a capstone in order to be effective, a creative assessment must involve a degree of innovation from the student. For instance, it is not enough for the major assessment for the Anthropology capstone to ask students to review a more creative ethnographic monograph; it is not a creative task until students are asked to respond to the monograph creatively. A further important consideration is to avoid advantaging those students who have already mastered creative tools in the existing environment by permitting a variety of means of creative expression and scaffolding creative skill acquisition where necessary (Daniel, 2010). Teaching modes of expression alternative to the essay form need not become a distraction from the need to teach disciplinary content – especially where creative representations of learning involve acquiring digital literacy. Digitally literate graduates can access issues of interest to their home disciplines more deeply and with greater discernment and are equipped to carve out space for their disciplinary knowledge in a digital landscape. Our work in the History and Media and Communication capstones presents an argument for an expanded definition of digital literacy to include creative media production alongside more traditional forms of networked communication literacy and digital scholarship (Löwgren and Reimer, 2014). This vision of communication as a complex, mediated act that requires its own set of standards and requirements better reflects media flows in a variety of professional settings and in turn expands the expectation of digitally literate curricula. The critical difference between traditional modes of assessment and new forms of mediated outputs is that they are designed to adhere to criteria that are strongly influenced by industry standards that have currency in the job market. Just like an artist with a portfolio, a musician with an EP, or a film graduate with a show reel, a HASS graduate with a series of published outputs or production credits can demonstrate a range of connectedness capabilities. Whether this takes the form of a simulated news environment, the publication of a webzine or a hybrid interactive text, the production of a podcast or a short-form documentary, or a curated exhibition via a web portal or mobile app, each of these outputs represents evidence-based outcomes that fulfil certain industry standards (e.g. Goodyear and Jaskot, 2014). By their nature, they provide a permanent archival link that potential employers or industry networks can readily access and evaluate. The challenge, of course, is resourcing and supporting such acts of mediated creativity that are increasingly dependent on technology.

Creativity should be seen as much more than an act or attribute. Rather, it is a conduit between authentic assessment design and the process of reflection and critique. It should be directed towards celebrating what makes an academic discipline unique and towards affirming that the act of learning is inherently creative.

4.   THE CELEBRATORY CAPSTONE EXPERIENCE

A capstone subject should be a challenging, shared experience, but it also must come to a suitable conclusion that showcases the skill and endeavour of its students and staff (Lee and Loton, 2017). It is critical that students and staff work collaboratively; in the ideal arrangement, a closing event might include representatives from industry, local government and communities who can welcome students into the fold. A higher-education capstone experience is the culmination of three to four years of study for students and their academic mentors, and as such deserves exposure outside of the walls of academe; certainly, beyond the confines of a rubric or an LMS site. The inclusion of a public celebratory element should be factored into the narrative of the unit from the very beginning, since it can increase the authenticity of the final assignment's design. Anticipating the event's public nature provides impetus for students to focus from the outset on the production of quality, industry-standard output: in their project groups, the students' task is not only to respond to a brief, but to respond with outcomes that can feature publicly at the end of semester event (Scavitto, 2016). In addition, seeing the diversity and ingenuity of peers' responses to a brief within the parameters of the discipline can be educative in itself. The outcome should be visible and enduring.

The Anthropology capstone marks the end of semester by combining group presentations with a careers forum. In earlier iterations of the subject, presentations were done in ordinary lecture time across successive weeks. Combining the presentations into a full-day event (set at the end of semester when there is little possibility of timetable clashes) fostered a sense of celebration and belonging, rather than the mundane fulfilment of an academic duty. The event took place in a non-teaching space typically reserved for casual staff events, helping to break down the formality of the presentations, while affording a sense of occasion and collegiality. Following the presentations, the careers forum included recognition of students' achievements. Similarly, the Creative Writing capstone culminates in a literary festival that takes place one evening in the penultimate week of the semester. The event celebrates students' connections with the wider community and with creative industries that value their disciplinary skills, and is promoted to students' families and friends, the unit's industry partners, coordinators of other capstone subjects and heads of programs, prospective Creative Writing graduate and undergraduate students, and Creative Writing students and staff from other universities. Students share responsibility with the coordinator for programming a creative showcase that, given the high degree of exposure, continues the students' service to the community collaborators on whose briefs they collaborate during semester. (The public nature of the celebration also gives the discipline an opportunity to celebrate the achievements and hard work of their faculty.) In both these units, the closing event cements and celebrates the prospect of being active and valued members of communities beyond university life and is therefore integral to the units' meaningfulness. We have recommended the introduction of a similar event for the History capstone that asks students to co-opt the teaching and informal spaces of Arts West as exhibition spaces in order to share their projects with an audience made up of disciplinary colleagues, family members, industry partners, potential employers and members of the public.

It must be said that, as with similar multi-modal arts events, such projects are only as stable as the organisational and administrative structures that support it. For instance, the Creative Writing unit's literary festival is a complex and often improvised undertaking, with a 200-strong guest list, catering, after-hours security and IT assistance, printed programs and poster advertising, all of which require monetary and personnel support from beyond the unit's own purse. Therefore, the coordinator and students must grapple with structures where it is not always clear where lines of responsibility begin and end in orchestrating an event, and which sometimes struggle to appreciate the value of celebration as a mode of public relations. There are other, practical considerations, too: the venue requires the technology to simulcast or display the student's work in the best possible light. An online presence is worthwhile, not only to socialise the work to a wider audience but to provide an archival record. Traditional press releases still work, personal email invitations are even better; street posters and stickers have currency alongside timely social media bursts. Setting up a publicity eco-system is a key component of a capstone intending to celebrate its connectedness; incorporating this task into student group work is justified by the fact that the labour can generate a valuable database of email addresses, social media accounts and phone numbers from industry, government, academia, local business and other networks, which becomes an ideal resource for any graduate in search of a job.

The value of the practical (and visible) outcomes of a professionally managed event cannot be understated. They have cross-promotional value to industry, the public and potential HASS students alike. Ideally, outcomes would demonstrate the expertise of the graduating students; the discipline spread – and flexibility – of HASS fields; the ability of students to integrate their learning into the workplace; and the dynamic and varied nature of the professional outcomes made possible by HASS programs.

5.   THE NETWORKED CAPSTONE EXPERIENCE

Networked education enables the development of disciplinary skills and industry connections that empower students to independently seek out and extend upon their communities (Bridgstock, 2019a; see Chapter 1 in this volume). This is typical of HASS disciplines that have evolved into a digital eco-system, as Burdick et al. point out:

> Networks connect us, they are social technologies. As scholarship moves from the library and the lecture hall to digital communication networks, it takes on expanded social roles and raises new questions. New modes of knowledge formation in the digital humanities are dynamically linked to communities vastly larger and more diverse than those to which the academy has been accustomed. These communities increasingly demand and delight in sociable and intellectual interactions, in which critique manifests as versioning, and thinking, making, and doing form iterative feedback loops. (Burdick et al., 2012, p. 75)

A networked capstone experience, however, should also pursue professional, community and industrial networks; external partners who actively expose students to authentic workplace practices onsite and on campus (Jackson, 2015). There are a number of challenges to the collaborative development and delivery of an industry-focused curriculum, especially where industry and government linkages require ongoing engagement and facilitation. Of course, the benefit to students of relationships with partners with professional or community standing is much greater if such relationships can be maintained and nurtured over time (McLachlan, Fleming and Pretti, 2016). Therefore, a critical first step is ensuring external collaborators are aware of the timelines that universities work to and to contextualise the structure of teaching delivery and expectations around assessment milestones. And the potential benefits of a networked experience work both ways. Professional partnerships can embolden a student team to attack the project brief with enthusiasm and creativity, thus creating outputs that can, for example, raise an organisation's visibility, create complementary content, provoke a rethink on policy, foster change in a local community or make recommendations for possible new directions in an organisation (Daniel, 2010; Fleischmann, 2015).

But for HASS disciplines with particularly strong academically-oriented professional identities, engaging with external partners in a professional industry context can be especially challenging. An important aspect in the creation of a networked capstone – and sometimes the most limiting factor to its implementation – is the capstone coordinator's own professional identity and how this intersects with external, industrial trends. For instance, the unit coordinators of the Creative Writing and Media and Communication capstones have extensive professional networks that bring students into contact with external partners including media organisations, production houses, local government departments, human rights organisations, cultural organisations and arts advocacy groups, museums, not-for-profits, festivals, archives, community media and artist-run initiatives. Professional identity is of course a complex beast and is developed over time often through unconventional pathways. Conceptions of identity generally rest on attributes commonly associated with members of a group that might include personal, vocational and professional elements. In disciplines where professional identities rely heavily on research achievement, there tends to be less focus on such an industrial identity. Therefore, membership of, and access to, associated professional networks and/or government policy fora is difficult if the coordinating academic has not been involved (or not recently) with such groups. As a result, many academics focus on fostering a research-oriented identity for their students, reinforcing a trajectory they themselves feel comfortable with.

The focus instead should be on tangible, industry-relevant outcomes to ensure that students are not only reflecting back on their individual skills development and discipline knowledge but also looking beyond the academy to how they may apply them in professional and social environments. Throughout the capstone unit, professional standards and expectations should be continually reinforced to ensure students understand how these standards and expectations operate within their chosen field and the complementary networks they intersect with.

TACTICS FOR A CONNECTED CAPSTONE EXPERIENCE

The five principles therefore provide a conceptual framework for curriculum design in relation to capstone units that seeks to overcome the limitations inherent in the WIL-focused capstone model discussed at the beginning of this chapter. When considering the practicalities of classroom delivery, it is worth reiterating some of the practical ways this can be achieved:

- Clearly articulate to students how the enterprise of research and critical thinking and the building of academic networks link in practical terms with career pathways, industry expectations and professional networks;
- Talk about the desired outcomes at the very start of the unit – *what are we here to achieve?* Explain the value of incorporating a public facing launch event to accompany any such outcome;
- Make sure any such event engages both industry (possible employers) and public (new audiences) giving students a sense of professional accomplishment and individual exposure;
- Classroom discourse should attempt to synthesise, wherever possible, academic requirements with industry expectations in relation to project outcomes and event design;
- Build production milestones into the classroom schedule that lead directly towards the final outcome both in terms of the individual student and the broader collaborative endeavour;
- Structure each session in the service of constructive outcomes, to train focus on the 'doing' part of the project: discussing/planning/researching/making/managing/communicating/resourcing/networking, etc.;
- Consider facilitating collaboration between students from more than one discipline. The interdisciplinary benefits are amplified and the experience more realistic if collaboration involves complementary assessment and/or project provision from outside of the discipline;
- Consider devoting a portion of the curriculum to building professional attributes: portfolio preparation, professional communication methods, managing interdisciplinarity, structuring a career and entrepreneurship;
- Build in opportunities for student reflection on their own process and its outcomes, as well as for student feedback on the unit's pertinence to their networks.

THE LAST WORD

We would like to see a shift in HASS disciplines where connectedness skills are introduced in earlier years so that a connected capstone is scaffolded by the structure of the degree and students are supported to develop relevant skills over time (Healey et al., 2013). This relies on careful, long-view curriculum design; on academic practitioners placing value on the pedagogical principles we have outlined here; and on revisiting the intended graduate attributes and learning outcomes of capstone units with a more nuanced lens. This lens should of course emphasise an industrial perspective but also remain cognisant of the expectations of a HASS graduate as a well-rounded community engaged citizen scholar (Arvanitakis and Hornsby, 2016; Watson, 2008).

To support the work of their staff, universities need to build reliable and enduring partnerships with industry, government and community to develop projects that are practical, substantive and sustainable over time. Where practical, external collaborators should also be involved in the teaching space – not just as guest lectures or practical workshop training, but also in the evaluation of project milestones, participating in assessment moderation and contributing to feedback. Universities must also incentivise professional development and capacity-building initiatives: often, our team has observed reluctance to use alternative forms of assessment – such as video essays, timelines, social media campaigns, podcasts, infographics or annotated media – due to the perceived need for extra support and a persistent scepticism regarding their academic merit (Timmis et al., 2016). Designing alternative assessment tasks that depend on technology integration can be unfamiliar to a seasoned academic, as may be new teaching techniques involving a mix of seemingly exotic software or conventional equipment used in more sophisticated ways.

The benefits to students' learning and to students' ongoing holistic development, however, are immeasurable. The more a student interfaces with industry and community, the more genuine a student feels their learning experience has been. This can have an empowering influence on the cohort at the culmination of study – a potentially challenging time. Therefore, when we think about designing capstone experiences, we should not only seek to leverage the key design principles detailed here – authenticity, reflection, creativity, celebration and networking – but we should also find ways to harness these principles to provide practical guidelines that can alleviate student anxiety around career trajectories and foster a sense of professional connectedness and personal accomplishment.

REFERENCES

Arvanitakis, J. and Hornsby, D. J. (2016). *Universities, the Citizen Scholar and the Future of Higher Education*. New York, NY: Palgrave Macmillan.
Baik, C. and Larcombe, W. (2016). Enhancing student wellbeing: Resources for university educators. Retrieved on 1 December 2017 from http://unistudentwellbeing.edu.au.
Biggs, J. B. and Tang, C. S. K. (2011). *Teaching for Quality Learning at University: What the Student Does*. Buckingham, PA: Open University Press.

Bozalek, V. and Zembylas, M. (2017). Diffraction or reflection? Sketching the contours of two methodologies in educational research. *International Journal of Qualitative Studies in Education, 30*(2), 111–127.

Bridgstock, R. (2016). Educating for digital futures: What the learning strategies of digital media professionals can teach higher education. *Innovations in Education and Teaching International, 53*(3), 306–315.

Bridgstock, R. (2019a). Graduate Employability 2.0: Education for work in a networked world. In J. Higgs, G. Crisp and W. Letts (eds), *Education for Employability: The Employability Agenda* (pp. 268–282). Rotterdam: Sense-Brill Publishers.

Bridgstock, R. (2019b). *Graduate Employability 2.0: Enhancing the Connectedness of Learners, Teachers and Higher Education Institutions. Final Report of the National Senior Teaching Fellowship.* Canberra: Department of Education and Training.

Burdick, A., Drucker, J., Lunenfeld, P., Presner, T. and Schnapp, J. (2012). *Digital Humanities.* Cambridge, MA: MIT Press.

Cleary, M., Flynn, R., Thomasson, S., Alexander, R. and McDonald, B. (2007). Graduate Employability Skills. Retrieved on 28 June 2018 from http://apo.org.au/node/80859.

Coll, R., Eames, C., Paku, L., Lay, M., Hodges, D., Bhat, R. ... Martin, A. (2009). An exploration of the pedagogies employed to integrate knowledge in work-integrated learning. *Journal of Cooperative Education and Internships, 43*(1), 14–35.

Craft, A. (2005). *Creativity in Schools: Tensions and Dilemmas.* London: Routledge.

Cullen, T. (2017). Capstone units and the transition from university to professional life. *Australian Journalism Review, 39*(1), 89–98.

Daniel, R. (2010). Career development and creative arts students: An investigation into the effectiveness of career theory and WIL experiences on practice. *Australian Journal of Career Development, 19*(2), 14–22.

Dewey, J. (1998). *How We Think: A Restatement of the Relation of Reflective Thinking to the Educative Process.* Boston, MA: Houghton Mifflin.

Edwards, S. (2017). Reflecting differently. New dimensions: Reflection-before-action and reflection-beyond-action. *International Practice Development Journal, 7*(1), 1–14.

Fernandez, N. P. (2006). Assessment matters: Integration, reflection, interpretation: Realizing the goals of a general education capstone course. *About Campus, 30*(3), 431–454.

Fleischmann, K. (2015). Developing on-campus work-integrated learning activities: The value of integrating community and industry partners into the Creative Arts curriculum. *Asia-Pacific Journal of Cooperative Education, 16*(1), 25–38.

Gannaway, D. (2016). *WIL-ing the BA: Work Experience Opportunities in the Australian Bachelor of Arts.* Brisbane, Australia: The University of Queensland.

Goodyear, A. C. and Jaskot, P. B. (2014). Digital art history takes off. Retrieved on 1 June 2018 from http://www.collegeart.org/news/2014/10/07/digital-art-history-takes-off/.

Haney, S. (2017). Exploring the use of personalized learning plans in the journalism capstone environment. *Teaching Journalism and Mass Communication, 7*(1), 22–33.

Hauhart, R. C. and Grahe, J. E. (2010). The undergraduate capstone course in the Social Sciences: Results from a regional survey. *Teaching Sociology, 38*(1), 4–17.

Hauhart, R. C. and Grahe, J. E. (2015). *Designing and Teaching Undergraduate Capstone Courses.* San Francisco, CA: Jossey-Bass.

Hayles, N. K. (2012). *How We Think : Digital Media and Contemporary Technogenesis.* Chicago, IL: University of Chicago Press.

Healey, M., Lannin, L., Stibbe, A. and Derounian, J. (2013). *Developing and Enhancing Undergraduate Final-year Projects.* York: The Higher Education Academy.

Holdsworth, A., Watty, K. and Davies, M. (2009). *Developing Capstone Experiences.* Melbourne, VIC: The University of Melbourne.

Houghton, L. and Stewart, H. (2017). Using the 'engagement' model of problem solving to assist students in capstone learning. *Systemic Practice and Action Research, 30*(5), 471–485.

Hwang, R. H., Hsiung, P. A., Chen, Y. J. and Lai, C. F. (2017). Innovative project-based learning. *International Symposium on Emerging Technologies for Education* (pp. 189–194). Cham, Switzerland: Springer.

Ito, M., Gutierrez, K., Livingstone, S., Penuel, B., Rhodes, J., Salen, K. … Watkins, S. C. (2014). Connected learning: An agenda for research and design. Retrieved on 23 May 2017 from http://dmlhub.net/publications/connected-learning-agenda-for-research-and-design/.

Jackson, D. (2015). Employability skill development in work-integrated learning: Barriers and best practice. *Studies in Higher Education, 40*(2), 350–367.

Jarman, M. R. and Wiley, K. (2007). *Benchmarking capstone projects in UTS Faculty of Engineering.* Paper presented at the ATN Evaluation and Assessment Conference 2007, Brisbane Australia.

Jorre de St Jorre, T. and Oliver, B. (2018). Want students to engage? Contextualise graduate learning outcomes and assess for employability. *Higher Education Research and Development, 37*(1), 44–57.

Leahy, K., Phillips, D., Debartolo, E., Brackin, P., Chenoweth, S. and White, A. (2017). Encouraging creativity in capstone design. *International Journal of Engineering Education*, *33*(5), 1468–1484.

Lee, N. and Loton, D. (2015). *Capstone Curriculum Across Disciplines: Synthesising Theory, Practice and Policy to Provide Practical Tools for Curriculum Design.* Sydney, NSW: Office for Learning and Teaching, Department of Education and Training.

Lee, N. and Loton, D. (2017). Capstone purposes across disciplines. *Studies in Higher Education*, Online Article.

Löwgren, J. and Reimer, B. (2014). *Collaborative Media: Production, Consumption, and Design Interventions.* Cambridge, MA: The MIT Press.

Matthews, K. E., Andrews, V. and Adams, P. (2011). Social learning spaces and student engagement. *Higher Education Research and Development*, *30*(2), 105–120.

McLachlan, K., Fleming, J. and Pretti, J. (2016). *Developing a Framework for Sustainable Work-Integrated Learning (WIL) Relationships.* Sydney, NSW: Macquarie University.

McNamara, J., Field, R., Coe, S., Butler, D., Brown, C. and Kift, S. (2015). Capstones as transitional experiences. *Legal Education Review*, *25*(1), 7–28.

Moon, J. (2004). *A Handbook of Reflective and Experiential Learning: Theory and Practice.* New York: Routledge Falmer.

Neary, M., Saunders, G., Hagyard, A. and Derricot, D. (2014). *Student as Producer: Research Engaged Teaching and Learning: An Institutional Strategy.* York: Higher Education Academy.

Olejarz, J. (2017). Liberal Arts in the data age. Retrieved on 1 September 2017 from https://hbr.org/2017/07/liberal-arts-in-the-data-age.

Race, P. (2014). *Making Learning Happen: A Guide for Post-Compulsory Education.* Los Angeles: Sage.

Reyna, J., Hanham, J. and Meier, P. C. (2018). A framework for digital media literacies for teaching and learning in higher education. *E-Learning and Digital Media*, *15*(4), 176–190.

Rheingold, H. (2018). Networked publics: Learning and creating as global, interconnected, interactive community enterprise. Retrieved on 28 June 2018 from https://dmlcentral.net/networked-publics-learning-creating-global-inter-connected-interactive-community-enterprise/.

Rowles, C. J., Koch, D. C., Hundley, S. P. and Hamilton, S. J. (2004). Toward a model for capstone experiences: Mountaintops, magnets, and mandates. *Assessment Update*, *16*(1), 1–2.

Ryan, M. and Ryan, M. (2013). Theorising a model for teaching and assessing reflective learning in higher education. *Higher Education Research and Development*, *32*(2), 244–257.

Ryan, M. D., Tews, N. M. and Washer, B. A. (2012). Team-teaching a digital senior capstone project in CTE. *Techniques: Connecting Education and Careers, 87*(2), 52–55.

Scavitto, D. (2016). The power and pedagogy of place: St. Johnsbury Academy's freshman Humanities capstone. *Vermont History, 84*(1), 9–25.

Schedin, S. and Hassan, O. A. B. (2014). An integrated learning model in collaboration with industrial partners [Conference Paper, peer reviewed]. *Proceedings of the 10th International CDIO Conference, Universitat Politècnica de Catalunya, Barcelona, Spain.* Retrieved on 6 July 2018 from https://ezp.lib.unimelb.edu.au/login?url=https://search.ebscohost.com/login.aspx?direct=trueanddb=edssweandAN=edsswe.oai.DiVA.org.umu.977 20andsite=eds-liveandscope=site.

Schön, D. A. (1983). *The Reflective Practitioner: How Professionals Think in Action.* London: Temple Smith.

Sharpe, R. and Beetham, H. (2010). Understanding students' uses of technology for learning: Towards creative appropriation. In R. Sharpe, H. Beetham and S. de Freitas (eds), *Rethinking Learning for a Digital Age: How Learners Shape their Experiences* (pp. 85–99). New York: Routledge.

Shulman, J. (2017). A good job for humanists. *Shared Resource Blog.* Retrieved on 1 September 2017 from https://mellon.org/resources/shared-experiences-blog/good-job-humanists/.

Siemens, G. (2005). Connectivism: A learning theory for the digital age. *International Journal of Instructional Technology and Distance Learning, 2*(1), online at http://itdl.org/Journal/Jan_05/article01.htm.

Smith, C. (2012). Evaluating the quality of work-integrated learning curricula: A comprehensive framework. *Higher Education Research and Development, 31*(2), 247–262.

Susskind, R. E. and Susskind, D. (2015). *The Future of the Professions: How Technology Will Transform the Work of Human Experts.* Oxford: Oxford University Press.

The University of Melbourne. (2015). Growing esteem 2015–2020, from https://about.unimelb.edu.au/strategy/growing-esteem.

The University of Melbourne. (2017). The Melbourne Way, from https://melbourne-cshe.unimelb.edu.au/resources/resources/teaching-and-learning/teaching-in-practice/the-melbourne-way.

Timmis, S., Broadfoot, P., Sutherland, R. and Oldfield, A. (2016). Rethinking assessment in a digital age: Opportunities, challenges and risks. *British Educational Research Journal, 42*(3), 454–476.

Upson-Saia, K. (2013). The capstone experience for the Religious Studies major. *Teaching Theology and Religion, 16*(1), 3–17.

van Acker, L., Bailey, J., Wilson, K. and French, E. (2014). Capping them off! Exploring and explaining the patterns in undergraduate capstone subjects in

Australian business schools. *Higher Education Research and Development*, 33(5), 1049–1062.

von Treuer, K. M., Sturre, V. L., Keele, S. M. and McLeod, J. E. (2010). Evaluation methodology for work integrated learning-placements: A discussion paper. *ACEN 2010: Proceedings of the 3rd Biannual Australian Collaborative Education Network National Conference* (pp. 489–497). Perth, Australia: Australian Collaborative Education Network (ACEN).

Walker, D., Boud, D. J. and Keogh, R. (1985). *Reflection, Turning Experience into Learning*. London: Kogan Page.

Watson, D. (2008). The university in the modern world: Ten lessons of civic and community engagement. *Education, Citizenship and Social Justice*, 3(1), 43–55.

Williamson, A. and Nodder, C. (2002). Extending the learning space: Dialogue and reflection in the virtual coffee shop. *ACM SIGCAS Computers and Society*, 32(3), 1.

10. Curriculum transformation for graduate connectedness and employability: perspectives from the University of Wollongong

Simon Bedford and Kenton Bell

INTRODUCTION

Globally, there continue to be intense discussions and reports (e.g. Manyika et al., 2017; Smith et al., 2018) surrounding the employment, career markets and future roles of graduates in light of significant technological, economic and social changes. While these influences are already making themselves felt, the future impact of these factors is currently hard to predict, even as higher education moves towards a renewed focus on capabilities that may prepare graduates for the challenge of lifelong learning and relearning. It is agreed that university graduates need to be adaptable and innovative to successfully navigate the evolving workforce (Hagel et al., 2014). There is also increasing recognition that traditional, content-driven and teacher focused approaches to higher education are not particularly effective in developing the capabilities required for future life and work (Ernst and Young, 2012). Rather, it may be more productive for universities to focus on educational techniques and methods that allow complex kinds of learning to take place in authentic environments that have been expressly designed to develop the future-orientated employability capabilities of learners.

The University of Wollongong (UOW) Curriculum Model represents a university-wide attempt to transform curriculum, pedagogy and assessment practices, with a view to the types of learning that are conducive to the development of twenty-first century capacities for employability. From 2014 onwards, the Curriculum Model was (and continues to be) embedded in all courses at UOW. The model and its roll-out to date are discussed in this chapter with a specific focus on the connectedness learning that is occurring within the five transformational pedagogic practices at the heart of the Model, and how these pedagogic practices are being translated into learning and teaching experiences throughout the university.

CONTEXT OF THE RESEARCH

This chapter describes the design and implementation of whole-of-course curriculum transformation initiated by UOW. As illustrated in Figure 10.1, the UOW Curriculum Model was developed to build on and enhance the institution's reputation for quality teaching and learning. The curriculum transformation takes a whole-of-institution approach, emphasising a selection of course design features that have a demonstrable impact on the student learning experience and can assist in preparing students for twenty-first century graduate destinations. The stated mission of UOW curriculum transformation is to "*develop a career-ready culture with a shared responsibility across UOW, where career development and employability practices are embedded and integrated throughout the learning experience, contributing to graduate success and lifelong learning*" (University of Wollongong, 2016a).

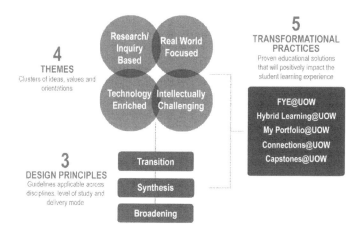

Figure 10.1   The UOW Curriculum Model

The UOW Curriculum Model is comprised of three overarching Design Principles, four Themes, and five Transformational Practices (University of Wollongong, 2016b). The Curriculum Design Principles are research-based guidelines, which apply to curriculum design across disciplines, levels of study and modes of delivery. These are:

- *Transition:* A curriculum-integrated approach that enables a smooth, supported shift into higher education and a successful transition from UOW to the world of work and lifelong learning.
- *Synthesis:* A curriculum-integrated approach that provides multiple, connected and sequenced opportunities for students to share, synthesise and integrate their learning.
- *Broadening:* A curriculum-integrated approach that compels a breadth of focus for learning beyond the student's primary area of study and recognises the interconnected nature of today's global challenges and the value multi-disciplinary teams bring to the modern workplace.

Curriculum Themes are broad clusters of ideas, values and orientations, which characterise the curriculum. The four guiding curriculum themes are:

- *Research/Inquiry Based:* The UOW curriculum will induct students into a rich set of research and inquiry processes that may include empirical, interdisciplinary, practice-based and creative research activity. This will develop connections between learning, academic research, critical inquiry and problem-solving. It will offer students opportunities to engage ethically with global challenges and to undertake mutually beneficial research related to professions and communities.
- *Real-world Focused:* The UOW curriculum will engage students with key professional or disciplinary scenarios and skill sets that model, simulate or address real-world practice. This focus brings the world into the classroom and takes students out into the community or profession. They progressively develop skills, aptitudes and values that equip UOW graduates to operate confidently and responsibly in a diverse range of complex situations.
- *Technology Enriched:* The UOW curriculum will be technology-enriched in its delivery and content and will prepare graduates to be digitally literate, technologically-engaged professionals. Students will use a wide range of technologies, media, tools and platforms to learn, create and connect with peers, teachers, researchers, communities and professions.
- *Intellectually Challenging:* The UOW curriculum will challenge students to think broadly and critically within and outside their disciplines and apply this knowledge to a range of complex questions and/or diverse situations. Carefully designed learning activities and open, flexible curriculum structures will empower students to be adventurous in their learning by exploring unfamiliar and challenging subject matter and pressing global questions.

At the heart of the delivery of the Curriculum Model are the Transformational Practices, a set of proven pedagogical practices, which have a significant positive impact on the student learning experience. The five transformational practices are:

- *FYE@UOW* – discipline-specific, curriculum-integrated first-year experience that enables students to learn 'how to learn' and provides a critical foundation for future academic success.
- *MyPorfolio@UOW* – courses incorporate digital processes and practices that allow students to reflect on, document, evidence and share their achievements and their evolving understanding of, and progress towards, key disciplinary and professional concepts and practices.
- *HybridLearning@UOW* – courses incorporate a variety of hybrid learning experiences, combine a range of approaches, strategies and delivery methods, providing students with a rich range of learning opportunities and the capacity to manage their own learning.
- *Connections@UOW* – students engage with diverse ideas and new contexts, through integrating an omnibus of cross-cultural understandings, global connections, Indigenous knowledges and cross- and interdisciplinary connections.
- *Capstones@UOW* – through a major project, workplace or other authentic experience, students will integrate and apply knowledge and skills gained throughout their course.

The curriculum model was embedded in course curricula through the comprehensive five-yearly course review cycle, commencing in 2014. As each course has come up for either course review or curriculum renewal (sometimes combined with professional re-accreditation) the curriculum appraisal tool has been used to evaluate how they are tracking against the five transformational practices and related areas, with a set of developmental action plans created to move towards full integration by the next review. As a rolling implementation approach has been adopted, the full impact of these curriculum renewals will not be evident until 2019–2020 and beyond, when graduates have passed through the renewed course curricula. However, enough of the model has now been implemented that both the process of implementation in specific courses and its impact can start to be explored in a preliminary way. This chapter will do this, using the lens of Connectedness Learning.

CONNECTING UOW CURRICULUM TRANSFORMATION WITH CONNECTEDNESS LEARNING

The UOW Curriculum Transformation process is a comprehensive institutional strategy to transform student learning and maximise success through the implementation of an integrated framework for student learning and experience. The process explicitly addresses curriculum and pedagogic approaches for employability, acknowledging graduate outcomes as a dimension of student success, and placing specific emphasis on the development of skills, aptitudes and values for graduate employability (University of Wollongong, 2016b). It could be argued, however, that the scope of the process extends beyond graduate employability alone, with the Principles, Themes and Practices that guide the model all being indicative of a broader higher educational approach, which strongly aligns with the key pedagogic elements identified within the Connectedness Learning Approach (see Chapter 1 in this volume).

The four Curriculum Themes link directly with Connectedness Learning in several ways, identifying specific avenues through which Connectedness Learning Pedagogies can be implemented. First, the model's commitment to student research and inquiry employs mutually beneficial research which spans communities and professions to connect students with global and ethical issues. This necessarily involves both staff and students moving beyond the institutional boundaries, especially at more advanced levels of learning, directly mapping this theme against key connectedness pedagogies of *Connected Learning* and *Work Integrated Learning*. The potential porosity of institutional boundaries in pedagogic practice is even more evident when considering the theme of real-world focus, whereby learning explicitly "*brings the world into the classroom and takes students out into the community or profession*" (University of Wollongong, 2016b); as a key pedagogic strategy outlined in the Connectedness Learning Approach, *Work Integrated Learning* has a demonstrated capacity to forge connections between higher education and industry, creating authentic and valuable learning experiences.

Second, direct links with the Connectedness Learning Approach can be found in the model's commitment to provide open, flexible, curriculum structures and technology-enriched learning, through which students are supported in using a wide range of technologies, media, tools and platforms to learn, create and connect with others, both within and beyond the university. These themes align with key pedagogical practices identified in the Connectedness Learning Approach, namely *Social Media and ePortfolios* and *Connectedness Learning Pedagogies*.

The three core design principles of transition, synthesis and broadening that guide the curriculum transformation strategy are underpinned by Kift, Nelson and Clarke's (2010) transition pedagogy (O'Donnell et al., 2015). For first year students, the emphasis on learning is fostering connections with their cohort, course and university. As students move through the course, learning experiences progressively broaden to encompass multi-disciplinary activities. Over time these become increasingly complex and interconnected, adopting global perspectives that extend learning beyond the walls of the institution. Through this process, students are supported in building their connections, starting with networks inside their cohort, before transitioning across discipli-nary boundaries and courses to develop sustainable and authentic connections with professional industry networks. This learning is evident in several of the key pedagogies identified in the Connectedness Learning Approach, includ-ing *Work-Integrated Learning, Industry Teaching and Engagement, Student Partnerships* and *Connected Learning.*

Some of the most direct links between the UOW Curriculum Transformation model and the Connectedness Learning Approach can be seen in the five trans-formational practices which are being embedded across all UOW courses. In the following section of this chapter, each of these five practices is discussed, outlining evidence for its inclusion in the Curriculum Transformation Model, identifying specific cases of practice and preliminary evaluative statements concerning its implementation, and exploring direct links to Connectedness Learning which identify how each pedagogical approach can support students in building, maintaining and making the most of their personal and profes-sional networks.

FYE@UOW: THE FIRST YEAR EXPERIENCE

Although the UOW Curriculum Model recognises transition as a whole of course principle, it emphasises the critical role that the first year experience plays in capacity building and establishing initial student narratives of purpose. FYE@UOW is designed to ensure that as students transition into university learning, they are supported through a structured, integrated approach which guides them in the development of essential academic skills, knowledge and values (University of Wollongong, 2016b). Consistent with the University's assessment and feedback principles, the first year experience includes an enhanced focus on formative assessment, which aims to introduce students to the cycle of evaluation, feedback, reflection and improvement that is vital to university and lifelong learning. FYE@UOW scaffolds opportunities for students to engage in research-led, real-world focused, digitally-enriched learning beginning from the first year of study. This process equips students with the knowledge and capabilities (and literacies) they need to become active learners and take strategic control over their learning as they transition into more complex academic work. Explicit connections made across subjects and the identification of pathways to future learning assist students in building a framework through which they are able to transition across the course and into the workforce.

Grounded in Kift and colleagues' transition pedagogy (Kift, Nelson and Clarke, 2010), the first year experience at UOW draws upon the professional development framework '*Six First Year Firsts: Critical Curriculum Points*' in highlighting the importance of six critical moments that significantly impact on first year students' transitions into university: first subject, first week, first class, first assessment, first feedback, and first final (Harden-Thew and Dean, 2015). These six points underscore the enormous psychosocial adjustment and volume of cultural learning that students undergo during their first semester as they become accustomed to 'being a student'. In this short time, students must determine both what they should learn, and how they should learn. This knowledge includes understanding the academic expectations and standards they are required to meet, acquiring strategies for interpreting, tackling and learning from feedback and assessment, and developing individual skills to effectively manage workloads and assessment stress. For many students, the transition to higher education marks a significant increase in the informational and academic literacy that they require. During this time, students must also learn how to access and make the most of the academic, personal and profes-sional help that is available to them through formal university support services. The social connections that first year students develop during this time, both with support providers and also with their peers and teachers, may be critical to their academic success (Krause, 2005).

In the first year experience, connectedness is evident in the connections that students form with their peers, teachers and the university as a whole. One example of how FYE@UOW has attempted to foster this cohesion can be found in the Law School, where all first year students are required to complete a set of carefully sequenced subjects, whereby each learning activity feeds into further support activities in other subjects. As part of this course, all students are allocated to a 'pod' – a group with whom they study all subjects – to increase cohesion and peer support. In Connectedness Learning terms, the pod approach supports learners in developing, strengthening and working with their peer connections to support their learning and wellbeing. The pod concept was developed by La Trobe University for pre-service teachers (Masters and Donnison, 2010), capitalising on the well-documented evidence which shows that social integration and community building offer significant benefits towards first year student transition and retention (Krause, 2005). Social networking strategies, such as scavenger hunts or 'meet and greet' ses-sions with fellow students, are commonly used at the beginning of a student's first year, particularly at Orientation. Sustained measures that strengthen these initial social connections among first year students are also widespread in many higher educational institutions, including activities such as ongoing peer mentoring and the provision of course or faculty social events. The classroom is also recognised as a central site for building community, through the implementation of within-class team-building strategies (Zhao and Kuh, 2004). The pod concept is one example of a strategy that can be employed within the classroom, whereby small classes of students learn together for the entire first year of study (common first year). It has been hailed as a remarkably successful way to build community, social cohesion and social capital among first years. Indeed, the community building aspect of the pods can become a 'selling point' for attracting future students (Masters and Donnison, 2010). In initialising students' first professional networks, such activities set the way in encouraging students to build and make the most of their connections to support academic growth and wellbeing.

HYBRIDLEARNING@UOW: BLENDING ONLINE AND OFFLINE MODES OF LEARNING

Combining face to face teaching with online, digital activities, HybridLearning@ UOW offers students a range of carefully selected learning opportunities, identified according to learner and curricular needs that aim to encourage authentic and active participation (University of Wollongong, 2016b). The amalgamation of face-to-face interactions with online learning activities and opportunities for collaboration is used widely in higher education as a means of aligning learning and teaching with today's digitally connected society (Francis and Shannon, 2013). At UOW, hybrid learning has been implemented across all courses in a variety of guises, including through collaborative and flexible learning tasks hosted on digital platforms, online tools which can be used to enhance communication and collaboration, integrated social media and open web resources to supplement learning, creative tasks and assessments including group-work, combinations of work-based and classroom learning, and real-time and virtual simulated professional practice (University of Wollongong, 2016b). This range of experiences is intended to provide students with multiple learning opportunities that build their capabilities to manage their own learning, aligning learning practice with the diversity of communication and collaboration evident in the contemporary workplace.

In wider practice, such learning approaches can range from the basic integration of technology to support face-to-face teaching, through to immersive online experiences which are delivered with minimal or no face-to-face interaction (Jones et al., 2009) known more traditionally as blended learning. Keeping pace with the fast rate of technological development, modern blended learning incorporates elements of socially networked, collaborative learning to supplement students' learning experiences, including interactive and shared media, artificial intelligence, simulations and augmented and virtual reality. Although heavily reliant on unitary learning management systems, universities are increasingly delivering modern blended learning through integrated virtual learning experiences which comprise multiple interacting systems and platforms to offer students an authentic learning experience. The use of learning analytics to measure, collect and analyse data about learners and their contexts also offers the potential for students to be given personalised learning experiences, which can be adapted to optimise learning and the environment in which it occurs (Siemens, 2013).

Meta-analyses on the efficacy of traditional blended learning in higher education suggest that it can be beneficial in improving students' engagement and performance (e.g. Means et al., 2013; US Department of Education, 2010), however, such outcomes must be tempered by considering that blended learning is often a more cost-effective approach than face-to-face teaching (Maloney et al., 2015), thus may be employed by universities primarily for financial rather than academic benefits. Although many students see blended learning as a valuable approach to supporting educational outcomes, inconsistencies in how it is used and a lack of formal training among educators may impact on its efficacy (Osgerby, 2013; Pillay and James, 2014). The effectiveness of any form of blended learning is highly contingent on the time and resources allocated to it, requiring appropriate resource allocation and the promotion of best-practice exemplars at the institutional level, while also ensuring individual schools provide sufficient time, professional development and resources for staff to understand and implement the approach effectively (Francis and Shannon, 2013). Furthermore, consideration must be given to the balance of face-to-face and online activities. Shannon, Francis, and Torpey (2012) found that blended learning was perceived most positively when it was used to supplement the traditional delivery of courses, as students valued the direct social interaction this offered, while retaining the opportunity to develop face-to-face communication skills.

It is through facilitating communication and the exchange of information between learners that the connectedness benefits of hybrid learning become most evident. Situating traditional learning experiences within socially networked, collaborative communities of practice can enhance connectedness through offering a broader scope of possible interactions and more abundant opportunities for students to share and discuss information (Arnold and Paulus, 2010; Rovai and Jordan, 2004). The accessibility of virtual learning environments allows students to interact with peers at any time, building and using their inter-group connections to support their learning outside of the classroom environment. For distance or online only learners, as well as students who are reluctant to speak up in class, hybrid learning provides heightened opportunities for increased participation, collaboration and connectedness among students who may otherwise have felt isolated from their peers (DeSchryver et al., 2009; So and Brush, 2008). Further, integration of social networks into virtual learning environments opens up potential interactions with alumni, industries and employers through which students can begin to build and use their professional networks.

HybridLearning@UOW has been deployed in varying forms across the university, however its potential for enhancing connectedness and students' networking capabilities is evident in the following example. The 'Business Integrative Capstone – Simulation of a Socially Innovative Enterprise' uses hybrid learning to provide experiential learning and responsible decision-making within a culminating capstone subject. The capstone is delivered in a 'half-flipped' format, with more face-to-face interaction at the start than at the end, as students move from theory to practice within a simulated business world. Students work in social teams, assigning roles and solving problems where they have to make weekly key decisions on product price, marketing and advertising to sell a product in the marketplace. Once students have graduated, they typically maintain connections with the course via the capstone by providing professional activities and examples and acting as mentors to the next generation. Delivering the subject through a hybrid learning simulation, students learn to work collaboratively and test their communication, problem-solving and critical thinking skills within an authentic, albeit simulated, real-world environment. The continued connections with alumni open the course to additional input from industry representatives, providing opportunities for students to witness how the skills they are developing can be employed outside of the university, while at the same time connecting them directly to industry and potential employers.

MYPORTFOLIO@UOW: EPORTFOLIOS AS LEARNING RECORDS

Internationally, portfolios are used extensively in higher education as a way of increasing the quality of learning and enhancing the value of educational outcomes to benefit students' employability and career success (Hallam, Harper and McAllister, 2012). Portfolios variously comprise students' coursework, individual achievements, prior learning, evidence of planning and reflection, skills and competencies, and assessments, either self, peer or teacher (Jwaifell, 2013), serving as an ongoing repository or record which documents how learners' skills and capabilities have been acquired and developed over time (Rennie and Morrison, 2013). The culminated collation of information spanning one's progress through a course and beyond means that portfolios represent a combination of both product and process which articulates the learner's experiences, achievements and learning (Gray, 2008).

As part of the curriculum transformation at the University of Wollongong, electronic learning portfolios are being embedded into all courses as a way of giving students the opportunities, skills and resources to develop and display a diverse set of 'real-world', authentic, digital artefacts, including the ability to reflect on their learning progress (University of Wollongong, 2016b). Courses have been designed to include assessments, whereby students produce professional work which can be included within their electronic portfolio. Additionally, as the course progresses, students select additional material gathered through extra-curricular and co-curricular activities to provide further evidence of their achievement and engagement in socially networked, connected activities (such as mentoring, collaborative problem-solving and networked learning). Accordingly, across the institution, portfolio learning has been delivered as part of a networked learning approach, whereby links with specific co-curricular and extra-curricular activities that are missing or underrepresented in the course have been used to enhance the core academic curriculum. Portfolios run through the backbone of the course, so that, upon graduation, students' portfolios will document not only their increased capabilities but also the learning journey they have taken to get there.

The use of portfolios to support student learning requires significant resources, including time commitment, staff professional development, adequate digital literacy and a reliable technological infrastructure which can support their integration into learning activities (Hallam, Harper and McAllister, 2012). Student engagement is a concern, with research suggesting that unless used for assessment purposes, students are unlikely to engage in portfolio development. Emmett (2011) found that in one assessment task where ePortfolios were encouraged but not required, 87 per cent of students did not use portfolios, suggesting that their motivation to pass the assessment was greater than their desire to enhance their learning or employability. There are also concerns around the application of portfolios towards future employment, as evidenced by mixed attitudes among employers towards their usefulness (Gray, 2008). From an institutional perspective, inconsistent usage, whereby portfolio learning is employed without any overarching strategic direction can significantly hamper the cohesion and effectiveness of the approach; portfolios should be deployed as part of an integrated curriculum to have sufficient impact on developing students' reflective and employability skills (Hallam, Harper and McAllister, 2012).

Although formal evaluation of portfolio learning within the UOW is yet to be performed, initial feedback suggests that the success of portfolios may be contingent on adapting their application according to discipline specific criteria. In integrating portfolios into their curricula, course designers chose to take different approaches. Some used learner portfolios (e.g. nursing degrees) as a means of collecting evidence for professional practice, including the identification and documentation of specific skills that have been obtained at crucial points within the curriculum. This approach involved students submitting parts of their portfolio for assessment and receiving feedback at regular intervals. In contrast, others linked students' portfolio learning specifically to employability by including a range of modules produced by the careers service, including building a professional LinkedIn profile, attending employer showcasing events, or engaging with alumni and graduates, as a way of building students' professional connections and relationships. This approach extends the application of portfolios by using them as a tool through which students can build and strengthen their professional networks, communicating evidence of their skills and capabilities to potential employers through social media or other networking avenues.

Linking portfolio development with other pedagogical approaches may further potential benefits. In the School of Psychology, course designers have focused on using portfolios within the capstone experience at the end of the course. Content to be captured and curated in the portfolio is nominated in selected third year subjects. These pieces of work will be selected on the basis that they reflect student skills which will serve as evidence for subsequent employment. The contents of the portfolio will be assessed in the capstone subject, whereby students will be required to appraise their skill profile (including their capacity to receive feedback and make improvements based on that feedback) and reflect on their achievements to date. This process will form the basis of team work that occurs in the context of a real-world problem that students will respond to in a series of additional assessments. Through the process of creating and maintaining their portfolios while simultaneously learning and enhancing their digital literacy skills, students are given the opportunity to engage in a continued cycle of exploration, connection and reflection through which they can develop their individual brand and identity (Bridgstock, 2019a).

Where implemented appropriately, portfolios can enhance graduate employability by providing a portable body of evidence displaying a graduates' skills and capabilities, which can migrate between courses, institutions and workplaces. Although this is a significant benefit in itself, the opportunities that portfolios provide for reflective learning are perhaps their most valuable asset. The narrative that spans their creation helps learners self-construct their personal identity through a combination of learning and feedback, providing opportunities to reflect on 'who they are and what they have learned' (Bennett et al., 2016; McAlpine, 2005). Kolb and Kolb (2005) suggest that systematic reflection is necessary to translate experience into learning, and portfolios guide leaners in identifying and substantiating their learning progress.

Through the process of collating and reviewing, portfolios help students move beyond the state of knowing *what* they have learned to consider *how* they have learned (Hallam, Harper and McAllister, 2012). By carrying these skills for self-reflection into their professional career, graduates can continue using their portfolio to support career transitions and identify professional development needs over the course of their working life (Gray, 2008).

CONNECTIONS@UOW: CROSS-CULTURAL AND INTERDISCIPLINARY LEARNING

Connections@UOW represents a set of pedagogic approaches that aim to connect learners with the world beyond traditional, single-discipline course experiences. In engaging students with diverse ideas and new contexts, the approach intends to broaden essential critical thinking skills, enriching students' global awareness, intercultural knowledge, and understanding of professional ethics. Connections@UOW integrates a whole of course omnibus of cross-cultural understandings, global connections, Indigenous knowledges and cross- and interdisciplinary connections. Structured interactions are embedded into each course, challenging students to situate their disciplinary knowledge within broader perspectives. This transformative practice often employs direct experience in combination with dialogic learning, an egalitarian dialogue in which students observe or directly participate in discussions where arguments are made based on validity claims. Examples of how Connections@UOW is being employed across disciplines include the use of: subjects from other discipline areas; subjects specifically designed to provide a wider perspective within the discipline; international case studies; international collaborations; study abroad opportunities; explorations of global issues around human rights and sustainable futures; and, learning for human diversity and intercultural understanding.

An example of how Connections@UOW is being used to support graduate connectedness can be found within the Engineering courses. A suite of subjects delivered in the Sustainable Engineering Integrated Learning Space combines project-based professional skills development with a reflective focus on sustainability and humanitarian issues. This combination provides both a broadening perspective and a specific focus that spurs students to produce innovative and creative professional work that is engaged with social and environmental justice issues. Another example is from Public Health, which offers an integrated set of curricular and co-curricular learning experiences where students engage authentically with community either on- or off-campus. One of its new subjects, *Community Development and Engagement for Social Change*, utilises the School simulation lab space and equipment to allow students to learn communication with media and professional/community partners through role-play activities. Students are also actively encouraged to join the Illawarra Public Health Society, which was established to promote health within the university and community populations. Community members, staff and students participate jointly in garden projects, as well as the utilisation of the food and nutrition laboratory. Through these co-curricular and extra-curricular community-based projects, graduates are equipped with the skills and attributes to apply innovative approaches to food education, promotion and advocacy in the local community.

The terms 'connections' and 'connected' mean somewhat different things when used in reference to Connections@UOW and the Connectedness Learning Approach (and also in Connected Learning, which is something else again – see Ito et al., 2014), but the approaches seem highly complementary. Connections@UOW aims to connect students with the world beyond disciplinary learning, fostering twenty-first century capabilities for economic and social engagement, as well as lifelong health and wellbeing. The Connectedness Learning Approach discussed in this book emphasises the social dimensions of connecting students to the world, which seems a necessary and indeed central element of developing intercultural, interdisciplinary, global, and indigenous awareness, knowledge, and skills. As Grossman and colleagues (2015) have argued, these capability sets might have at least one key underlying learning construct in common – what they term critical social thinking, or the ability to recognise, interpret, and respond appropriately in complex social situations. A complex social situation can be defined as any setting in which there might be actors representing diverse identities, motives, and behavioural styles, who must interact in order to achieve their respective objectives. Critical social thinking has multiple roles to play in Connections@ UOW, through social learning processes: learning from observation of others, learning through acting with others, and learning through dialogue with others.

CAPSTONES@UOW: CAPSTONE EXPERIENCES

Capstone courses provide students with a way of integrating and applying knowledge and skills gained throughout their courses of study. They are substantial culminating and celebratory learning experiences that occur towards the end of the course, often in the final semester (Lee and Loton, 2015). Capstones are also a way of demonstrating overall course quality by showing the attainment of course level learning outcomes (Krause et al., 2014). It is also commonly agreed that capstone courses should involve authentic practice, usually through addressing complex 'real-world' problems in professional settings, using professional methods and approaches (Healey et al., 2013; Herrington, Reeves and Oliver, 2014).

Capstones@UOW is intended to provide all students at UOW with the opportunity to experience a significant final-year integrative learning experience characterised by relevance, complexity and independence in application to real-world, intellectually challenging situations and problems. Capstones experiences at UOW can involve a combination of independent research projects, client-based projects, work-engaged learning projects and internships or professional placements. They are supported in many courses by 'cornerstones' (subjects that bring together learning from a sequence of study) throughout the degree, as well as the use of portfolio learning through MyPortfolio@UOW and other showcasing opportunities. The UOW Curriculum Transformation Model recommends that capstones include a showcase experience to provide students with opportunities to share their achievements with a broader audience beyond the peer group and discipline (University of Wollongong, 2016b). Healey et al. (2013) suggest that showcasing student work potentially has a number of important benefits: it is a simple way to ensure the deepening and integration of student learning; in itself an authentic element of professional life; and it has reputational benefits for the student and institution. Types of capstone showcases promoted by UOW include: posting prototypes or posters on a virtual platform; competitions; presenting findings or ideas at a student event or as part of an academic or professional forum; and, showcasing prototypes and solutions at an event aimed at industry professionals.

One example of how capstones are being used to support connectedness is occurring in the UOW Business School, whereby students are offered a suite of final year subjects, including an independent research project, a group work simulated business development project and an internship. Thus, different capstone experiences are offered to meet different learning needs of students across Business and Commerce undergraduate courses. Each of the subjects is designed to integrate and apply the degree's overarching focus on socially responsible practice. Another example from a journalism course is the third year newsroom practice capstone subject, which employs an iterative approach to learning, whereby students play a number of different roles, including: editorial content managers, reporters across different media modes, editors and mobile reporters. Collaboratively, they produce a weekly online publication in a deadline-driven environment (Latukefu et al., 2013).

While the journalism capstone is a key subject that brings together a range of different skills and processes so that students work in a collaborative, structured and reflective way (Latukefu et al., 2013), it is important to note the progressive development of this approach across the curriculum rather than merely within the capstone subject. This course is preceded by a second year subject, in which students learn video skills and then produce a multicomponent, multimedia website. Although the final journalism artefact is an individual project, it is produced in a collaborative environment in which students are encouraged, through a range of structured classroom activities, to reflect on and critique each other's evolving projects. This prepares students to engage in both the multimedia and team-based aspects of the capstone. The central idea of a newsroom editorial process, whereby students collectively engage in a news conference and are allocated a story task to complete by the end of the day, is introduced in a first year newsroom subject. Thus, the capstone course represents the culmination of a learning journey for students, and also the considered application of a whole-of-course approach to curriculum design, something that is agreed to be a key determinant of success for capstones, but which can also represent enormous complexities and challenges for curriculum designers (Lee and Loton, 2015).

Lee and Loton (2015) propose six principles for successful capstone design: (1) integration and extension of prior learning; (2) authentic and contextualised experiences; (3) challenging and complex problems; (4) student independence and agency; (5) a concern with critical inquiry and creativity; and (6) active dissemination and celebration. While possibly implied to some extent in the principles of authenticity and dissemination, a commitment to fostering connectedness (particularly through networking and interaction with professional networks, and interdisciplinary practice with peers) could also be argued to be an important principle for capstones. Lee and Loton (2015), as well as others (Hauhart and Grahe, 2015), have found that the most common capstone curriculum models are project or problem-based (89 per cent in Lee and Loton's study), and feature a combination of individual and group work, often in interdisciplinary topic areas (Rowles et al., 2004), in partnership with industry or community. About half of the capstones in Lee and Loton's research were described as Work Integrated Learning. As such, capstones represent an unparalleled opportunity in programs to foster students' professional networks, hone their collaborative skills across disciplinary areas, and refine their connected identities before moving into the world of work. The implications of connectedness learning for capstone practice are discussed in more detail by Goodwin et al., in Chapter 9 of this volume.

CONCLUSION

The global discussion around employability indicates that university graduates need to be adaptable and innovative (Hagel et al., 2014). The University of Wollongong Curriculum Model attempts, through institutional change, to course curriculum, pedagogy, and assessment practices towards the development of twenty-first century capacities. It demonstrates that to facilitate the future employability of students, explicit measures need to take place to assist them in developing a social network literacy and 'brand' awareness of their professional identity to grow, work with, and maintain connections. These changes need to be embedded as part of a "*processual approach in which responsibility ... is shared*" (Bennett et al., 2017, p. 59) across the entire institution (i.e. academics, professional staff, students) using a whole of curriculum approach, as the UOW Curriculum Model and its integration into courses is starting to do.

However, to make this successful, a long-term strategy for its integration outside the institution is also required. Specifically, identifying and making strategic connections with employers, alumni and community partners to serve as a 'pipeline' for student employment and foster an interdisciplinary discussion between key stakeholders to eliminate silos to improve efficacy and institutional uptake (Bridgstock, 2019b). While still ongoing, the opportunity of using the University of Wollongong work as a case study can guide other institutions internationally on ways to achieve curriculum renewal and foster graduate employability in a sustainable and progressive way.

ACKNOWLEDGEMENTS

The authors would like to acknowledge the contributions of Sibylle Schwab, Jake Holman, Margaret Wallace, Anne Melano, Marcus O'Donnell, Learning, Teaching and Curriculum and Faculty staff, for this work which would not have been possible without them.

REFERENCES

Arnold, N. and Paulus, T. (2010). Using a social networking site for experiential learning: Appropriating, lurking, modeling and community building. *The Internet and Higher Education, 13*(4), 188–196.

Bennett, D., Knight, E., Divan, A., Kuchel, L., Horn, J., van Reyk, D. and Burke da Silva, K. (2017). How do research-intensive universities portray employability strategies? A review of their websites. *Australian Journal of Career Development, 26*(2), 52–61.

Bennett, D., Rowley, J., Dunbar-Hall, P., Hitchcock, M. and Blom, D. (2016). Electronic portfolios and learner identity: An ePortfolio case study in music and writing. *Journal of Further and Higher Education, 40*(1), 107–124.

Bridgstock, R. (2019a). Employability and career development learning through social media: Exploring the potential of LinkedIn. In J. Higgs, D. Horsfall, S. Cork and A. Jones (eds), *Challenging Future Practice Possibilities*. Rotterdam: Sense-Brill Publishers.

Bridgstock, R. (2019b). *Graduate Employability 2.0: Enhancing the Connectedness of Learners, Teachers and Higher Education Institutions. Final Report of the National Senior Teaching Fellowship*. Canberra: Department of Education and Training.

DeSchryver, M., Mishra, P., Koehleer, M. and Francis, A. (2009). *Moodle vs. Facebook: Does using Facebook for discussions in an online course enhance perceived social presence and student interaction?* Paper presented at the Society for Information Technology and Teacher Education International Conference.

Emmett, D. J. (2011). *Student engagement with an ePortfolio: A case study of pre-service education students.* Doctoral dissertation, Queensland University of Technology.

Ernst and Young. (2012). *University of the Future: A Thousand Year Old Industry on the Cusp of Profound Change.* Australia: Ernst and Young.

Francis, R. and Shannon, S. J. (2013). Engaging with blended learning to improve students' learning outcomes. *European Journal of Engineering Education, 38*(4), 359–369.

Gray, L. (2008). *Effective Practice with E-portfolios.* Bristol: Higher Education Funding Council for England.

Grossman, R., Thayer, A. L., Shuffler, M. L., Burke, C. S. and Salas, E. (2015). Critical social thinking: A conceptual model and insights for training. *Organizational Psychology Review, 5*(2), 99–125.

Hagel, J., Brown, J., Mathew, R., Wooll, M. and Tsu, W. (2014). *The Lifetime Learner: A Journey Through the Future of Postsecondary Education.* Deloitte, TX: Deloitte University Press.

Hallam, G., Harper, W. and McAllister, L. (2012). Current ePortfolio practice in Australia. In D. Cambridge (ed.), *E-portfolios and Global Diffusion: Solutions For Collaborative Education* (pp. 129–148). Hershey, PA: IGI Global.

Harden-Thew, K. and Dean, B. A. (2015). *Focusing on six first year firsts: A professional development framework supporting teachers of first year subjects.* Australia: Students Transitions Achievement Retention and Success: STARS Conference.

Hauhart, R. C. and Grahe, J. E. (2015). *Designing and Teaching Undergraduate Capstone Courses.* San Francisco, CA: Jossey-Bass.

Healey, M., Lannin, L., Stibbe, A. and Derounian, J. (2013). *Developing and Enhancing Undergraduate Final-year Projects.* York: The Higher Education Academy.

Herrington, J., Reeves, T. C. and Oliver, R. (2014). Authentic learning environments. In J. M. Spector, M. D. Merrill, J. Elen and M. J. Bishop (eds), *Handbook of Research on Educational Communications and Technology* (pp. 401–412). New York, NY: Springer.

Ito, M., Gutierrez, K., Livingstone, S., Penuel, B., Rhodes, J., Salen, K. ... Watkins, S. C. (2014). Connected learning: An agenda for research and design. Retrieved on 27 March 2018 from http://dmlhub.net/publications/connected-learning-agenda-for-research-and-design/.

Jones, N., Chew, E., Jones, C. and Lau, A. (2009). Over the worst or at the eye of the storm? *Education+Training, 51*(1), 6–22.

Jwaifell, M. (2013). A proposed model for electronic portfolio to increase both validating skills and employability. *Procedia–Social and Behavioral Sciences, 103*, 356–364.

Kift, S. M., Nelson, K. J. and Clarke, J. A. (2010). Transition pedagogy: A third generation approach to FYE: A case study of policy and practice for the higher education sector. *The International Journal of the First Year in Higher Education, 1*(1), 1–20.

Kolb, A. Y. and Kolb, D. A. (2005). Learning styles and learning spaces: Enhancing experiential learning in higher education. *Academy of Management Learning and Education, 4*(2), 193–212.

Krause, K. L. (2005). Understanding and promoting student engagement in university learning communities. Paper presented as keynote address: Engaged, Inert or Otherwise Occupied, 21–22. Retrieved on 20 March 2019 from https://www.liberty.edu/media/3425/teaching_resources/Stud_eng.pdf.

Krause, K. L., Scott, G., Aubin, K., Alexander, H., Angelo, T., Campbell, S. … Pattison, P. (2014). Assuring learning and teaching standards through inter-institutional peer review and moderation: Final report of the project, 15. Retrieved on 27 March 2018 from https://www.westernsydney.edu.au/__data/assets/pdf_file/0007/576916/External_Report_2014_Web_3.pdf.

Latukefu, L., O'Donnell, M., Burns, S. G., Hayes, J. E., Ellmers, G. N. and Stirling, J. (2013). Fire in the belly: Building resilience in creative practitioners through experiential and authentically designed learning environments *The CALTN Papers: The refereed proceedings of the Creative Arts Learning and Teaching Network Symposium, Hobart, Australia: Tasmanian College of the Arts, University of Tasmania and the Creative Arts Learning and Teaching Network* (pp. 61–90).

Lee, N. and Loton, D. (2015). *Capstone curriculum Across Disciplines: Synthesising Theory, Practice and Policy to Provide Practical Tools for Curriculum Design.* Sydney, NSW: Office for Learning and Teaching, Department of Education and Training.

Maloney, S., Nicklen, P., Rivers, G., Foo, J., Ooi, Y. Y., Reeves, S. … Ilic, D. (2015). A cost-effectiveness analysis of blended versus face-to-face delivery of evidence-based medicine to medical students. *Journal of Medical Internet Research, 17*(7), e182.

Manyika, J., Chui, M., Madgavkar, A. and Lund, S. (2017). Technology, jobs, and the future of work. *McKinsey Global Institute.* Retrieved on 18 July 2018 from https://www.mckinsey.com/featured-insights/employment-and-growth/technology-jobs-and-the-future-of-work.

Masters, J. and Donnison, S. (2010). First-year transition in teacher education: The pod experience. *Australian Journal of Teacher Education, 35*(2), 87–98.

McAlpine, M. (2005). E-portfolios and digital identity: Some issues for discussion. *E-Learning and Digital Media, 2*(4), 378–387.

Means, B., Toyama, Y., Murphy, R. and Baki, M. (2013). The effectiveness of online and blended learning: A meta-analysis of the empirical literature. *Teachers College Record, 115*(3), 1–47.

O'Donnell, M., Wallace, M., Melano, A., Lawson, R. and Leinonen, E. (2015). Putting transition at the centre of whole-of-curriculum transformation. *Student Success, 6*(2), 73–79.

Osgerby, J. (2013). Students' perceptions of the introduction of a blended learning environment: An exploratory case study. *Accounting Education, 22*(1), 85–99.

Pillay, S. and James, R. (2014). The pains and gains of blended learning–social constructivist perspectives. *Education+ Training, 56*(4), 254–270.

Rennie, F. and Morrison, T. (2013). *E-learning and Social Networking Handbook: Resources for Higher Education.* New York: Routledge.

Rovai, A. P. and Jordan, H. (2004). Blended learning and sense of community: A comparative analysis with traditional and fully online graduate courses. *The International Review of Research in Open and Distributed Learning, 5*(2), 1–13.

Rowles, C. J., Koch, D. C., Hundley, S. P. and Hamilton, S. J. (2004). Toward a model for capstone experiences: Mountaintops, magnets, and mandates. *Assessment Update, 16*(1), 1–2.

Shannon, S., Francis, R. and Torpey, G. (2012). *Barriers to adoption of blended learning and online feedback and assessment by sessional staff.* Paper presented at the ASA 2012 Conference, Griffith University, Gold Coast.

Siemens, G. (2013). Learning analytics: The emergence of a discipline. *American Behavioral Scientist, 57*(10), 1380–1400.

Smith, M., Bell, K., Bennet, D. and McAlpine, M. (2018). Employability in a global context: Evolving policy and practice in employability, work integrated learning, and career development learning. Retrieved on 20 March 2019 from https://cica.org.au/wp-content/uploads/Employability-in-a-Global-Context.pdf.

So, H. J. and Brush, T. A. (2008). Student perceptions of collaborative learning, social presence and satisfaction in a blended learning environment: Relationships and critical factors. *Computers and Education, 51*(1), 318–336.

University of Wollongong. (2016a). Student career development and employability strategy and plan. Retrieved on 18 July 2018 from https://www.uow.edu.au/curriculum-transformation/SCDE/index.html.

University of Wollongong. (2016b). UOW Curriculum Model. Retrieved on 18 July 2018 from https://www.uow.edu.au/content/groups/public/@web/@cedir/@man/documents/doc/uow185464.pdf.

US Department of Education. (2010). *Evaluation of Evidence-Based Practices in Online Learning: A Meta-Analysis and Review of Online Learning Studies*. Washington, DC: US Department of Education, Office of Planning, Evaluation and Policy Development.

Zhao, C. M. and Kuh, G. D. (2004). Adding value: Learning communities and student engagement. *Research in Higher Education*, *45*(2), 115–138.

PART III

Institutional enabling strategies

11. Institutional enabling strategies
Ruth Bridgstock and Neil Tippett

INTRODUCTION

Over the preceding chapters we have explored the importance of connectedness capabilities for graduates and also identified the pedagogic approaches which can be used within higher education to foster students' connectedness capabilities and networks. In this final section of the book, we address the larger question of how degree programs, organisational areas such as Faculties or Divisions, and universities more broadly, can enable connectedness learning.

Seeking to characterise the extent of connectedness learning and teaching in higher education institutions, Bridgstock (2019b) conducted in-depth interviews with 71 higher education staff, university alumni, and employers/recruiters throughout Australia. Two key thematic challenges to higher education connectedness emerged. First, the university was often seen as a 'walled garden', with relatively limited and mostly transactionally-based interaction between the institution and entities outside of it. Second, the university could be depicted as a 'series of silos' in which staff, programs, and organisational areas all have relatively little interaction with each other, even inside departments, and interactions/collaborations are hampered by structural and bureaucratic factors. Although these challenges were seen to be consistent across the higher education sector, there are many approaches that universities can use to overcome these institutional barriers, and this chapter will discuss some of these. Following this, the chapter then outlines seven enabling institutional strategies that can be used by universities to create, grow and maintain inter- and intra-institutional connectedness, which in turn create conditions for the development and use of connectedness pedagogies and capabilities. Finally, the chapter introduces three empirical chapters, which explore how these enabling strategies are being integrated within and across different higher education institutions, and the impact they have had towards enhancing graduates' connectedness capabilities.

THE CONNECTED INSTITUTION

If we are to support students to develop connections and then to learn from them, work with them and build productive and meaningful careers and lives, it follows that universities should also be well connected. This argument can be made at a number of levels. Foremost, in a practical sense, if the university maintains productive relationships with industry, community, researchers and teachers within and beyond the institution, it can leverage these to offer distinctive and enriched collaborative learning experiences that also grow students' connectedness capabilities and networks (Bridgstock, 2019a). In so doing, the institution models reciprocal connectedness practices and capabilities at the level of staff and organisational behaviour, infusing connectedness within the anatomy of the university itself. This modelling requires both professional learning and a shift in organisational culture, which can be further strengthened and propagated through connectedness practice. Thus, through building a culture of connectedness, the institution starts to enrich its own knowledge and practices, and enhance its external reputation (Cooper, Orrell and Bowden, 2010). These benefits can also extend beyond the institutional walls, contributing to the enrichment of knowledge and practices among the university's partners.

The notions of knowledge transfer and knowledge exchange between universities and industry are by no means new (Jongbloed, Enders and Salerno, 2008), however, the literature in this space still tends to focus on research, commercialisation, and to some extent community service activities (the 'third mission'), with teaching and student involvement lagging somewhat behind (Xia, Caulfield and Ferns, 2015). Indeed, in comparison, learning and teaching seemingly suffer from a lack of strategic or systematic development and management of external engagement and partnerships, such as client relationship management approaches. The rise of work integrated learning and the associated need to manage partner relationships for large numbers of student placements means that this is changing, albeit slowly (Fleming, 2016; O'Leary, 2013; Tran, 2016).

Anticipating the changing role of the higher education sector, Bridgstock (2017) suggests a utopian vision of the future university as the hub of a knowledge network, demonstrating potential benefits of the connected university to students, teachers, industry, professionals, users and university researchers. She conceptualises the future university as being based on overarching, accessible, empowering, dynamic, global, communally constructed frameworks of open materials and online platforms (Tapscott and Williams, 2010) that are continually evolving and adapting in response to external and internal changes. The hub acts as both a conduit and knowledge integrator for the latest university and industry generated research and practice trends that students, professionals and communities alike can access as needed. Learning occurs authentically through experiential practice, embedded into communities and networks, with learners able to search out task-relevant knowledge and information from the knowledge network, with the support and facilitation of teachers.

This utopian vision offers a counterpoint to the highly bounded bureaucratic institutions that universities are today. Many universities are set up in ways that actively work against developing better networks (Ankrah and Al-Tabbaa, 2015). Social networks are based on the open sharing of information, learning, and connections; however, universities still tend to cautiously guard their research, curriculum and staff/students by keeping them inside of the walled garden, limiting their access to the outside world. Minocha, Hristov and Reynolds (2017) reviewed practices across UK higher education for graduate employability, concluding that university–industry interaction represented a significant opportunity for growth and strengthening. Risk management and the protection of data and intellectual property are part of the reason for this practice being underdeveloped, however, by engaging in highly protective behaviour, universities limit the opportunity for reciprocal and trusting relationships to develop; relationships which can form the foundation for effective collaborative work.

Industry stakeholders can also find that universities are difficult to work with as institutions. Universities can work at a different pace to other organisations, and their processes and administrative requirements can be barriers to engagement. In addition, many higher education institutions have not yet adopted integrated and strategic stakeholder engagement and management practices. These institutions continue to engage in low-value, short-term transactional interactions with external partners (such as sending students for placements each semester, with little acknowledgement or interaction with the partner otherwise), and purely bottom-up, academic-led small collaborations that are based on individual relationships and disappear when the staff member moves elsewhere. Different parts of the institution may make multiple bottom-up uncoordinated approaches to potential partners.

A key challenge and concurrent opportunity for universities is to engage in strategic, deeper long-term and highly reciprocal collaborations with external partners that are multi-pronged (teaching, research, commercialisation, community). Each prong of activity can complement the others in building knowledge and practice, fostering a symbiotic relationship between partners. For success, common goals to collaborative work that address mutual benefits to all stakeholders need to be developed, with both partners working towards the goal through a close partnership (Choy and Delahaye, 2011; Cooper, Orrell and Bowden, 2010; Peach, Larkin and Ruinard, 2012). The benefits of such partnerships must be reciprocal, including enriching authentic learning experiences for students, reputational effects for universities, providing a 'talent pipeline' for industry, exposure to fresh new ideas for all partners through research and practice, and improved curriculum.

Another key challenge for universities is silo-busting. Inter-disciplinary teaching, collaborations between teaching and research, and shared endeavours to build external partnerships are all highly valuable activities, and yet many in universities find it difficult simply to share knowledge and practice (Al-Kurdi, El-Haddadeh and Eldabi, 2018). In 2005, Friedman et al. lamented, "it is unfortunate that universities, while they may ideally be teaching organisations, generally do not have any of the characteristics of learning organisations. There is little knowledge sharing; ten different faculty members may teach the same course, but they will not work together to share ideas. There is still very little team teaching in a typical university" (see Friedman and Kass-Shraibman, 2017, p. 295).

Many scholars agree that inter-disciplinary interaction and collaboration could be increased inside universities, to the benefit of many (Örtenblad and Koris, 2014). As students learn to connect with others through scaffolded authentic practice, so too many university staff will benefit from professional learning opportunities that support them to collaborate effectively with others in the university for mutual benefit. Some researchers have found that academics have generally positive attitudes towards knowledge sharing and collaborative practice but may be inhibited in doing so by individualistic organisational culture, instrumentalism, inconsistent leadership and messaging, and barriers in terms of information technology and organisational structure (Fullwood, Rowley and Delbridge, 2013). Strong disciplinary affiliations and long-held beliefs about curriculum and pedagogy can also be barriers to collaboration and sharing. Cultural change is required in order to foster connections inside higher education institutions across disciplinary and functional silos, and to support institutions to work effectively with stakeholders outside the organisation.

INSTITUTIONAL ENABLING STRATEGIES FOR CONNECTEDNESS

At present, higher education institutions clearly struggle in using connectedness to move beyond walls and silos to establish more strategic, integrated and sustainable approaches to education. The Connectedness Learning Approach outlines seven enabling strategies that can be used by universities to create, support and maintain partner, collaborator and network engagement plans and practices to cultivate better connected programs, organisational area and institutions. Implemented institution-wide, these enabling strategies can help ensure that structures, processes, teaching staff, curricula and pedagogic practices are all aligned in supporting students to develop connectedness for life and work. The seven institutional enabling strategies are:

1. *Develop an integrated suite of connectedness pedagogies and partners:* build an integrated program of connectedness pedagogies. Maximise the benefit of connections by partnering across multiple pedagogic approaches where appropriate. Partner with stakeholders across multiple pedagogies where appropriate.
2. *Identify, develop and strengthen key relationship broker roles:* which individuals and teams will be responsible for developing and maintaining extra- and intra-university/program connections and partnerships? What level of resourcing (including workload allocation) will be required? How will the benefits of personal points of contact be balanced with the risks of individually brokered connections?
3. *Reduce institutional barriers to extra-university connectedness:* streamline processes, create simple, responsive and personal points of contact, reduce forms and 'red tape', and simplify and standardise intellectual property, legal and insurance processes.
4. *Identify, make and grow strategic extra-university connections:* identify key industry and community partners in line with strategic plans, actively seek connections for consultation and engagement, offer genuine value to connections (e.g. continuing professional education and networking opportunities, a pipeline of excellent students/graduates for employment, access to facilities, research expertise) and manage connections sensitively.
5. *Strengthen and maintain extra-university connections:* develop deeper stakeholder engagement strategies, moving from finite and transactional to long-term partnerships and collaborating on mutually beneficial tasks (e.g. knowledge exchange activities, investment and building trust, keeping one another 'in the loop').
6. *Foster intra-university connectedness:* ensure that networks of individuals and programs engaged in similar or related practices (e.g. alumni engagement program leaders, faculty stakeholder engagement managers) are built across organisational areas to maximise learning, knowledge exchange and connection sharing.
7. *Use connectedness-enabling digital tools, platforms and infrastructure:* where possible, choose digital technologies that support and enable connectedness – for instance, those that are industry-authentic, open and connected into wider networks beyond the university (e.g. social media, blogs, industry-authentic online portfolios), and adopt data management strategies to support this.

To guide the effective implementation of these strategies, the Connectedness Learning Approach also outlines eight learning principles that support institutions in applying connectedness across programs, organisational areas and the university as a whole. These principles are:

- The program is 'plugged in' to wider professional, industry and interest groups and networks.
- The program seeks out and develops new relationships in a strategic way, according to principles of reciprocity.
- The program deepens the relationships it has in effective ways, including through valuing its connections.
- Interactions and communications are straightforward and effective.
- Processes are simple and straightforward, with 'red tape' minimised.
- Partnerships and networks within the university (intra-university connections) are present and optimised.
- There are enough resources (people, workload, funding) to foster sustainable connectedness.
- There is an evaluation plan in place that covers the above dimensions.

This volume includes three chapters that focus explicitly on various institutional enabling strategies that support connectedness learning, and the development of connectedness capabilities among students and staff.

In Chapter 12, Kerr, Wright and Barraud consider how universities and schools can work together to support the development of learners' twenty-first century skill sets by documenting the design and delivery of a co-curricular design-led social entrepreneurship program initiated by a secondary school and developed through collaboration with a university partner in Queensland, Australia. Discussing the creation, implementation and evaluation of this program, the authors provide a practical account of how inter-institutional partnerships can be developed and maintained for mutual benefit. The chapter provides evidence of how the program was able to support connectedness learning among both students and teachers, and in doing so, create opportunities for further learning and collaboration.

In Chapter 13, Hammer et al. describe a pilot initiative to integrate enabling strategies into institutional program review and enhancement processes at a regional Australian university. Comprising a cross-disciplinary project team which included careers and employability staff, the authors use documentary analysis to map existing connectedness learning within the Creative Arts and Engineering programs. Subsequent interviews with selected stakeholders were used to determine the effectiveness of these approaches, and identify strengths, gaps and opportunities for unit and program enhancement. In discussing the findings, the authors address the challenges that universities face in embedding connectedness learning into institution-wide review and enhancement processes, yet also provide recommendations and examples of good practice which can support educators in integrating connectedness learning pedagogies within their own disciplines.

In Chapter 14, Kitto et al. consider how universities can start using systemic enabling strategies to deliver connectedness learning at scale, and over a lifetime. Drawing upon the lessons learned from two ongoing projects at the University of Technology, Sydney, the authors explore institutional barriers to large scale connectedness learning. With a specific focus on student data, institutional connectivity and digital infrastructure, the chapter provides a series of practical recommendations that could be generally applied within any university looking to move towards a model of lifelong connectedness learning.

REFERENCES

Al-Kurdi, O., El-Haddadeh, R. and Eldabi, T. (2018). Knowledge sharing in higher education institutions: A systematic review. *Journal of Enterprise Information Management, 31*(2), 226–246.

Ankrah, S. and Al-Tabbaa, O. (2015). Universities–industry collaboration: A systematic review. *Scandinavian Journal of Management, 31*(3), 387–408.

Bridgstock, R. (2017). The university and the knowledge network: A new educational model for 21st century learning and employability. In M. Tomlinson (ed.), *Graduate Employability in Context: Research, Theory and Debate* (pp. 339–358). London: Palgrave Macmillan.

Bridgstock, R. (2019b). *Graduate Employability 2.0: Enhancing the Connectedness of Learners, Teachers and Higher Education Institutions. Final Report of the National Senior Teaching Fellowship.* Canberra: Department of Education and Training.

Bridgstock, R. (2019a). Graduate Employability 2.0: Education for work in a networked world. In J. Higgs, G. Crisp and W. Letts (eds), *Education for Employability: The Employability Agenda.* Rotterdam: Sense-Brill Publishers.

Choy, S. and Delahaye, B. (2011). Partnerships between universities and workplaces: Some challenges for work-integrated learning. *Studies in Continuing Education, 33*(2), 157–172.

Cooper, L., Orrell, J. and Bowden, M. (2010). *Work Integrated Learning: A Guide to Effective Practice.* London: Routledge.

Fleming, J. (2016). *Collaborating with WIL Stakeholders: Success factors for sustainable relationships.* Paper presented at the 2nd International Research Symposium on Cooperative and Work-Integrated Education, Victoria, BC.

Friedman, H. H. and Kass-Shraibman, F. (2017). What it takes to be a superior college president: Transform your institution into a learning organization. *The Learning Organization*, *24*(5), 286–297.

Fullwood, R., Rowley, J. and Delbridge, R. (2013). Knowledge sharing amongst academics in UK universities. *Journal of Knowledge Management*, *17*(1), 123–136.

Jongbloed, B., Enders, J. and Salerno, C. (2008). Higher education and its communities: Interconnections, interdependencies and a research agenda. *Higher Education*, *56*(3), 303–324.

Minocha, S., Hristov, D. and Reynolds, M. (2017). From graduate employability to employment: Policy and practice in UK higher education. *International Journal of Training and Development*, *21*(3), 235–248.

O'Leary, S. (2013). Collaborations in higher education with employers and their influence on graduate employability: An institutional project. *Enhancing Learning in the Social Sciences*, *5*(1), 37–50.

Örtenblad, A. and Koris, R. (2014). Is the learning organization idea relevant to higher educational institutions? A literature review and a 'multi-stakeholder contingency approach'. *International Journal of Educational Management*, *28*(2), 173–214.

Peach, D., Larkin, I. and Ruinard, E. (2012). *High-risk, high-stake relationships: Building effective industry-university partnerships for work integrated learning (WIL).* Paper presented at the Australian Collaborative Education Network (ACEN) National Conference, Deakin University, Geelong.

Tapscott, D. and Williams, A. D. (2010). Innovating the 21st-century university: It's time. *Educause Review*, *45*(1), 16–29.

Tran, T. T. (2016). Enhancing graduate employability and the need for university-enterprise collaboration. *Journal of Teaching and Learning for Graduate Employability*, *7*(1), 58–71.

Xia, J., Caulfield, C. and Ferns, S. (2015). Work-integrated learning: Linking research and teaching for a win–win situation. *Studies in Higher Education*, *40*(9), 1560–1572.

12. Developing a connected learning community for social entrepreneurship through university and high school collaboration

Jeremy Kerr, Natalie Wright and Timothy Barraud

INTRODUCTION

Increasingly, international research suggests that developing twenty-first century skills in the K-16 education pipeline (Partnership for 21st Century Learning, 2015; Trilling and Fadel, 2012; World Economic Forum, 2015), in particular the disposition of adaptivity, will minimise disengagement and prepare learners, teachers and school leaders to successfully navigate the shifting milieu and attain lifelong employability (Hung, Lim and Lee, 2014). Established curricular, disciplinary and educational system boundaries have enculturated students and educators with narrow understandings of learning, misaligned with the practices of the real-world domain (Voogt et al., 2013). In response, education researchers, policy makers and practitioners have highlighted the value of connecting learning across school, university and community contexts, and bridging formal and informal transdisciplinary learning to empower creative agency and active citizenship (Kumpulainen, 2014; Lee et al., 2014). Achieving this requires upskilling teachers to become both partnership brokers and brokers-of-learning, encouraging metacognitive development to facilitate links across contexts, and foster transferable attitudes, skills and knowledge (Lee et al., 2014).

Despite recent focus, connected learning linking schools with universities has been recognised as beneficial since the late 1980s (Edwards, Tsui and Stimpson, 2009). Researchers have identified advantages for both institutions in engaging in inter-sectoral collaboration (Aydın et al., 2018; Mullen, 2009; Stevens, 1999), which has also been recommended as an approach to achieving educational reform (Dyson, 1999). Increasingly, literature conceptualises school–university partnerships as more collaborative models such as communities of practice (Day, 1998; Martínez, Sauleda and van Veen, 2000; Sutherland, Scanlon and Sperring, 2005) and (professional) learning communities (Edwards, Gilroy and Hartley, 2005; Snow-Gerono, 2005).

However, university–school partnerships have tended to focus on pre-service teacher education (Brady, 2002; Goodlad, 1993; Rayner and Corkill, 2015), alongside continuing teacher professional learning. It is only in recent years that community stakeholders and school students are becoming a central focus in these initiatives, with a key motivation to increase the capacity building of school students, rather than focusing on formal teacher education (though this may still be a part of such projects). Examples include programs to assist culturally and linguistically diverse school students (Wesley, 2015), increase STEM engagement for female school students (Shewmaker and Lee, 2015), and develop unique student mentorship relationships (Wasburn-Moses and Noltemeyer, 2018). This movement has subsequently led to a demand by educators for scholarly guides and practical illustrations about how such initiatives are developed and facilitated (Parker and Zenkov, 2017).

In this chapter, we outline an Australian example of connected, student-centred learning that spans educational contexts and sectors. The program, co-developed by Indooroopilly State High School (ISHS) and Queensland University of Technology School of Design (QUT), incorporated "understandings of design thinking, metacognition and the social construction of knowledge" (Hung, Lim and Jamaludin, 2014, p. 5), and the combined participation of teachers, outside experts and students, to develop a co-curricular, networked, design-led social entrepreneurship initiative for middle school students and teachers. By investigating this epistemic shift towards student-centred, participatory, connected learning, the program aimed to give learners the autonomy to practise and refine their soft interpersonal skills in a meaningful, 'safe' and authentic context.

This chapter examines the strategies used to create and implement this learning initiative, recounting the establishment of a connected learning community and the design process, and evaluating the effectiveness of this approach, with consideration of student and teachers' connectedness capabilities. It then examines the potential reciprocity and transferability of the model in building connectedness capabilities and graduate employability in higher education.

BACKGROUND TO THE PROJECT

The obligation for educators to broaden entrepreneurship and enterprise education programs to include the acquisition of a broader set of lifelong skills and enterprise capacity (not simply training for business startup), has long been acknowledged as a requisite to prepare students for the economy in which they will operate and their contribution to society (Commission of the European Communities, 2003; Gallaway et al., 2005; Sexton and Kasarda, 1992). This has seen an increase in the development of these programs in both schools and universities internationally in recent times (Birdthistle, Hynes and Fleming, 2007; Nielsen and Stovang, 2015; Uleanya and Gamede, 2017; Val et al., 2017), despite the fact that entrepreneurship skills are best learnt through an integrated and experiential general learning experience, rather than a didactic one (Weaver, 1999).

For this reason, a design thinking approach to entrepreneurship education is being recognised as one which not only develops the cognitive-related skills (i.e. opportunity identification, assessing business ideas, business development, strategy growth) but also the non-cognitive skills including creativity, risk-taking, collaboration, communication, problem solving and personal development (Nielsen and Stovang, 2015; Val et al., 2017). Consequently, this represents an educational paradigm shift involving a "radical change in curriculum, teaching methods, teaching style, teacher–student relations, teaching space and assessment" (Nielsen and Stovang, 2015, p. 987), which necessitates teacher training and continuous evaluation for both sectors.

ISHS is committed to producing ethical, global twenty-first century learners. It aims to provide quality learning schoolwide through embedding four pedagogic principles: Critical Thinking; Creative Problem Solving; Connectedness; and Collaboration, which are aligned to the P21 Learning and Innovation Skills (Partnership for 21st Century Learning, 2015; Trilling and Fadel, 2012). In preparation for the senior phase of learning, all Year 10 students are offered the opportunity to engage with a co-curricular Social Entrepreneurship Project (SEP) focused on 'Connectedness'. SEP encourages students to investigate career planning and pathways by working collaboratively in small teams to: design a solution for a social need; create a prototype fit for market; and, learn the skills of design thinking and enterprise to accelerate their own entrepreneurial creations. The 17-week, predominantly teacher-led program, is comprised of lectures, feedback sessions, a pitch-off and an Innovation Expo, whereby projects are demonstrated to the school and local community.

Whilst largely a successful endeavour in 2016, opportunities for improvement and development were identified through a school-initiated online survey, which indicated that teachers lacked the necessary skills in design thinking and enterprise to best foster the development of their projects. Identifying the value that external consultants could bring to this program, ISHS enacted a partnership with QUT motivated by the research of Wright and Davis (2014), to redesign the SEP curriculum in 2017, seeking to use the value of cross-sectoral connected learning to embed the school's four pedagogic principles, through a design-led framework.

DESIGN OF THE PROJECT

SEP was developed over two distinct phases: (1) the formation of a connected learning community to guide the project, and (2) the creation of the SEP curriculum.

Phase 1: Developing a Connected Learning Community

Prior to developing the SEP curriculum, a series of key steps were taken in partnership between the university and the high school to ensure a culture of collaboration and innovation. With the school's larger strategic ambition to build a culture of practice in connected design-led educational innovation (Wright and Wrigley, 2017), a Memorandum of Understanding (MOU) was co-signed in order to recognise the formation of a mutually beneficial cross-sectoral learning community called the 'Innovation Hub'. The school identified key priorities, including professional development opportunities for the upskilling of teachers and the development of curriculum to enrich student engagement and benefit skills growth. Similarly, the MOU identified the university's focus on collaborative research, allowing for the collection of data from teachers, students and other stakeholders, for evaluation and publication.

The 'Innovation Hub' served as a vehicle to guide the implementation of a series of critical enabling strategies for cross-institutional connectedness. It became a means through which the institutions could negotiate institutional barriers impacting the collaboration (e.g. the procedures for ethics clearance), as well as an opportunity to clarify key roles and responsibilities in the partnership. The 'Innovation Hub' envisioned experimentation, educational innovation and transformational change, with a premise that all aspects of the school could potentially become the focus of 'Innovation Hub' projects, including curriculum design, extracurricular activities, school facilities and school systems.

The first initiative undertaken by the 'Innovation Hub' was an all-of-teaching-staff professional development (PD) program, which served to ensure teachers understood the design thinking process, had the foundational skillset and mindset to support its implementation, and were able to apply a design-led approach for use across the school and in the SEP. Feedback following the experiential workshops indicated that teachers gained a deeper, practical understanding of design thinking, and began to 'trust' the approach. Critically, teachers began to foster relationships with university staff, creating a culture of collaboration between the university and school, upon which to build the student-centred SEP project.

Over the course of the project, the learning community, and therefore the MOU remit, was broadened to allow for greater cross-university engagement opportunities for school students and teachers during both school and on-campus visits, thereby enabling multiple avenues for reciprocity and added value. The project acted as the impetus for the establishment of a state government-funded student entrepreneurship competition called *Gen[in]: Shaping Queensland Entrepreneurs* (Queensland Government, 2018), which allowed all QUT stakeholders to broaden state-wide extra-university networks with other institutions and industry partners beyond the SEP. At the same time, this opportunity fostered intra-university connectedness, by widening the network to include the sharing of transdisciplinary, intergenerational, and experiential knowledge of both students and academics from QUT.

Phase 2: Developing the SEP Curriculum

The redevelopment of the SEP curriculum was underpinned by the necessary extension of the learning community that brought missing perspectives and knowledge bases to what is an emerging, transdisciplinary area. Initially consisting of high school teachers and QUT School of Design staff, networking activities grew the learning community to include facilitators (academics and students) from additional university departments and research centres, and affiliated experts. Significantly, each stakeholder had a different focus and expertise in the development and support of enterprises and innovation, leading to the challenge of integrating all into a cohesive learning experience for students.

The development of learning strategies and content for the program began with the preparation of a draft schedule by the key partners, inviting direct participation into the course from each member of the extended learning community. Ideas were typically raised by a participant or brainstormed by groups of participants and then distributed for feedback across the learning community. It was through this process that various content and pedagogies were able to be integrated into the learning program. Collaboration was either asynchronous and email-based, or synchronous using teleconferencing social media or face-to-face meetings, but resultant in the digital sharing of resources, which easily allowed teaching material to be developed and distributed.

As the learning community solidified, the value it offered to high school teaching staff became increasingly apparent. Due to the transdisciplinary nature of social entrepreneurship, essentially overlapping the fields of design, business, social and cultural studies, and the environmental sciences and emerging technologies, most teachers only had general understandings, and those with deeper knowledge of specific areas, felt less confident in teaching others. While experts and facilitators from the university were to deliver some of these aspects of the program, teachers, as facilitators at the centre of the learning community and the 'teaching process', gained more in-depth understandings of content, perspectives and pedagogies from the greater learning community. The multidisciplinary expertise that they had access to and acquired across the learning community, contrasts directly with standard teacher-driven programs, which can be solitary and siloed in their knowledge bases (Kyndt et al., 2016).

THE SOCIAL ENTREPRENEURSHIP PROGRAM

Following the design phase, the reconceptualised SEP was delivered in two terms, over a 17 week period. The program involved 243 students, distributed into 9 classes, and supported by 11 teachers from various school subject areas. Regular SEP classes/sessions occurred on a weekly basis in scheduled 70-minute after-school sessions on Monday afternoons. Concurrent scheduling allowed for some classes to be held with the entire cohort together in the large school hall, while others sessions were facilitated by a school teacher in classes of approximately 27 students.

The program was framed as a competitive 'Social Entrepreneurship Challenge', wherein all students would work in teams of 3–5 to develop a sustainable social enterprise start-up prototype, and compete for prizes that would assist in making their 'pitch' a future reality. In this way, the program built upon the first SEP iteration, but 'raised the stakes' and opened future potential pathways for students beyond the program itself. The 'Challenge' intended to give the non-assessable co-curricular program a heightened focus, increasing motivation and authenticity for students.

To create landmarks and specific short-term goals, several defining 'learning events' were created outside of the scheduled classes. Firstly, a reconceived 'Innovation Expo' was held in the school auditorium, wherein all student groups showcased and promoted their initial social business start-up prototypes in individual expo stalls, in order to receive diverse constructive feedback from visitors. This event moved connectedness learning beyond the immediate learning community encompassing the two institutions, to include students from other year groups, parents, local businesspeople, community members and guests from the university and allied groups. As part of this learning event, students competed to have the most visitors fill in short feedback forms as a type of user testing/market research, highlighting project strengths and offering areas for improvement for the next iteration of their prototype. With the event drawing over 1,500 visitors, students received various and often mixed feedback from both peers and experts, thereby gaining an authentic understanding of the complexity of testing market responses as a start-up designer.

The next milestone students worked to was creating a prototype video of their revised project to be presented within each class in a 'video pitch off'. Each class then voted for a representative start-up group to compete in a culminating 'QUT Shark Tank' event at the university campus. This showdown event, which was promoted across the school and university via social media, saw each finalist team present to a panel composed of participating program mentors and facilitators. As it was hosted on campus at the university, selected SEP students were able to physically connect their learning to the outside, 'real' world and future study and career pathways, made visible though a tour of the university campus.

Outside of the milestone learning experiences, the regular Monday SEP sessions utilised a number of distinct approaches to further allow connected learning to occur. In the first week, all students were introduced to social entrepreneurship through an interactive presentation communicating design thinking as a framework for project creation. Following this, students worked through a series of class-based workshops codesigned by university educators and high school teachers. These required students to reflect on their passions, interests and social concerns in order to connect with like-minded students to form teams. Scaffolded workshops then assisted students in applying a design thinking process to develop their projects. Intermittently, workshop sessions were interrupted by presentations from business mentors, sometimes in the form of Q&A forums, which allowed the 'business end' of social entrepreneurship to be considered in tandem with the 'creative' and 'design' front-end of project development. Figure 12.1 illustrates the resulting extended learning community that was formed for this connected, adaptive and event-focused program. It explicitly distinguishes the program from other traditional co-curricular school programs which consist solely of a teacher and class group.

To further illustrate the scope and nature of the connected learning program, a SEP student journey map is presented in Figure 12.2. This summarises the chronological program experience and serves to demonstrate how the connectedness curriculum was conceptualised and developed throughout the design phase. Utilising the central metaphor of a student journey, the cross-institutional and multidisciplinary team was able to give continued focus and priority to the student experience while reconciling their different pedagogies, knowledge bases and course content. Conceptualisation of a program or service through a journey map reinforces the value of visual thinking as a distinctly 'designerly' way to approach course development.

EVALUATING THE SEP

Research Design

To evaluate the SEP and capture the multiple perspectives of stakeholders, a variety of research tools were utilised. Prior to implementation of the program, a descriptive survey was distributed to each of the stakeholder groups – students, teachers and facilitators. The questionnaire, containing both quantitative and qualitative questions related to each stakeholder group,

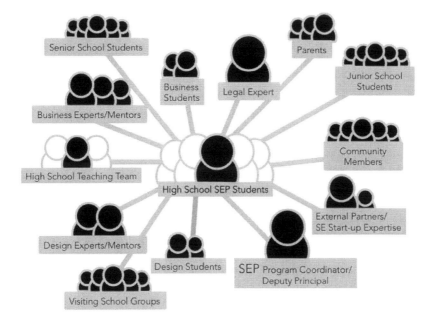

Figure 12.1   SEP stakeholder map

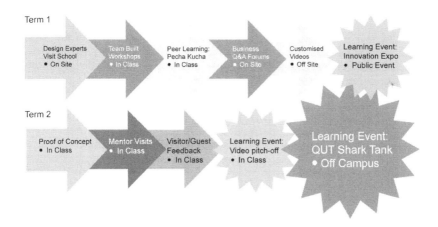

Figure 12.2   Student connected learning journey map

employed a quantitative five-point Likert scale to gauge perceptions of the value of the program across two areas: (1) Education to prepare students for the twenty-first century workforce, and (2) The Social Entrepreneurship Program.

In addition, surveys for students and facilitators included an additional section to gauge perceptions of the value of design thinking for innovation. A total of 186 students (76 per cent), four teachers (36 per cent) and three facilitators (50 per cent) responded to the survey. During the program itself, all participating students completed visual diaries. Semi structured interviews were also undertaken with selected staff (n=3) at the 'Innovation Expo' event, which occurred midway in the SEP.

At the completion of the program, students selected to compete in the 'QUT Shark Tank' event (n=25 in 9 groups) were asked to summarise their group experience visually via a journey map. They also participated in four 10–15-minute face-to-face focus groups conducted at QUT. The focus groups provided an opportunity for them to discuss three core issues: (1) their experiences and evaluations of the SEP; (2) their understanding of the importance of skills learnt (including design thinking) in workplace futures; and (3) the importance of networks and 'connectedness' in social entrepreneurship. Additionally, teachers (n=6) discussed similar issues in a 30-minute face-to-face focus group conducted at ISHS. All focus groups were video-recorded and then transcribed. Informally, teachers led a general discussion of student experience in a final class and recorded key observations. The school also undertook a final digital evaluation survey with 68 student participants.

When analysing survey questionnaires, numerical percentages were calculated to provide an overview of perceptions. The transcripts from the multiple sources of qualitative data (open-ended comments in the survey, focus groups and student and staff journals) were read closely, and the main themes were identified. This was followed by the coding process: categorising, sorting data, separating, labelling, and also adding the visual data from student journals and exercises. The data from the various sources was analysed using Constas' (1992) category process development approach which focuses on the combination of views from literature and the study. In this process, transcripts were tabled against key indicators related to the Connectedness Learning Approach (Chapter 1 in this volume) to ascertain more in-depth patterns in the data. Multiple extracts of raw data (specific quotes) are purposefully included to enable the reader to understand the evaluation.

FINDINGS

In evaluating the program, it was apparent that stakeholders viewed it overall as a valuable and positive experience. The numerous pedagogical approaches and transdisciplinary content had been successfully integrated and applied, producing identifiable emerging connectedness capabilities across key stakeholder groups, in particular for SEP students and the school teaching staff. The following provides an evaluation of the specific connectedness pedagogies employed within the program, and an assessment of the resulting connected capabilities amongst students and teachers.

Co-curricular Activities

The co-curricular foundation of the program was cited as an essential component of the learning, despite some students finding it difficult at times to balance with other time commitments and obligations for assessable schoolwork. In particular, teachers described that the co-curricular context allowed students to actively take risks and experiment with approaches to problem-solving, not often possible in curriculum-based school subjects.

Teachers emphasised that assessment (of sorts) was still occurring widely throughout the program, with associated learning emerging in much more meaningful ways. Assessment was informal and formative, rather than focused on a final evaluation of work. Teachers indicated that this allowed for greater emphasis on the feedback from external stakeholders, particularly industry experts. It was also noted that the informal assessment structure provided greater flexibility for stakeholders to provide student feedback. As expected, teachers strongly acknowledged that students appreciated and more highly valued feedback from external participants who they regarded as aspirational and experts in the field.

The value of the co-curricular nature of the program, was also recognised across all student surveys and focus groups. One student observed that it was within this context that he could "discover and explore a more non-educational side of thinking" and that he was "developing character qualities that are actually more adapted to the modern society". Another student described that it allowed her to develop "a broader range of skills" that might help to "fill in the gaps in what we learn in class, with things such as persistence, collaboration and initiative".

Industry Teaching and Engagement

Across all program feedback, the value of the presence of industry partners, was recognised. Students preferred when this occurred in face-to-face contexts, such as school visits from experts and the on-campus judging panel experience for the 'QUT Shark Tank' event. When the industry partners' participation occurred in digital format, through customised videos for example, the experience was still valued, but less popular than the physical visits. Face-to-face connectedness – even when it is one-to-many – was preferred over digital connectedness. In this regard, students described that they appreciated "seeing someone talk to me who has been there" and the "face behind the idea".

Students particularly cited the Q&A forum format as an effective opportunity to maximise learning from experts.

General student impressions regarding the impact of mentor teaching, are epitomised in the statement, "It was really important to see that they could have been in our position and reached a point like that". Students appreciated not only the level of success of the mentors and their industry insights, but also the candour that many displayed, indicating that the students could be in their position if they were to work hard, explore certain approaches and take risks. This emerged as a key component in building students' capabilities.

Student Partnerships

While students were aware of the increased learning opportunities they gained from experts, they also valued working with fellow students. In fact, students working closely together was cited as one of the most enjoyable aspects of the co-curricular project, second only to industry guests. A small group of students reported that they had made friends in the program with others they "wouldn't have otherwise". This indicated connections emerging similar to workplace relationships.

The strength of the team-based activity in developing new capabilities within students was highlighted across all teacher feedback. Teachers indicated that they saw first-hand how students often struggled in group-based learning scenarios, but ultimately resolved issues and thereupon developed new social and leadership skills.

Giving students the opportunity to self-select an area to develop team projects was seen as a positive, beneficial experience. It was, however, problematic for a small group of respondents who recounted instances of teams swapping members due to interests in projects changing through early stages, and this causing disruption. Such occurrences can be a risk of team-based learning, though it could be argued that such situations represent key opportunities for adaptive and advanced social skill development.

Connected Learning

The two key authentic 'learning events' in the program – the 'Innovation Expo' and the 'QUT Shark Tank' – proved the most memorable and defining aspects for participants, as demonstrated on journey maps drawn by both students and teachers. All maps were constructed with these elements at the forefront, highlighting their significance and key developmental role in the program. The significance of these events and their learning impact was reiterated across all group reflections upon completion of the program.

Staff identified that the reconceptualised tone and scale of the Expo made for exciting learning that placed reasonable pressure on students to perform. It was noted that prior to the Expo, groups were at various stages of prototype development, but on the eve of the event, most students put in additional effort in order for their projects to be feedback-ready. Teachers expressed some apprehension around students' preparedness, but on the day most had advanced their work and represented themselves professionally. It was noted that the Expo, in exposing student teams to other team projects – some of which were of a very high calibre – also pushed them to work more creatively and constructively throughout the remaining sections of the program.

The 'QUT Shark Tank' event was also highly regarded as a 'milestone' moment. Of greatest perceived impact, by both students and teachers, was that the students' projects were seen as viable beyond the school context and not simply a 'school project'. The authentic feedback from the expert panel was valued, encouraging the students to continue to develop their projects as tangible social businesses. It was observed that this represented a pivotal point wherein the experts were developing further ties with the students and potentially embedding future career pathways.

CONNECTEDNESS CAPABILITIES

All stakeholder groups provided evidence that the experience had been beneficial in growing skills and capabilities. For students, this was a result of being the central participant in the extended connected learning community of the SEP (Figure 12.1), while for the teachers, this occurred through the integration and interaction with learning community members during the design and delivery of the SEP.

Student Connectedness Capabilities

Feedback data indicated that student connectedness capabilities were not developed from participation in one specific activity, but from a culmination of the learning experiences provided by the new, complex learning ecosystem. Over the course of the program, students sought to build their own connected identities by actively developing and publicly presenting a professional self, which required skill building in self-expression and communication. Most significantly, through their interest-driven activities and research, supported by informal mentorship, students acknowledged that they built increased empathy for stakeholders. As one student described, "this program taught us to think about other people and consider their perspectives".

Further, both staff and students identified that through the development of the project, students did not just learn about issues, but became agents for social change. When students presented their projects to the public and peers in different contexts they were not simply summarising an issue, but championing a cause and advocating change. This is consistent with literature on 'connected civics' learning (Cohen and Kahne, 2012; Ito et al., 2015). Teachers acknowledged this aspect of the course was highly satisfying, with one describing that the program had "tapped into a sense of social justice and even service". It was noted that many students learn about and discuss social, cultural and environmental issues through social media, but never become connected or affiliated with a cause beyond this. One teacher observed that the program had challenged them by asking "but what are you going to do about it?" and provoked further connection to a community with which they may have already had an affinity and empathy.

The growth in communication skills necessary to present this connected identity was mentioned by both teachers and students. Students were offered multiple contexts in which to learn the art of professional, persuasive public speaking. Their skills were sharpened principally through reflection on audience feedback, and through the act of repeating and actively refining arguments. Teachers and students both indicated that students had learnt how to more appropriately present a thoughtful argument and engage an audience. Business mentors in particular, were identified by students as providing key 'turning points' in their communication skill development, emphasising that innovators have to present themselves 'front and centre' at the same time as their projects in order to 'sell' their idea. One student appropriately para-phrased the mentor's expression, "ideas are cheap but it's your team and how you sell your team that will make you stand out".

Students came to understand the value of feedback, realising that it was not a criticism of them, but an essential stage in honing strong ideas and projects. As such, students became more relaxed when receiving feedback, and demonstrated a clear understanding of the feedback loop in the design/ innovation process. This increased receptiveness to feedback was highlighted by one student who explained that the most enjoyable aspect of the program was "making our idea and then seeing what people thought".

The program offered students various opportunities to collaborate and grow their connections. When reflecting on growth of their connectedness capabilities within the program, students described areas such as "building skills in leadership", being more mindful "to consider lots of viewpoints" and developing an ability to critique an idea constructively, without being con-cerned about causing offence. Furthermore, they noted development of skills in teamwork and perseverance, including how to manage opposing viewpoints. Student journey maps explicitly emphasised an experience of the project as a unified group of individuals. It was noted by teachers that in final presentations, students operated as united and cohesive teams, demonstrating a level of increased professionalism.

Finally, at the conclusion of the program, students displayed a desire to continue strengthening and maintaining their connections outside of the SEP environment. This was summarised by one student who suggested that "if we do want to pursue this, we now have lots of people to talk to". Importantly, students saw potential in continuing connections and believed that they possessed the ability do this independently.

Teacher Connectedness Capabilities

Teachers also identified personal benefits gained through the application of the Connectedness Learning Approach. Whilst the collaboration's enabling strategies ensured there were mutual benefits for all stakeholders to encourage buy-in, the extent to which teachers felt they had developed their own twenty-first century skillsets was notable. Integral to this was the consideration of teachers as part of the extended learning ecosystem, and not simply as school contributors and facilitators. As such, teachers benefited from the informal learning opportunities provided, including ongoing support, knowledge transfer, and mentoring.

Throughout this collaboration it was evident that teachers were able to build their own connected identities, both with the QUT educators, as well as with their student cohort, through their engagement in the co-curricular activities. Significantly, it was those 'first steps' including building the Innovation Hub and Design Thinking PD, which led to teachers feeling that their contribution was meaningful. Teacher feedback indicated that these initiatives were critical in demonstrating that QUT was invested in working with the school to foster a culture of long-term pedagogical exchange. Survey feedback received prior to the start of SEP, indicated the significant relationship building and skills development that had occurred through the initial establishment process. Teachers noted that through their experiential involvement in the Design Thinking PD, they developed confidence to begin teaching students through a new pedagogical framework.

In engaging and leading students through the experimental program, teachers demonstrated a level of calculated risk-taking that all stakeholders expected of the students. Teachers indicated an enjoyment of the entire process – collaborating and learning with external experts and facilitating the course itself – and felt their skills and knowledge base had increased in diverse ways. All expressed increased confidence in supporting transdisciplinary knowledge creation across the program. No collected data indicated that teachers felt 'out of their depth' or unprepared to provide input and support classes throughout the program. With teachers assuming the disposition of a student learner in their absorption of content and mutual co-creation of cultural products (McWilliam and Haukka, 2008) (thereby also building empathy for others), a significant finding of the research is that much of the learning and capacity-building experienced by students, was also experienced by teachers.

CONCLUSIONS

It is apparent that Connectedness Learning provides considerable potential benefit in preparing adaptive students equipped for the demands of the twenty-first century workforce. This SEP project incorporated a complex application of many core elements of the Connectedness Learning Approach, and consequently, was a testing ground for its viability and potential for success. Furthermore, this project also developed new approaches for its practical application, showcasing pathways for other educational partnerships. In understanding the study's potential contribution in inspiring others to apply aspects of the Connectedness Learning Approach to reconceptualise their learning programs and foster new types of collaborations, this chapter concludes with a series of observations and suggestions for educators.

Certainly, a key determinant of project success was the commitment of all involved to explore new types of learning and partnership synergies. For the project team, this was exemplified in the adoption of a design mindset (Wright and Wrigley, 2017), or at least an endeavour to exercise experimental, collaborative, human-centred and metacognitive design mindshifts (Goldman et al., 2012). A commitment to assuming this mindset, led the team to take calculated speculative risks and 'prototype' ideas, with the expectation of refinement along the way. This mindset was mirrored throughout the learning community, creating a culture ripe for educational innovation. The fact this project was able to develop and attract the support of so many diverse participants is testament to a common vision for creating responsive learning models for our changing world.

The team also found advantage in consolidating a relationship prior to formal program collaboration. The Connectedness Learning Approach outlines a series of key enabling strategies that foster connectedness which were employed across the SEP project, with the establishment of such specific elements like an MOU recognising the formation of a dedicated learning community, and PD workshops based around new pedagogies. All of these served to not only empower and educate partners, but to build the relationships that were essential in forming a foundation for the extensive program to be undertaken.

With regards to building the connected learning community and developing the curriculum, the Stakeholder Map and Student Journey Map presented in this chapter serve as useful reference points for educators during conceptualisation and ideation. True to a design-led approach, such tools allow simplified visual representation of ideas to support effective collaboration and communication.

It is important to note that the co-curricular nature of this project allowed significant scope to experiment with the application of many of the defining pedagogies of connectedness learning, demonstrating their compatibility. Thus, connectedness learning is not necessarily about choosing one or a few approaches but integrating as many aspects into learning experiences as is meaningful. Furthermore, it is important educators consider what aspects of the Connectedness Learning Approach are likely to be most beneficial for each context. As an example, this project aimed to explore the use of digital technologies for connectedness, however outcomes illustrated how intrinsic face-to-face experiences were for meaningful learning to occur.

Approaching education design through the lens of connectedness learning can directly benefit all involved in the partnership, fostering a culture of enriching networked and interdependent educational practice (Fullan, 2015). The project described in this chapter represents just one way that cross-institutional and cross-sectoral collaboration can occur. Other ways might include embedding high school teachers into universities, and bringing secondary and tertiary students together to work on informal enterprise projects. Once the institutional barriers are broken down, there are many dynamic and exciting ways that connectedness learning can occur.

REFERENCES

Aydın, U., Tunç-Pekkan, Z., Taylan, R. D., Birgili, B. and Özcan, M. (2018). Impacts of a university–school partnership on middle school students' fractional knowledge: A quasiexperimental study. *The Journal of Educational Research*, *111*(2), 151–162.

Birdthistle, N., Hynes, B. and Fleming, P. (2007). Enterprise education programmes in secondary schools in Ireland: A multi-stakeholder perspective. *Education+Training*, *49*(4), 265–276.

Brady, L. (2002). School university partnerships: What do the schools want? *Australian Journal of Teacher Education*, *27*(1), 1–9.

Cohen, C. and Kahne, J. (2012). *Participatory Politics: New Media and Youth Political Action*. Oakland, CA: YPP Research Network, Mills College School of Education.

Commission of the European Communities. (2003). Green Paper: Entrepreneurship in Europe. Retrieved 6 June 2017 from http://ec.europa.eu/invest-in-research/pdf/download_en/entrepreneurship_europe.pdf.

Constas, M. A. (1992). Qualitative analysis as a public event: The documentation of category development procedures. *American Educational Research Journal*, *29*(2), 253–266.

Day, C. (1998). Re-thinking school–university partnerships: A Swedish case study. *Teaching and Teacher Education*, *14*(8), 807–819.

Dyson, L. L. (1999). Developing a university-school district partnership: Researcher-district administrator collaboration for a special education initiative. *Canadian Journal of Education/Revue canadienne de l'éducation*, *24*(4), 411–425.

Edwards, A., Gilroy, P. and Hartley, D. (2005). *Rethinking Teacher Education: Collaborative Responses to Uncertainty*. London: Routledge Falmer.

Edwards, G., Tsui, A. B. M. and Stimpson, P. G. (2009). Contexts for learning in school–university partnership. In A. B. M. Tsui, G. Edwards, F. Lopez-Real, T. Kwan, D. Law, P. Stimpson, R. Tang and A. Wong (eds), *Learning in School–University Partnership: Sociocultural Perspectives* (pp. 3–24). New York, NY: Routledge.

Fullan, M. (2015). Leadership from the middle. *Education Canada*, *55*(4), 22–26.

Gallaway, L., Andersson, M., Brown, W. and Whittam, G. (2005). *The Impact of Entrepreneurship Education in Higher Education*. Edinburgh: Heriot-Watt University.

Goldman, S., Carroll, M. P., Kabayadondo, Z., Cavagnaro, L. B., Royalty, A. W., Roth, B. ... Kim, J. (2012). Assessing d.learning: Capturing the journey of becoming a design thinker. In H. Plattner, C. Meinel and L. Leifer (eds), *Design Thinking Research: Measuring Performance in Context* (pp. 13–33). Berlin, Heidelberg: Springer Berlin Heidelberg.

Goodlad, J. I. (1993). School–university partnerships and partner schools. *Educational Policy*, *7*(1), 24–39.

Hung, D., Lim, K. Y. and Jamaludin, A. (2014). An epistemic shift: A literacy of adaptivity as critical for twenty-first century learning. In D. Hung, K. Y. Lim and S. S. Lee (eds), *Adaptivity as a Transformative Disposition: For Learning in the 21st Century* (pp. 3–14). Singapore: Springer.

Hung, D., Lim, K. Y. and Lee, S. S. (2014). *Adaptivity as a Transformative Disposition: For Learning in the 21st Century*. Singapore: Springer.

Ito, M., Soep, E., Kligler-Vilenchik, N., Shresthova, S., Gamber-Thompson, L. and Zimmerman, A. (2015). Learning connected civics: Narratives, practices, infrastructures. *Curriculum Inquiry*, *45*(1), 10–29.

Kumpulainen, K. (2014). Pedagogies of connected learning: Adapting education into the twenty-first century. In D. Hung, K. Y. Lim and S. S. Lee (eds), *Adaptivity as a Transformative Disposition: For Learning in the 21st Century* (pp. 31–41). Singapore: Springer.

Kyndt, E., Gijbels, D., Grosemans, I. and Donche, V. (2016). Teachers' everyday professional development: Mapping informal learning activities, antecedents, and learning outcomes. *Review of Educational Research*, *86*(4), 1111–1150.

Lee, S. S., Hung, D., Lim, K. Y. and Shaari, I. (2014). Learning adaptivity across contexts. In D. Hung, K. Y. Lim and S. S. Lee (eds), *Adaptivity as a Transformative Disposition: For Learning in the 21st Century* (pp. 43–60). Singapore: Springer.

Martínez, M. A., Sauleda, N. and van Veen, D. (2000). Participation in the discourse of a community as the nucleus of learning. *Teacher Development*, *4*(2), 257–269.

McWilliam, E. and Haukka, S. (2008). Educating the creative workforce: New directions for twenty-first century schooling. *British Educational Research Journal*, *34*(5), 651–666.

Mullen, C. (2009). *The Handbook of Leadership and Professional Learning Communities*. New York, NY: Palgrave Macmillan.

Nielsen, S. L. and Stovang, P. (2015). DesUni: University entrepreneurship education through design thinking. *Education+Training*, *57*(8/9), 977–991.

Parker, A. and Zenkov, K. (2017). Preface. In D. Yendol-Hoppey, D. Shanley, D. C. Delane and D. T. Hoppey (eds), *Working Together: Enhancing Urban Educator Quality Through Partnerships* (pp. ix–xiv). Charlotte, NC: Information Age Publishing.

Partnership for 21st Century Learning. (2015). P21 framework definitions. Retrieved 2 May 2017 from http://www.p21.org/storage/documents/docs/ P21_Framework_Definitions_New_Logo_2015.pdf.

Queensland Government. (2018). Gen[in]. Retrieved 12 January 2018, from https://www.studyqueensland.qld.gov.au/genin.

Rayner, G. and Corkill, P. (2015). Building greater capacity in science education: A partnership between a secondary science school and a research-intensive university. In B. Cozza and P. Blessinger (eds), *University Partnerships for Community and School System Development (Innovations in Higher Education Teaching and Learning, Volume 5)* (pp. 99–117). Bingley, UK: Emerald Group Publishing.

Sexton, D. L. and Kasarda, J. D. (1992). *The State of the Art of Entrepreneurship*. Boston, MA: P.W. Kent Publishing Co.

Shewmaker, J. W. and Lee, S. K. (2015). Distributed leadership in a university–school collaborative partnership to build the STEM pipeline for girls. In B. Cozza and P. Blessinger (eds), *University Partnerships for Community and School System Development (Innovations in Higher Education Teaching and Learning, Volume 5)* (pp. 195–209). Bingley, UK: Emerald Group Publishing.

Snow-Gerono, J. L. (2005). Professional development in a culture of inquiry: PDS teachers identify the benefits of professional learning communities. *Teaching and Teacher Education*, *21*(3), 241–256.

Stevens, D. D. (1999). The ideal, real and surreal in school–university partnerships: Reflections of a boundary spanner. *Teaching and Teacher Education, 15*(3), 287–299.

Sutherland, L. M., Scanlon, L. A. and Sperring, A. (2005). New directions in preparing professionals: Examining issues in engaging students in communities of practice through a school–university partnership. *Teaching and Teacher Education, 21*(1), 79–92.

Trilling, B. and Fadel, C. (2012). *21st Century Skills: Learning for Life in Our Times*. New York, NY: John Wiley and Sons.

Uleanya, C. and Gamede, B. T. (2017). The role of entrepreneurship education in secondary schools at further education and training phase. *Academy of Entrepreneurship Journal, 23*(2), 1–12.

Val, E., Gonzalez, I., Iriarte, I., Beitia, A., Lasa, G. and Elkoro, M. (2017). A design thinking approach to introduce entrepreneurship education in European school curricula. *The Design Journal, 20*(S1), S754–S766.

Voogt, J., Erstad, O., Dede, C. and Mishra, P. (2013). Challenges to learning and schooling in the digital networked world of the 21st century. *Journal of Computer Assisted Learning, 29*(5), 403–413.

Wasburn-Moses, L. and Noltemeyer, A. (2018). Effectiveness of campus mentors, an alternative school–university partnership. *Preventing School Failure: Alternative Education for Children and Youth, 62*(3), 190–197.

Weaver, R. Y. (1999). Society, educational systems and entrepreneurship. *Industry and Higher Education, 13*(6), 376–381.

Wesley, T. (2015). Changing demographics: Using university–school partnerships to support the instruction of culturally and linguistically diverse student populations. In B. Cozza and P. Blessinger (eds), *University Partnerships for Community and School System Development (Innovations in Higher Education Teaching and Learning, Volume 5)* (pp. 179–194). Bingley, UK: Emerald Group Publishing.

World Economic Forum. (2015). New vision for education: Unlocking the potential of technology. Retrieved 2 May 2017 from http://www3.weforum.org/docs/WEFUSA_NewVisionforEducation_Report2015.pdf.

Wright, N. and Davis, R. M. (2014). Educating the creative citizen: Design education programs in the knowledge economy. *Techne Series: Research in Sloyd Education and Craft Science A, 21*(2), 42–61.

Wright, N. and Wrigley, C. (2017). Broadening design-led education horizons: Conceptual insights and future research directions. *International Journal of Technology and Design Education, 27*(4), 1–23.

13. Integrating connectedness learning into institutional program review processes in an Australian regional university

Sara Hammer, Peter Ayriss, Marita Basson, Beata Batorowicz, Jo Devine, Melissa Forbes, Alexander Kist, Tessa McCredie, Amanda McCubbin and Bill Wade

INTRODUCTION

University stakeholders including students, employers and government, continue to demand accountability from universities related to graduate employability and employment outcomes. This is particularly the case for regional universities that are in areas where unemployment rates are typically higher than in metropolitan centres. Currently, in Australia, employment outcomes for graduates are worsening (Australian Government Department of Education and Training, 2018), which is creating greater pressure on universities to better prepare their graduates for the world of work, and the world at large.

In this chapter, we evaluate a pilot of an institutional curriculum review and enhancement process at a regional Australian university. We applied two enabling strategies from the Connectedness Learning Approach (Chapter 1 in this volume), *fostering intra-university connectedness* and *reducing institutional barriers to connectedness*, to the mapping and development of connectedness learning pedagogies within existing institutional review and design processes for Creative Arts and Engineering programs. These two areas of study offer particular interest since they sit at opposite ends of the employment outcomes scale: Australian Engineering graduates demonstrate some of the highest levels of employment four months after graduation, while in comparison, Creative Arts graduates are among the lowest (Australian Government Department of Education and Training, 2018). Our aim was to develop a collaborative, multi-disciplinary approach to the review and design of program curricula using connectedness learning as a focus for program enhancement. If adopted more widely, this would enable our institution to integrate, strategically, the review and assurance of connectedness learning outcomes and capabilities for our graduates as part of regular accreditation and re-accreditation review cycles.

BACKGROUND

The University of Southern Queensland (USQ) is a post-1970s, regional university with a large non-traditional student population. The majority of students are mature-aged, studying part-time and online, with a significant number coming from low socio-economic backgrounds, and/or being the first in their family to attend higher education. Many students come to USQ in order to improve their professional standing or life prospects, and for this reason, the employability and employment capabilities of graduates is of particular importance to the University.

With the aim of integrating Connectedness Pedagogies into institutional program review and enhancement processes in the Creative Arts and Engineering programs at USQ, a project team was established which comprised: the project lead; three learning and teaching team members from a centralised program support unit; a Careers and Employability Director; two learning and teaching coordinators and one discipline coordinator from Engineering; and, two discipline coordinators from Creative Arts. At the time the project commenced, the Creative Arts program was preparing for institutional re-accreditation and the Engineering program was working towards attaining professional re-accreditation.

In both programs, connectedness pedagogies were used as a review lens to identify existing good practice and address curriculum gaps. This would enable programs to provide greater connectedness with industry partners, enhance graduate employability through fostering students' professional networks, and develop students' professional identities. Each discipline faced a different set of challenges. For Creative Arts students, the difficulty lay in navigating the complex, disjointed career pathways which are common to this discipline, whereby even high-profile career pathways can still result in unstable employment. For USQ students, this is often further exacerbated by the professional isolation and lack of career opportunities arising from the University's regional context. Growing students' connectedness capabilities and forging links with industry partners were seen as potential avenues through which students could overcome the geographical and disciplinary barriers which hamper their potential employability.

For the Engineering program, a prior professional accreditation review had resulted in Engineers Australia making specific recommendations that the program provide greater opportunities for industry engagement. The industry engagement focus used by the Engineering program encapsulated aspects of the Connectedness Learning Approach, which itself illustrated how authentic learning experiences and greater industry engagement could help students to enhance their career capabilities, once these were embedded within the program in response to the Engineers Australia recommendations.

LITERATURE REVIEW

The desired graduate outcomes to be developed and assured in our case study were students' *connectedness capabilities* (Chapter 1 in this volume). We locate the Connectedness Learning Approach within employability, which according to Fugate, Kinicki and Ashforth (2004, p. 18) is a broad psycho-social construct representing the "synergistic collection of individual characteristics that is energized and directed by an individual's career identity". Employability is influenced by the affordances associated with social and human capital. For example, career identities, provide a mental frame of reference that enables individuals to shape and regulate their behaviour in line with their 'desired self', including the implications of particular activities for that self. Additionally, individual activities take place against a backdrop of social networks, which are a key indicator of 'social capital' and the ability for individuals to access information, and career opportunities (Fugate, Kinicki and Ashforth, 2004).

There is some evidence to show that 'developmental networks', or networks of experienced professional peers that provide support to an early career individual, can have a positive impact on career identity and employment (for example Hoye, Hooft and Lievens, 2009). Engagement with developmental networks shifts individual activity away from atomistic, self-referential processes, and can provide an effective means of support for achieving job outcomes in which individuals seek weak, yet high status ties within their network (Hoye, Hooft and Lievens, 2009). The Connectedness Learning Approach (Chapter 1 in this volume) identifies the affordances that digital networks offer in enabling individuals to connect with an exponentially greater number of people: creating and maintaining those weaker, high status ties that provide greater access to new information and resources, and can serve as a vehicle for promoting one's career identity.

Using the university curriculum to foster students' employability skills requires a concomitant focus on program quality and the assurance of university graduate outcomes, such as graduate attributes, professional standards or employability (Barrow et al., 2010; Bath et al. 2004; Farquharson, 2013;

Oliver, 2013). The assurance of learning outcomes associated with particular programs of study is a requirement for self-accrediting universities, both within Australia and internationally (European Association for Quality Assurance in Higher Education, 2015). Australian higher education standards (Australian Government Department of Education and Training, 2015) require that universities identify, assess and externally benchmark student achievement of expected learning outcomes. For a program to deliver on desired outcomes, the curriculum, or elements thereof, must be fit-for-purpose, including that individual courses align with designer intentions. One of the technical methods that universities use for assuring program quality is curriculum mapping.

A practice originating in American secondary schools (Plaza et al., 2007), curriculum mapping can be defined as:

- a consideration of the relationship between intended program outcomes;
- assessments that evidence the desired learning; and,
- the learning and teaching strategies at both the course and program level required to support it.

In higher education, curriculum mapping is most commonly found in accounts or studies that focus on the development of university graduate attributes. A notable example was reported by Oliver et al. (2007) who outlined a systematic, five-phase, mapping support model. This was situated within a comprehensive program review process and aimed to provide an authentic learning experience for students, based around the progressive development of graduate attributes. Existing programs of study were mapped to assess alignment with the University's graduate attributes, including external accreditation competencies where applicable. Revisions were made to address gaps identified in students' graduate attribute development, and ensure a sufficient spread of assessment types and experiences that would become increasingly sophisticated as the degree progressed (Oliver et al., 2007).

In Australia and internationally, curriculum mapping occurs as part of a collaborative curriculum review and design approach. In the US, Truesdale, Thomson and Lucas (2004) emphasise the role of curriculum mapping in facilitating a cohesive educational community. Canadian authors Jacobsen et al. (2018) found that a key outcome of their curriculum mapping exercise was the development of a disciplinary 'community of practice'. Indeed, Hubball and Burt (2004) argue that enhancing university curricula requires, amongst other things, an inclusive approach to program design. This call is echoed in the Australian context (Lawson et al., 2011) although to date there are relatively few examples (Hammer, McDonald and Forbes, 2014; Oliver et al., 2007).

Curriculum mapping activities themselves often require different, more collaborative ways of working within universities and must contend with established disciplinary and organisational norms. This is also true of changes made to the curriculum itself. In the case of the Connectedness Learning Approach, facilitating the development of students' network-related capabilities as part of their university study may have wider cultural and organisational implications for educational providers. One example is the requirement to move from a traditional focus on students' cognitive development towards the integration of student identity development work throughout a student's program of study (Daniels and Brooker, 2014). In another example, Langrish et al. (2010) found that moving beyond the usual approach of adding occasional industry lectures towards a more sustained, structured approach enabled a greater focus on genuine industry engagement and student-industry networking. Their work also considered how industry engagement can be addressed as part of 'business as usual processes' such as the review and development of program curricula, including the design of assessments and learning and teaching activities.

PROJECT DESCRIPTION

The aim of our project was to enhance opportunities for students to connect with industry partners and promote their career identity through integrating connectedness learning pedagogies into two phases of existing program quality, review and enhancement processes. The two programs used in this project were selected because they were due to begin a detailed institutional, quality review and enhancement process in 2017 and represented two contrasting accreditation scenarios for universities. The Bachelor of Creative Arts had no professional accreditation standards, while the Bachelor of Engineering (Hons) required professional re-accreditation with Engineers Australia (EA). This industry body had recently provided feedback to the Engineering disciplines recommending that greater exposure to industry was required for the program to receive EA re-accreditation. This presented the team with an opportunity to apply elements of the Connectedness Learning Approach as a lens through which to conduct quality review and enhancement processes across two different disciplinary contexts. Furthermore, the Approach had the potential to be used as a lever for breaking down institutional silos, facilitating a multi-disciplinary approach to program review and enhancement.

One facet of incorporating a connectedness learning viewpoint into existing program quality and enhancement activities at our institution was to facilitate greater inclusion of Careers and Employability staff, enabling career development activities to be more deeply embedded into program design and design processes. This was achieved by incorporating Careers and Employability staff into research team activities, including through mapping current generic career development activity use within programs, and through viewing curriculum map findings to indicate where they could be able to support faculty colleagues in addressing current gaps. Program developers were also able to promote careers and employability in Engineering workshops; however, this was not possible for Creative Arts.

As this project involved integration within *existing* business-as-usual activities, our process would necessarily involve differences and unplanned variation, both in terms of which connectedness pedagogies were represented and applied, and in terms of how curriculum review and development activities were implemented according to the preferences of each school.

Of the four program review and development phases, only Phase 1 *Awareness raising*, and Phase 2 *Curriculum mapping and design* were employed as part of this project. Phases 3 (implementation) and 4 (evaluation) were not included within the scope of this process. Activities which relate to each of these phases are described below:

Phase 1: Awareness Raising

The awareness raising phase included consultation with Heads of School, the formation of teams for each program, and an initial team briefing session. The project lead was also invited to address a Creative Arts forum about the Connectedness Learning Project, however, no similar event took place within Engineering.

Phase 2: Curriculum Mapping and Design

Following the awareness-raising phase, we collected unit curriculum data from academics in each program using different collection instruments and processes.

Creative Arts: For Creative Arts we were able to develop a project-based, purpose-built online survey instrument, which we sent to individual members within each discipline within the Program; the instrument referenced the full range of Connectedness Pedagogies (see Chapter 6 in this volume). Responses and curriculum mapping were analysed over a period of a few weeks and discipline leaders received a report before the initial curriculum workshop. The survey, developed using Google Docs, aimed to collect data from Creative Arts academics about their existing use of all Connectedness Pedagogies, which included activities grouped under the following categories:

*   Industry teaching;
*   Student partnerships;
*   Connected learning;
*   Work Integrated Learning (WIL);
*   Co-curricular activities;
*   Alumni engagement;
*   Social media and ePortfolios.

Engineering and Surveying: Schools generated a paper-based questionnaire, which they sent to every academic, including lecturers in the Program under study. A narrower range of connectedness pedagogies, referred to as *industry exposure activities*, were mapped and analysed over a period of two months. Review and reporting activities took place concurrently with repeat workshop activities, which occurred over a number of months. Industry exposure activities and their alignment with aspects of the Connectedness Learning Approach are shown in Table 13.1.

Table 13.1   Industry exposure alignment with connectedness pedagogies

Connectedness Learning Approach: Connectedness Pedagogies	Industry Exposure Activities
Industry teaching	Invited guests (f2f and online)
	Interviewing of practicing professionals
	Dialogue (f2f and online) with hardware and software suppliers, or their representatives
Student partnerships	Use of mature-aged students' knowledge (f2f and online)
	Mini-case studies, Comprehensive case studies
	Use of standards
Connected learning	Use of industry-relevant hardware and software
	Open access, online material from reputable sources
	Real-time capture of projects
	Site visits including virtual site visits
Work Integrated Learning	Community projects

The data collected using each method was used to generate a curriculum map for each program. The structure of each map included a list of units in order of recommended student enrolment patterns along the vertical axis, with connectedness pedagogies/industry exposure learning and teaching activities along the horizontal axis. Engineering and Surveying academics were asked whether industry exposure activities were captured in unit learning outcomes, topics or assessments.

EVALUATION METHOD

We applied a qualitative, social constructionist (Mallon, 2013), multi-methods approach to determine whether the integration of connectedness learning approaches with our program quality enhancement processes was effective, based on the following research questions:

1. How did the connectedness learning/industry exposure integration within program review and development process work for each discipline? How effective was it?
2. What were participants' experience of applying the connectedness learning/industry exposure lens to their program review process?

RESEARCH PARADIGM

We have located our study within the social constructionist research paradigm. Social constructionism is applicable to our case because of the potential impact of disciplinary and even sub-disciplinary practices and shared beliefs on the program quality and enhancement process. Social constructionists argue that knowledge and therefore practices are socially situated and co-created based on the shared understandings of particular groups (Andrews, 2012). There are obvious cultural and pedagogical differences between Creative Arts and Engineering disciplines. Coupled with the different conceptions and approaches evident in each of the curriculum quality and enhancement processes under study, applying a social constructivist viewpoint enables us to foreground disciplinary differences and similarities and their possible influence on the direction and effectiveness of each case.

METHOD

The multi-methods approach we used to determine the effectiveness of our process included the following stages:

1. Document analysis.
2. Curriculum map analysis.
3. Participant interviews.

Stage 1: Document Analysis

We applied a multi-methods approach to determine the effectiveness of our process in each instance. Document analysis was applied to the documentary artefacts involved in the program review and enhancement process in each case. Documentary analysis can be defined as "a systematic procedure for reviewing and evaluating documents – both printed and electronic ... material" (Bowen, 2009, p. 27). As with any text, documentary data can be analysed to explore concepts, issues or dimensions related to a particular phenomenon under study. It is generally used alongside other qualitative or quantitative methods, as a means of corroborating and enriching findings about a particular event. Documents analysed for this study included the following written arte-facts of the program review process:

• Workshop action lists or implementation plans;
• Curriculum maps and data collection forms;
• Curriculum reports.

These documents provided us with program review findings and recom-mendations, as well as intended actions arising from review processes. They enabled us to determine, first, the quality enhancement value and effectiveness of applying connectedness learning as a review lens; and, second, any doc-umented evidence of planned change to program curricula arising from its application. Documents were analysed using multiple iterations of deductive and inductive, thematic analysis (Braun and Clarke, 2006) applying mapping categories and report headings in combination with emergent themes.

Stage 2: Curriculum Map Analysis

Activities referred to by lecturers and captured in curriculum maps were verified by randomly selecting and reviewing curriculum documentation and Learning Management System (LMS) for a sample of units for each discipline major within the program. Our verification process focused on the following questions:

1. Is there evidence of the declared connectedness learning/industry exposure activity in the course documentation, or on the unit LMS? In particular, are there any documents such as unit specifications that represent a de facto contract between an institution and its students?
2. Does the declared activity align with the definition of a particular connect-edness learning pedagogy or industry exposure activity?
3. How transparent is the activity, and the purpose of the activity for students?
4. What is the currency and production quality of learning resources related to connectedness learning/industry exposure activities?

We triangulated these mapping results by incorporating a connectedness/ employability lens into our initial round of face-to-face, group program review activities, which were designed to shift participant conceptions from the indi-vidual unit-level to program level, and involved a program-wide 'Strengths, Connections, Interesting and Possibilities' (SCIP) analysis method. For Creative Arts this analysis took place in one combined session, with discipline teams presenting elements of their existing curriculum to their colleagues. For the Engineering program, this took place using multiple sessions for each discipline team: sessions were sometimes held more than once to capture missing participants or focus on year groupings. Any new data provided in workshops was incorporated into curriculum maps, which would be used to inform curriculum development processes for both programs.

Stage 3: Interviews

The perceived effectiveness of the program quality enhancement process was also assessed using qualitative, semi-structured interviews with volunteers who were research team members and at least one program team member who was not a member of the research team. Questions focused on participant roles, their perception of how the process worked for their program; the usefulness of the connectedness learning/industry exposure lens; the effectiveness of the process; what they believe it achieved; possible changes; and any future plans to access Careers and Employability support.

Participants were recruited via email, and interviews were carried out face-to-face by program development consultants, research team members who did not normally work with that discipline as part of their regular role: this measure was intended to provide participants with a greater level of distance from their interviewer and reduce the likelihood of undue influence on given responses. Interviews were recorded, transcribed and returned to participants for validation and further comment. Validated transcripts were inductively, thematically analysed by the principal researcher using multiple iterations of theme identification, re-analysis, and refinement (Braun and Clarke, 2006). Documents (including curriculum maps) and interview data were analysed separately, then together, to identify common themes. We also identified themes that were particular to each of the programs, and for careers and employability.

FINDINGS

For the curriculum mapping survey in Creative Arts we received responses for 50 per cent of the units within each major: overlap between the majors resulted in a total coverage of around 60 per cent within the Creative Arts program. A similar result was achieved in Engineering, with around 70 per cent of all units covered. As the lens and data collection process for each program was slightly different, this resulted in different appearing curriculum maps.

Once activities that fell within the scope of the project were complete, we recruited volunteers from the research team, and from among discipline coordinators in both programs. Seven participants volunteered to be interviewed, including five members of the research team, and one academic from each program team who was not a member of the research team. Written feedback was collected from the two program development consultants, who themselves conducted the interviews, using the same interview questions.

We identified three meaningful overarching themes from our analysis of the documentary and interview data, which we labelled: *'process strengths'*, *'externalities'*, and *'future fixes'*. Sub-themes sitting within each of these were divided again on the basis of whether they were:

- Common sub-themes – those that were common to at least the two program contexts and could be discerned across both data sources.
- Particular sub-themes – those specific to a single disciplinary context, including that of careers and employability.

Process Strengths

Common to both programs

One strength of the program review process, including the integration of Connectedness Pedagogies and the application of Connectedness Enabling Strategies, was that evidence collected enabled participants to identify strengths, gaps and opportunities for enhancing Connectedness Pedagogies; and the transformative potential of Connectedness Pedagogies as a curriculum lens. In the Creative Arts, participants reflected on the potential of the process for identifying existing strengths:

> Well I think it worked well because most did answer [the survey] ... people when they see these things are [saying to themselves]: "we do that already", which is nice because it helps identify that [existing good practice] ... (PGCA)

Analysis of curriculum mapping documents and participant interviews identified common gaps that required addressing, such as transparency and visibility of practices:

> I think that we all need to get better at being much more explicit about the ways in which we think we're doing this: as in, explicit when we're talking to students about it so it ... so kind of ... having a much stronger kind of metanarrative when we're teaching to say "well you know so and so is going to be working with you on this – what do you think you're going to get out of it?" (DCCA1)

Another gap the process identified was the lack of a previous systematic, whole-of-program approach to connecting students with industry:

> ... so we tend to think in terms of [units] and in terms of any visioning activities it certainly brought up the focus and made us think about: "well, is it up-to-date,

something's got to be useful for the students; is there another way we can leverage industries?". (DCENG1)

Curriculum review and practice mapping workshop action lists showed a greater focus on learning and teaching approaches than was previously the case.

Another strength common to both programs was the transformative potential of Connectedness Pedagogies as a curriculum lens, which allowed academics to look at their courses in a new light:

> My perspective is that it worked well in that it captured a lot of information and it galvanised people in terms of bringing it to front-of-mind, and everyone was looking at their courses with fresh eyes a little bit. (DCENG1)

Findings for Engineering suggest that application of the connectedness learning/industry exposure lens transformed the way some academics looked at their courses and sharpened their focus on providing industry learning opportunities for students. For others, this was expressed as a moral imperative:

> It's that thing that if you've heard it you can't unhear it and if you do ignore it, it is kind of like ... well it's almost unethical you know because you're not doing the best thing for your students. (DCCA1)

Particular to Creative Arts

Process-strength sub-themes which were particular to the Creative Arts program included: the need for an interdisciplinary approach, and the requirement to focus on regional, community connections for students. Both the workshop action list and participant responses highlighted the need for hybridity, interdisciplinarity and cross disciplinary and community collaboration:

> You've got TV and Radio, Visual Arts and you know like we could be doing documentaries ... and we've got Music – we could tap into each other a lot more successfully. (PGCA)

> I hope in the future we see a lot more interdisciplinary work with the Creative Arts where we aren't actually asking community or industry to come to us but we are actually going out, right? Um, and we're working with community groups or organisations. (DCCA1)

Creative Arts participant interviews suggested that a focus on Connectedness Pedagogies highlighted for them the need to facilitate regional, community connections for their students:

> ... and I think that's the other thing, um we really need to really consider the strength of the regional community that we have, because it's building, and it's actually built

on our students or past students. So we do have past students running artist-run spaces and collectives that our former students are now participating [in] and building on .... (PGCA)

Particular to Engineering and Surveying

For Engineering and Surveying participants, process strengths included its alignment with disciplinary, industry-oriented values, the opportunity to promote Careers and Employability services in face-to-face workshops, and the value of collaborative, disciplinary and year group sessions:

> I think overall it was quite successful ... I would say the biggest surprise for me is the, the sharing of it and just "Oh, I didn't know you're doing that in your [unit]" so it was a bit of a surprise because you're operating in silos in a technical field and so with the way they mixed examiners together you know ... it was an opportunity for us to sit down and learn from each other as well as doing the audit at the same time. (DCENG2)

Particular to Careers and Employability

For the Careers and Employability participant, process strengths included the learning opportunity presented by their involvement in the project, and the alignment of the Connectedness Learning Approach with planned future directions in providing services to academics:

> ... I think it was really useful for our team to understand the process academics go through when they're identifying their connectedness activities ... it was something we hadn't been involved in before so we got a chance to look at a program level.... (CAEM)

In addition to process strengths, our analysis of documentary and interview data also highlighted issues that came about as a result of externalities: contextual factors that were not within the control of the project team.

Externalities

Common to both disciplines

Reviewing the mapping documentation and subsequent reports, it is clear that the sheer number of connectedness learning pedagogies or industry exposure categories resulted in extremely labour intensive, detailed documentation that required a substantial amount of interpretation on the part of learning and teaching staff to distil findings for program teams. This was affirmed by written feedback from Program development consultants who described the process as "tedious but enlightening" (PDC1).

Interview data suggested that two interrelated externalities significantly influenced the perceived effectiveness of the process. First, the process as driven by the School was perceived to be indifferent to disciplinary difference, and poorly communicated. Second, as a result of staff disquiet the program accreditation process was halted, pending a solution. For one participant, the result was that connectedness learning activities were trumped by their negative perception of the program re-accreditation process:

> I think people can understand it, people have been trying to do their best to do this but the people in our School who are not Creative Arts people who have been trying to run it … have not really been aware of what they're walking into. Even though people have told them it is not one-size-fits-all. (DCCA2)

That the program re-accreditation process was placed on hold was seen as a positive by another participant, from the perspective of the connectedness learning agenda:

> We had started the process but it wasn't a feature … it didn't seem to be formally part of that conversation and that process as I understand it has been put on hold so in a way that's good because we've got an opportunity to make sure this is somehow fed into that process …. (DCCA1)

Particular to Engineering

By contrast, the first sub-theme grouped under the externalities for Engineering related to the perceived overreliance on inductive, review activities with little direction and feedback from the top. One participant reflected that:

> I think the thing that would have been really useful to people would have been to have a better understanding of what it entails before we ask then to do the audit, and say what industry engagement that they had in their courses. To get buy-in from people at an earlier stage …. (DCENG2)

Another participant flagged a concern that an analysis report generated by the Project team and submitted to the two heads of school had not yet been disseminated:

> … they've all done the audits but I don't think they've seen what's come from the audits … it's always nice to see what the result is. It might give them some impetus to act on it … things tend to sit on [heads of school] desks sometimes because they're very busy people. (DCENG3)

Another sub-theme included the challenge faced by international colleagues in helping their students make connections with industry:

> … I think a problem for a lot of them is that they are not local people. You know they come from overseas. Some of them have language barriers; some of them have cultural barriers. To them it is quite a daunting task to engage with industry, espe-

cially local industry. They tend to have more international connections than they have local connections. (DCENG3)

Particular to Careers and Employability

School ownership of the process and limited access by support staff generally extended to Careers and Employability staff, which meant they perceived their engagement to be funnelled via academic staff within the project:

> It was very much, I guess, a support role to the academics in the work they did in this project … the project leader worked very closely, I guess, with the program areas … and we were very much involved in those discussions. We were involved to the point where we understood the mapping process, why it was happening, and how academics were identifying areas they were connecting with industry. (CAEM)

Future Fixes

Common to both programs

The overarching theme of *future fixes* captured ways in which the connectedness learning integration process could be improved in future, but also ideas about possible next-steps. Sub-themes common to the two programs included, first, the need to further unpack connectedness learning/industry exposure pedagogies prior to the review process:

> I think it would be really useful to have sessions where you step people, you know, if you're applying it in a particular discipline or group of disciplines: sessions where you talk through the framework and how it can be applied and all the possibilities of it with academic staff. (DCCA1)

Second, participants perceived the need for a greater focus on quality assurance, to ascertain the quality of individual practice:

> The quality: I think … we've identified the categories but how do we identify the quality of that and strategies for engagement? So it's about evidence building, archive, and that will help with the business case in terms of the [program] re-accreditation. (PGCA)

And to assure that agreed-upon actions are implemented and actioned:

> As a starting point yes; it generates new ideas: new opportunities to move to the next step. Whether they do it or not? We need, you know, another step. You know, another audit to see: "hey what have you guys done about it". (DCENG2)

A final sub-theme highlighted the need to better integrate Careers and Employability staff into the process, as exemplified by the following comments by the Careers and Employability participant who suggested that:

> Perhaps we could have had one meeting focused on careers and employability maybe, and how we map into the map. Things like that: maybe a suggestion for the future. (CAEM)

This was echoed by the program development consultant for Engineering:

> It could be worthwhile doing industry engagement mapping as another part of the [standard program review and enhancement] process. It is an interesting and relevant lens against which [units] and programs can be examined, particularly for those courses and programs that have poor [evaluation] and [graduate outcome] data. (PDC2)

Particular to Creative Arts

A particular future fix sub-theme for Creative Arts was the need to restart the process in a way that would generate more consistent disciplinary ownership and improve formal integration of Connectedness Pedagogies. One Creative Arts participant explained that:

> You see we've done two of these [re-accreditations] before and we all worked together and it was all generated by the then Head of School...although it was always a bit stressful you know … everyone got on. You know, you do the group work …. (DCCA2)

The Creative Arts program coordinator also emphasised the need for documentation and record keeping for the purposes of accreditation, but also as a resource to generate connectedness synergies within teams and across disciplines:

> Everyone's got their own method. Now it is how do we collate this information together? How do we know? How do we systematically archive and document our projects? There is so much potential for cross-overs. I don't think we've kind of really resourced … I think we work really well individually and now: we could resource each other a lot better. (PGCA)

Particular to Engineering and Surveying

The documentary review and interview data from Engineering and Surveying participants suggested the need for greater program level leadership and design coherence, moving forward:

> So this was a great opportunity for us to have a bit of an overview of "ok, these are some of the changes [that] we made … these are some of the good changes, bad

changes or whatever let's try to" … Maybe a next step is to align the full program as a cohesive, coherent ah, group of courses rather than in isolation. (DCENG2)

Particular to Careers and Employability

For careers and employability in particular, one sub-theme identified from interview data related to a wish that the process leverage future contact with and support for academics in the project by Careers and Employability staff:

> As a nice neat wrap-up I think it would be great for the academics who were involved in the project to be able to say yep okay – I can use the Careers and Employability team for those connectedness activities. (CAED)

DISCUSSION

Due to the inherent, socio-political complexity of program review processes in universities (Hammer, McDonald and Forbes, 2014) integrating Connectedness Pedagogies into existing re-accreditation support processes worked differently for each School. The project was also impacted by externalities over which it had little or no control.

The effectiveness of connectedness learning integration in future will be dependent on balancing top-down strategic vision and leadership, with a collaborative, inclusive approach to curriculum review and enhancement (Hubball and Burt, 2004). In our case, the top-down, School-led approach in Creative Arts was perceived by at least one participant as impacting negatively on review and enhancement activities. By contrast, Engineering audit activities were seen positively as offering opportunities for shared practice within disciplines and year groupings. Indeed, participant feedback suggests that the face-to-face workshop element of the industry exposure audit worked particularly well and promoted a positive atmosphere of peer learning. They also provided the program development consultant, who facilitated the workshops and who was part of the Research team, with the space to promote careers and employability support to academics. Yet participants also indicated that they lacked overarching vision and cohesiveness. These challenges notwithstanding, review activities attracted high return rates and face-to-face sessions were well attended, facilitated forms of peer learning, achieved their purpose on paper, and created a platform to implement positive change.

Our experience also highlighted the usefulness of the connectedness learning/industry exposure pedagogies review lens in identifying strengths, gaps and opportunities for unit and program enhancement. Whilst extensive mapping and analysis was required to validate declared academic activities, the process did identify where connections with industry or related pedagogies were enacted in programs, which created a platform for sharing good practice.

It also highlighted the often ad hoc, implied nature of current practice in this area, thus paving the way for a more systematic, whole-of-discipline approach to industry connection and career development moving forward.

Significantly, for our institution, one of the key findings of this project was the lack of *visibility* of existing connectedness learning/industry exposure pedagogy in both programs. Not only was there a lack of metanarrative to help students understand the importance of opportunities to connect with industry or community, the innovative approaches used in both programs were found to be largely invisible to stakeholders.

Project findings also highlighted the transformative potential of applying connectedness learning/industry exposure as a lens for curriculum review and enhancement. Academics in both programs were able to foreground innovative learning and teaching approaches, which departs somewhat from a typical program review focus on assurance of learning: which tends to privilege alignment of curriculum elements with unit learning outcomes. Indeed, the focus on industry connection led participants to view their own curriculum with 'fresh eyes' or to recognise the ethical imperative in providing such opportunities. As such, we believe that the process influenced how some participants conceived the role of their unit curriculum and their role as teachers or as advocates for industry engagement.

Positives arising from the process for Creative Arts in particular included the opportunity to consider connections with other internal and external disciplines, as well as the importance of facilitating local, regional connections for their students. All participants agreed that future graduates will require multi-disciplinary capabilities (Bennet et al., 2014). Also, as many graduates from our institution will go on to create their own small companies or artist-led spaces, providing existing students with opportunities to connect with successful graduates in this space enables them to develop nascent professional networks and career identities

In terms of the connectedness enabling component of our process, the integration of Careers and Employability staff produced mixed results. The Careers and Employability manager perceived significant value in their participation, and there appeared to be some positive impact in terms of future careers and employability practice, along with some intention on the part of participating academics to access their support. It is perhaps worth noting that more experienced participants with established professional networks seemed less enthusiastic about the value of engaging Careers and Employability support. Responses suggest that newer academics and international staff with fewer local contacts may benefit from such support. Yet the lack of access to academics combined with a lack of formal role in the program review and enhancement process at our institution made brokering participation difficult.

Recommendations for our institution arising from this project include the following: first, to ensure that learning and teaching approaches used in programs are made explicit in unit and program documentation, including relevant university web pages; second, to include Careers and Employability staff within program review teams.

Overall, our findings suggest that a small number of significant future fixes would enhance the effectiveness of connectedness learning/industry exposure pedagogies integration. These include greater guidance for program teams and disciplines to unpack individual pedagogies and develop shared understandings. This would improve curriculum mapping accuracy and required effort, as well as enabling consistent application and increased quality of outcomes for students, which could be further enhanced by assessing the quality of learning materials and incorporating processes for closing the loop on planned curriculum enhancements.

CONCLUSION AND NEXT STEPS

Connectedness learning/industry exposure integration with existing program review and development processes worked differently for Creative Arts and Engineering. As a lens, connectedness learning/industry exposure activity categories provided participants with a language to affirm existing good practice and identify practice gaps and opportunities. Participants were also able to reframe and reconceptualise the purpose and intent of their learning and teaching activities and strategies as creating connection with industry, community and other disciplines, and their own role as one of facilitating those connections for students. For participating Careers and Employability staff, the project created a foundation for future collaboration and enabled them to better understand academic practices of program review and enhancement, and to use this experience as one lever to revise their approach for providing support for academics at our institution.

Future iterations of program review and enhancement processes will ensure that there are opportunities for participating academics to unpack connectedness learning pedagogies from the perspective of their own disciplines. Other required components will include quality assurance measures, and a clear role for Careers and Employability staff, both as part of review and enhancement activities, and as part of follow-up support for academics.

REFERENCES

Andrews, T. (2012). What is social constructionism? *Grounded Theory Review*, *11*(1), 39–46.

Australian Government Department of Education and Training. (2015). Tertiary Quality and Standards Agency Act 2011: Higher Education Standards Framework (Threshold Standards) 2015. Retrieved on 2 March 2018 from https://www.legislation.gov.au/Details/F2015L01639.

Australian Government Department of Education and Training. (2018). *2017 graduate outcomes survey: National report*. Retrieved on 2 March 2018 from https://www.qilt.edu.au/docs/default-source/gos-reports/2017/2017_gos_national_report_final_accessiblea45d8791b1e86477b58fff00006709da.pdf?sfvrsn=ceb5e33c_4.

Barrow, R., Behr, C., Deacy, S., McHardy, F. and Tempest, K. (2010). Embedding employability into a classics curriculum: The Classical Civilisation Bachelor of Arts programme at Roehampton University. *Arts and Humanities in Higher Education*, 9(3), 339–352.

Bath, D., Smith, C., Stein, S. and Swann, R. (2004). Beyond mapping and embedding graduate attributes: Bringing together quality assurance and action learning to create a validated and living curriculum. *Higher Education Research and Development*, 23(3), 313–328.

Bennet, D., Coffey, J., Fitgerald, S., Petocz, P. and Rainnie, A. (2014). Beyond the creative: Understanding the intersection of specialist and embedded work for creatives in metropolitan Perth. In G. Hearn, R. Bridgstock, B. Goldsmith and J. Rodgers (eds), *Creative Work Beyond the Creative Industries: Innovation, Employment and Education* (pp. 158–172). Cheltenham, UK and Northampton, MA, USA: Edward Elgar Publishing.

Bowen, G. A. (2009). Document analysis as a qualitative research method. *Qualitative Research Journal*, 9(2), 27–40.

Braun, V. and Clarke, V. (2006). Using thematic analysis in psychology. *Qualitative Research in Psychology*, 3(2), 77–101.

Daniels, J. and Brooker, J. (2014). Student identity development in higher education: Implications for graduate attributes and work-readiness. *Educational Research*, 56(1), 65–76.

European Association for Quality Assurance in Higher Education. (2015). Standards and Guidelines for Quality Assurance in the European Higher Education Area. Retrieved on 7 September 2018 from https://enqa.eu/wp-content/uploads/2015/11/ESG_2015.pdf.

Farquharson, K. (2013). Regulating sociology: Threshold learning outcomes and institutional isomorphism. *Journal of Sociology*, 49(4), 486–500.

Fugate, M., Kinicki, A. J. and Ashforth, B. E. (2004). Employability: A psycho-social construct, its dimensions, and applications. *Journal of Vocational Behavior*, 65(1), 14–38.

Hammer, S., McDonald, J. and Forbes, M. (2014). Three perspectives on a collaborative, whole-of-program process of curriculum change. *Journal of Teaching and Learning for Graduate Employability*, 5(1), 47–62.

Hoye, G., Hooft, E. A. J. and Lievens, F. (2009). Networking as a job search behaviour: A social network perspective. *Journal of Occupational and Organizational Psychology*, *82*(3), 661–682. doi:doi:10.1348/ 096317908X360675.

Hubball, H. and Burt, H. (2004). An integrated approach to developing and implementing learning-centred curricula. *International Journal for Academic Development*, *9*(1), 51–64. doi:10.1080/1360144042000296053.

Jacobsen, M., Eaton, S. E., Brown, B., Simmons, M. and McDermott, M. (2018). Action research for graduate program improvements: A response to curriculum mapping and review. *Canadian Journal of Higher Education*, *48*(1), 82–98.

Langrish, T., See, H., Prince, R. and Hind, D. (2010). Industry associates: Moving toward a more structured learning and teaching interaction between industry and university. In *Chemeca 2010: Engineering at the Edge; 26–29 September 2010, Hilton Adelaide, South Australia* (pp. 3555). Barton, A. C. T: Engineers Australia.

Lawson, R., Taylor, T., Fallshaw, E., French, E., Hall, C., Kinash, S. and Summers, J. (2011). *Hunters and gatherers: Strategies for curriculum mapping and data collection for assurance of learning.* Paper presented at the ATN Assessment Conference, Perth, Western Australia.

Mallon, R. (2013). Naturalistic approaches to social construction. In E. N. Zalta, U. Nodelman, C. Allen and J. Perry (eds), *Stanford Encyclopedia of Philosophy* (Winter 2014 edn). Stanford, CA: Metaphysics Research Lab, Stanford University. Retrieved on 7 September 2018 from https://plato .stanford.edu/archives/win2013/entries/social-construction-naturalistic/.

Oliver, B. (2013). Graduate attributes as a focus for institution-wide curriculum renewal: Innovations and challenges. *Higher Education Research and Development*, *32*(3), 450–463.

Oliver, B., Jones, S., Ferns, S. and Tucker, B. (2007). Mapping curricula: Ensuring work-ready graduates by mapping course learning outcomes and higher order thinking skills. In *ATN Evaluations and Assessment Conference 2007*. Brisbane: Queensland University of Technology.

Plaza, C. M., Draugalis, J. R., Slack, M. K., Skrepnek, G. H. and Sauer, K. A. (2007). Curriculum mapping in program assessment and evaluation. *American Journal of Pharmaceutical Education*, *71*(2), 1–8.

Truesdale, V., Thomson, C. and Lucas, M. (2004). Use of curriculum mapping to build a learning community. In H. H. Jacobs (ed.), *Getting Results with Curriculum Mapping* (pp. 10–24). Alexandria, VA: Association for Supervision and Curriculum Development.

14. The connected university: connectedness learning across a lifetime

Kirsty Kitto, Julieanne Cutrupi, Mark Philips, Gabrielle Gardiner, Moein Ghodrati and Simon Buckingham Shum

INTRODUCTION

Learning happens across a lifetime. In a constant process of personal growth, individuals connect across a wide variety of spaces and in markedly different contexts: learning from their peers in classes, developing new skills when dealing with groups, applying skills learned in extracurricular activities to new contexts, and so on. As they gain confidence, those same individuals start to mentor, teach, and instruct other people in their network. Sometimes they decide to return to formal learning opportunities, sometimes not. This process of learning continues throughout a lifetime, not just during a finite period of formal education at the start of a person's career.

This means that an individual will experience a wide array of learning experiences throughout their lifetime, connecting with a broad cross-section of people and systems, both formal and informal. As was discussed in Chapter 1 of this volume by Bridgstock and Tippett, the last two decades have seen an increasing recognition of the importance of helping our students to develop the skills, mindsets and capabilities to connect; with each other, with academia, and with people who can help them to grow a professional identity. Multiple theories have formalised this need, described approaches for achieving it, and discussed its benefits. And yet it is difficult to find an example of a university that has achieved any form of connectedness learning at scale. We must start to ask why.

In this chapter we will step back, moving away from a consideration of individual cases of practice designed to encourage connectedness learning, to consider instead how the enabling strategies for achieving connectedness learning might be facilitated by a university's digital infrastructure. Reducing institutional barriers to connectedness is not an easy feat to achieve. Here, we will start to move beyond specific teams and individual universities and ask what type of information ecology (Davenport and Prusak, 1997) will help to facilitate connectedness learning across a lifetime of learning. We start with a brief examination of workforce disruption and transition to illustrate why lifelong connected learning is more important than ever.

EMPLOYABILITY IN AN AGE OF WORKFORCE TRANSITION

The modern conceptualisation of employment is rapidly shifting. While our parents planned to work for the same company for life, our children can expect to change career many times (Committee for Economic Development of Australia, 2015). As a range of social, economic and digital influences start to impact upon the workforce, few people can expect to stay in one career throughout their lifetime, with estimates emerging that the current generation of school leavers can expect to have around 17 jobs across five careers in their lifetime (McPherson, 2017).

This problem also affects employers. Many professions have problems with retaining a skilled workforce; people increasingly tend to move and transition to new opportunities if they find themselves bored or disenfranchised. More and more, methods dependent upon data and analytics are proposed as solutions to this problem: for recruitment, team formation, the calculation of KPIs, and other challenges being faced by Human Resources (HR) departments. Fields such as *HR Analytics* are increasingly claimed to help with recruitment processes and longer term professional development of staff (Bersin, 2018). However, such changes in HR practices can bring both invasions of privacy, and risks of poor automated generalisations about the capability of an individual. For instance, are our basic metrics and assumptions about performance correct? If they are not then the use of analytics and automated reporting will only serve to institutionalise bias and poor practice.

How does this play out in connectedness learning? The true value of connectivity has not traditionally been well recognised in the workforce. People use Personal Learning Networks (PLNs) (Richardson and Mancabelli, 2011) and social relationships to ask questions and seek information. These informal conversations lead to the sharing of information via weak ties (Granovetter, 1973), and are facilitated by supercooperators (Nowak and Highfield, 2011), who are key to the effective transmission of information in an organisation. Often an individual's essential dissemination and linkage role is not apparent until they move on and communication issues arise. However, few performance metrics reward such behaviour, and so recognition of these informal links is generally ad hoc. How might we start to surface some of these important characteristics in the metrics that are increasingly being used?

One of the fields that holds the most promise for developing new metrics of these complex competencies is Learning Analytics (LA), which has largely arisen from the field of Higher Education (HE) and so provides a natural avenue through which HE might start to influence these developments in the workforce. Perhaps there is an opportunity to start measuring behaviours that we actually value in the workforce, instead of the more common scenario where institutions reorient their KPIs to value the things that they can measure (Kitto, Buckingham Shum and Gibson, 2018).

LEARNING ANALYTICS FOR A LIFETIME OF CONNECTEDNESS

While HE was slow to adopt analytics when compared with other sectors, there is growing recognition of the importance of different kinds of Learning Analytics (LA) for helping to improve the quality of education (Siemens, Dawson and Lynch, 2013). However, institutional adoption has tended to be sporadic at best (Colvin et al., 2015) for a wide range of reasons, including: surprisingly low data literacy in many parts of the academic workforce; poor practices in data warehousing making it difficult to access necessary data; siloed policies and practices and so on. A number of new policy frameworks, leadership models and organisational structures have started to emerge in an attempt to address these problems (Buckingham Shum and Mckay, 2018; Dawson et al., 2018; Tsai et al., 2018).

One branch of LA, Social Learning Analytics (Buckingham Shum and Ferguson, 2012), could help to resolve problems associated with finding metrics of connectivity and contribution. Social Learning Analytics have been intensively studied over a number of years, with interesting tools starting to emerge from this research (Chen et al., 2018). Sensemaking tools that help people to think about their place in a network, and how they might leverage this to develop their careers seem to be just around the corner. Other avenues of work include developing student facing LA solutions that will help people to build other twenty-first century skills that prepare them for lifelong learning in a complex and uncertain world (Buckingham Shum and Crick, 2016). Skills like: critical thinking, creativity, collaboration, metacognition, and motivation are increasingly valued across all curricula (Lai and Viering, 2012) and LA is rising to the challenge of finding innovative ways to use data to encourage their development.

However, universities need to do more than support our students in developing a rich portfolio of attributes and skills; we also need to help them to *demonstrate* those attributes, in a manner that employers can understand and interpret. This in turn requires that students be able to make sense of their own learning records and digital traces, understanding what they are doing (and why) to the extent that they can use the artefacts of their learning as evidence of their capabilities. It is not just universities that need to map course learning outcomes to assessment tasks; our students also need to understand how their various subjects connect, and how what they are doing will connect them with their chosen profession. However, a lack of access to data means that LA is rarely applied at a whole of course level, let alone across a lifetime.

WHERE IS THE DATA?

In a lifetime model of learning, we immediately come across a problem that many universities have until now avoided: learning happens everywhere, at any time. People continuously plan for the future, upgrade their skills, interact with others who have different attitudes, beliefs, skills and so on, and encounter new sources of knowledge (both online and in the real world). Throughout a lifetime it is reasonable to expect that one person will interface with many different educational systems (e.g. K-12, higher education, and continuing professional development). Workforce disruption implies that university graduates will increasingly enter the workforce for a period and then return to formal education when they decide to upskill or retrain in a new profession. While participating in each of these different educational systems throughout their lifetimes, our students will leave digital traces in a large number of different IT systems: Student Information Systems (SIS); Learning Management Systems (LMS); Social Media; MOOC platforms; Human Resource Systems; and ePortfolios, among many others.

The digital traces that are relied upon for analytics by various communities are rarely connected at all. They are siloed in various different IT systems and organisational structures. Any analytics generated using these unconnected data silos will be partial at best and could well result in highly misleading conclusions. For example, if our curriculum pathways are not defined in a system that records student satisfaction scores then it will be hard to realise that a subject with very low student feedback scores and poor grades might be consistently linked to students who were granted an exemption from a prerequisite subject. Our data must be carefully curated and highly connected to enable insights beyond the single subject level. And yet it is rare to see a curriculum information system connected to data about either student satisfaction or grades. This means that analysis is often performed in isolated silos – telling only a very small chapter of a far more complex story. This problem becomes even more urgent in the context of university careers services as they shift to models that seek to generate connected communities (Dey and Cruzvergara, 2014). Such models consider all parts of a student's journey, aiming to help them plan, correct course or decide to seek specialised career advice. How might we start to join the dots along a student's lifetime of learning?

AN INSTITUTIONAL PERSPECTIVE: THREE UTS PROJECTS IN CONNECTED INTELLIGENCE

In 2011 the University of Technology Sydney (UTS) embarked on a strategy aimed at realising a *Data Intensive University*:

> [W]here staff and students understand data and, regardless of its volume and diversity, can use and reuse it, store and curate it, apply and develop the analytical tools to interpret it. (Ferguson et al., 2014, p. 138)

A high priority was learning to appropriately use data and evidence to support the decision making of all stakeholders, defined as the entire UTS community. Consultation with stakeholders suggested that the name of this strategy should be changed to *Connected Intelligence* because it provided a more 'inclusive' branding for non-STEM disciplines, as well as encapsulating the ideas of connecting people, data and processes, in an intelligent, evidence-based approach. In August 2014 The Connected Intelligence Centre (CIC – https://utscic.edu.au/) was formed to facilitate this strategy. CIC takes the form of an innovation centre (Buckingham Shum and Mckay, 2018), operating as a creative incubator to catalyse thinking about the impact of data and algorithms on education, research, and society more broadly, thus it is a focal point for the university as it tries to move towards achieving connectedness learning at scale. Here, we will explore the concept of lifelong connectedness learning from the perspective of three ongoing UTS projects that are supported by CIC: student facing analytics for lifelong learning; data portability; and understanding student outcomes in more detail than the Graduate Outcomes Survey (GOS) enables.

STUDENT FACING ANALYTICS FOR LIFELONG LEARNING

How can we help students to understand the value of the digital traces that they leave throughout a lifetime of learning? The value of those traces might become apparent to students if they can help a student to learn how to learn, so improving their capabilities as a lifelong learner. Existing LA solutions often fall short here, focusing more on reporting a student's rank in a cohort than aiming to provide them with insight about what they are doing as they study, and so helping them learn to learn more effectively (Lockyer, Heathcote and Dawson, 2013). Such insights require that the data describing student interactions with the relevant LMS be available at a very fine level of detail. Counts of how many times a student has posted to a discussion forum are not sufficient. We require an understanding of who said what, to whom, and when, so that we can make use of discourse analytics (Ferguson and Buckingham Shum, 2012) to help students think about the *quality* of their connections. For example, a student who merely posts "great idea" to a forum has not helped to develop that idea, or probed it for weaknesses. While it is important that peers learn to encourage one another, it is also essential that they learn how to challenge and question a line of thinking in a community of inquiry, and LA has provided methods for helping us to automate the analysis of this process (Kovanović et al., 2016). Similarly, what order a student completes a task in is important information that must be preserved in order to build up an understanding of which types of metacognitive processes and self-regulation strategies they are developing (Buckingham Shum and Crick, 2016).

Modern LMSs have started to deliver the data that is necessary for these types of analysis, but not all do. Furthermore, it can be difficult to use that data in LA that encourages the types of capabilities that universities are increasingly trying to develop in our students. Some LMSs provide Application Programming Interfaces (APIs) for data extraction, but many do not, and often the vendor delivered solutions do not make it easy for institutional teams to access data at the level of individual events. Analytics depends on the data (Bryant, 2017) but that data is frequently aggregated, inaccessible, or available only to people with administrative status. Tensions often arise between giving access to the teams that need the data, and maintaining the stability and security of systems that are core to university business.

Even if institutional practice has advanced to the point where the necessary LMS data can be collected, many students do the bulk of their learning 'in the wild' beyond the LMS, which means that information about the learning they do there (e.g. on YouTube, or in group-based Slack conversations, or MOOCs, and in various Blog sites), also provides an important source of information about their process of learning. Work in providing LA beyond the LMS (Bakharia et al., 2016; Kitto et al., 2015) has demonstrated that if care is taken in representing data interoperably using common standards then these sources too can be integrated, so helping to unify data from multiple places and spaces into a collection that tells a far more complete story about a student's learning journey.

Assuming that a university has managed to collect a rich set of data describing the student journey through their systems (no easy feat), the question of how it should be presented to students is largely unsolved. As Teasley (2017) has pointed out, one size does not fit all when it comes to student facing dashboards. It is essential to connect the LA with the pedagogical context that led our students to generate these digital traces. This provides an essential grounding for approaches using data and analytics; many subjects expect their students to be participating in profoundly different activities throughout the course of a semester and this leads to very different behavioural traces. However, generating this form of linkage requires ready access to the learning outcomes for a subject and assessment structure, along with the way in which it progresses over a teaching period (i.e. its learning design). Such data is rarely available to a team developing LA solutions; it is often locked up in spreadsheets and word documents in a variety of Faculty file systems (both physical and virtual).

CIC has an emerging focus on delivering LA that links to the learning design of a subject (Echeverria et al., 2018; Kitto et al., 2017) and is now working to build student facing dashboards that are both user configurable and connect to the learning design of a subject. In the first instance this work will be implemented in a postgraduate environment using the Canvas LMS (https://www.canvaslms.com/). This provides an interesting case in point for the issues discussed above. Canvas is a modern, open source and cloud based LMS which provides an API for data access (https://canvas.instructure.com/doc/api/). This makes it *in principle* possible to deliver real time student facing LA, but the Canvas LA solutions currently provide few insights that would help a student learn how to learn. At UTS, CIC is working with the postgraduate futures team to build a LA API which will provide access to the required data, via an intermediate layer. This will form the basis of a loose coupling between a number of core UTS IT systems and various analytics capabilities developed by CIC. This will be a significant advance, as it will move UTS beyond direct point to point connections of various IT systems, instead providing a safe and extensible way to rapidly develop and adopt new solutions that will help to facilitate connectedness learning across the university, that is, at scale.

DATA PORTABILITY

A related underlying infrastructure project emerges quickly when attempting to deliver LA that collects data over a lifetime. Specifically, in attempting to provide student facing analytics that uses data from multiple systems, and potentially over a lifetime of learning, a number of problems around *data portability* quickly become apparent. There is no guarantee that the data collected from multiple systems will make sense anywhere beyond where it was initially generated. However, new educational data standards have emerged, which offer us a rare opportunity to improve this situation (Griffiths, Hoel and Cooper, 2016), and key to the student facing LA dashboards currently being implemented is the recognition of the need to somehow unify the semantics of the data describing a wide range of social interactions (Bakharia et al., 2016). We shall return to this more global problem shortly.

INTERNSHIPS AND GRADUATE OUTCOMES BEYOND THE GOS

As with many other universities, UTS is working hard to understand the employment outcomes of its graduates. Data from the national Graduate Outcomes Survey (GOS – see https://www.qilt.edu.au/about-this-site/graduate -employment) is carefully tracked, but weaknesses in the associated methodology are well understood (see Jackson and Bridgstock, 2018). As with many other universities, UTS is looking for more nuanced ways of understanding the outcomes of our students and how they can be improved. This has led to a second collaboration across organisational units in an attempt to build better analytics describing graduate employability. At UTS the data related to this problem is shared across multiple units:

- The Planning and Quality Unit receives the GOS data and uses it to generate KPIs relating to how our graduates perform in the job market.
- The Careers Unit understands which students access their training services, internship opportunities and work.
- The Alumni Office has bought a dataset that matches past UTS students to profiles on LinkedIn at surprisingly high levels of accuracy (e.g. 40,000 profiles can be matched to UTS records with 98 per cent certainty that they are indeed the same student).
- The IT division maintains a data warehouse containing information about student demographics, courses completed, grades, use of the institutional LMS etc.

Each unit can analyse the data that they have direct access to in isolation, but the full and rich story about a graduate's employability only emerges when it is connected and analysed as a whole. However, this connection must be performed with care – who should have access to and stewardship of datasets like this? And how can they be appropriately analysed? The role of the CIC as a connection point between these different organisational units is leading to the careful linking up of datasets like this. Perhaps unsurprisingly to those who understand the importance of connectedness learning, analysis of this data has revealed a strong statistical link between undertaking an internship and positive graduate employment outcomes as measured by the GOS four months after graduation, across all degrees. Even students from cohorts that have traditionally struggled to find employment have much improved chances of doing so if they have completed an internship. For example, UTS' international students are often not as well connected to the domestic employment market via the soft connections that our domestic students leverage (see also Chapter 5 in this volume). This means that their employment statistics are normally substantially lower when compared to domestic students who have achieved similar grade profiles across the same degree. However, the outcomes for this cohort are markedly improved by undertaking an internship. Analyses like these have led UTS to aim for the provisioning of 'internship like' experiences for all students. This might take the form of many different models (e.g. a WIL project, capstone projects, industry posed problems in an 'innovation lab' and so on) and represents a massive organisational commitment that is still ongoing.

We see that connecting data across units has helped to support ongoing institutional investment in the Work Integrated Learning component of the Connectedness Learning Approach. An effort is now underway to generate additional actionable insights by connecting more data to provide richer stories about students' experience of UTS and beyond.

CONNECTING BETWEEN PROJECTS

All of these projects have the potential to dramatically change how UTS enables its students to experience connectedness learning. But connecting them together would provide even more options over a lifetime of learning. Consider, for example, a student facing LA tool that helps students to understand their current capabilities, storing evidence in an ePortfolio. What if they could explore the employment opportunities in a specific geographical region, using a LA dashboard to match their current skill sets to jobs that they were interested in, working out what skills and capabilities they had strong evidence for, and where they were weak. What if they could perform scenario-based modelling to try and work out the consequences of different curriculum choices that they were considering, linking this to a real time feed about the employment status of students who had followed a similar pathway? Perhaps they would start to use such tools to manage their careers, building a strong professional identity as they went. What would be required to build a suite of such tools?

First, we need authentic mappings of institutional curricula that can somehow be mapped to standard job advertisement datasets that are starting to appear in the HE sector (e.g. those provided by https://www.burning-glass.com and https://www.monster.com/). Curriculum mappings that are provided by sector wide efforts such as the formalised descriptors used to understand learning outcomes beyond single institutions might help. Examples include the Australian Qualifications Framework (AQF), Scottish Credit and Qualifications Framework (SCQF), and the German Qualifications Framework (Deutsche Qualifikationsrahmen, DQR) at the national level, and the European Qualifications Framework (EQF) at a regional level (Keevy and Chakroun, 2015). However, the mapping of learning outcomes into frameworks such as these is only the first step, and academic teams have often treated educational standards as a compliance exercise rather than an opportunity to ensure that information about student qualifications is indeed portable to other scenarios. How are we to map these sometimes poorly conceived curriculum descriptions to datasets that were created without reference to them? Partial solutions exist already, but we are yet to see any HE institutions attempt to implement them at scale. For example, it is possible to map curriculum documentation into widely understood educational constructs (e.g. Bloom's taxonomy) using simple stemming and text analysis (Gibson, Kitto and Willis, 2014) although it is possible to get far more sophisticated. Publicly available taxonomies of skills, competences, qualifications and occupations exist (e.g. https://ec.europa.eu/esco/resources/data/static/model/html/model.xhtml) which could be extended to qualifications frameworks using natural language processing. CIC is currently working to realise this type of mapping between various curriculum documents and taxonomies describing skills and qualifications more generally.

IS ONE UNIVERSITY ENOUGH?

Even if one university progresses to the point where it could provide this type of connectivity and data portability, will this be sufficient to enable a lifelong connectedness learning experience? E-portfolios require a significant curation effort, which can sometimes be exported to other platforms, but often not. Educators are increasingly moving to the course led curation of professional portfolio tools, such as LinkedIn, to mitigate against this problem (Bridgstock, 2019), but a largely unaddressed problem remains; standard ePortfolios do not currently link to evidence or proof of the claimed competencies, and so are not much more sophisticated than a traditional curriculum vitae, even if they provide many more options for connectivity. Digital badges are claimed to solve this problem because of the way that they can be linked to metadata about the awarding institution and information about the activities undertaken (Gibson et al., 2015), but they bring their own problems when we consider how they are currently collected and presented. Even within one institution it is rare to see badges carefully mapped out, and the mappings between digital credentials are still largely underspecified. Hickey and Willis (2017) provide some of the best practice scenarios where badges get aggregated at different levels to combine to larger awards, but much work remains to be completed. Across institutions we see this problem only grow in magnitude. A potential employer is unlikely to understand how the badges awarded by two different institutions relate to one another, which makes comparisons difficult. When the extra granularity of badges is considered (as compared with degrees) we see a further problem: across a lifetime an individual may collect hundreds of badges. How can they be curated into an interpretable story about an individual's skills and capabilities across multiple institutions?

The problem of lifelong educational data portability is large, and much work remains to be done.

RECOMMENDATIONS FOR SUPPORTING CONNECTED UNIVERSITIES

What has UTS learned from its Connected Intelligence strategy and its ongoing engagement with other universities? Experience throughout the Australian sector has led to a wealth of examples about what works, and what can go wrong, in creating a connected university. Here, we will try to explicitly state some of the lessons that CIC has learned along the way about the data, institutional connectivity, and IT infrastructure required to support lifelong connected learning. We will frame this discussion in terms of a set of recommendations that might be applied more generally by any university as it moves to a model of lifelong connected learning.

Local Organisational Structures Should not Dominate Decisions with Wide Impact

Who makes the decisions about software acquisitions at your university? Are all stakeholders equally represented? Or is one organisational unit responsible? The ability of a degree program to offer Connectedness Learning can be affected by decisions made by many different organisational units including: The teaching and learning arm of an institution; an IT division; project management procedures; and even specific faculty business processes. It is essential that organisations learn how to consider all stakeholders affected by various organisational decisions. Thus, an IT unit that decides to stop support of an institutional Google account, often for very good reasons such as data security, might shut down an entire connectedness learning program overnight. A decision to move core infrastructure such as a LMS or SIS to the cloud could be exceptionally well motivated from the perspective of security, maintenance, and modernity ... yet it can have severe repercussions in terms of the ability of other units to offer advanced LA solutions. The in-house and highly customised systems developed by many Australian universities are rapidly being replaced by cloud-based products which often provide marked improvements in usability, but Australian institutions often lack the global influence to demand changes or extensions of functionality. If missing functionality impacts upon the ability of other university units to deliver core functionality then this can become a significant problem. Thus, a failure to consider the broader context in which a system will be deployed can lead to highly adverse outcomes for approaches like connectedness learning that can break quickly if other units are not aware of team requirements beyond their own.

A related set of problems can arise if one organisational unit has core decision making capabilities over systems that affect other units. Organisational culture can mean that different units approach the same problem from markedly different perspectives. For example, do the KPIs associated with an expenses system reside in one unit? Other units might be profoundly affected by how that unit defines business processes. If decisions are made with reference to only one unit's needs then other programs can be profoundly handicapped. This problem often presents in the performance metrics and KPIs of an institution; it is frequently the case in an unconnected university that one unit optimises its own KPIs at the expense of another – this is a key symptom of the need for a change in lines of accountability.

Genuine Data Portability, Access and Control are Essential

The issue of what to do with data, who has the right to access and control it, and how interoperable it needs to be are widely debated (Duch-Brown, Martens and Mueller-Langer, 2017). Many universities are rightly concerned about the ways in which tech giants might misuse personal data (Chakravorti, 2018). Sometimes institutions attempt to regain control of their data through policy settings. For example, bans on the use of social media in teaching are likely to become more common in an attempt to protect the privacy of students. However, this form of action is rarely enforceable, leading academic teams to go underground. More importantly it does our students few favours. We need to teach them how their data is used by various corporations, governments and service providers, opening up the black box of algorithmic decision making and teaching them how to challenge inappropriate classifications (Kitto, Buckingham Shum and Gibson, 2018). If universities step away from the role of teaching our students about how their personal data is used then we might ask who will step into the gap? Connectedness learning offers a very real pedagogical opportunity for exposing students to the varying ways that technology makes use of data, and so improving their understanding of how it might be abused.

Emerging political pressures make this set of issues even more urgent. For example, the European General Data Protection Regulation (GDPR) will have a significant impact upon how we make use of data in HE. Of interest to us here, these laws list a set of eight rights that pertain to individuals with respect to the digital footprint that they leave as they interface with various IT systems throughout a lifetime, including rights to be informed; access data; object to records; and fix or erase them if incorrect etc. Many of these rights have been implemented by leading European HE providers,[1] but, one is proving difficult to realise; *the right to data portability*, which states that:

> The data subject shall have the right to receive the personal data concerning him or her, which he or she has provided to a controller, in a structured, commonly used and machine-readable format and have the right to transmit those data to another controller without hindrance from the controller to which the personal data have been provided. (https://gdpr-info.eu/art-20-gdpr/)

This right requires that European universities increasingly pay serious attention to the concept of data interoperability, as otherwise educational data will be largely useless beyond the specific institutional context in which it was generated. Even if every university were to adopt one educational data standard (and they do not) most universities would struggle to produce the entire record of a student's interactions within their IT systems. On the contrary, student data is commonly siloed across multiple systems, with markedly different data access protocols and a wide range of custodians in charge of different components (from academics, to administrative officers, counsellors, and librarians). Furthermore, institutions often use terms in different ways, making the portability of meaningful data between them problematic. For example, the AQF requires that graduate attributes are extensively mapped to learning outcomes in the Australian sector, which have been demonstrated to have a marked overlap (Oliver and Jorre de St Jorre, 2018). However, the complexity of identifying these commonalities makes these types of mappings very difficult, often taking a large amount of manual labour. Similarly, the definition of a part-time or low SES (socioeconomic status) student, and terms such as course, unit, subject, program and module can differ in ways that are subtle but promote ongoing misunderstandings between various stakeholders, especially when mapping to an international context. If genuine portability is to be enabled then we will also have to carefully consider the semantics of our data, ensuring that its meaning can be mapped between different institutions. This means that rather than just a set of issues to be navigated, the right to data portability offers a policy driven opportunity to 'get our house in order' and to work towards generating educational data that can be used to facilitate lifelong connected learning.

Standards Should be Followed

Data and technology standards have been developed for a reason. They facilitate the movement of information, metrics, data and analysis beyond the confines of one stand-alone system. Every time a vendor, institution or research group develops its own in-house solution to the representation of data, the specification of competency or the transmission of information, we have lost the ability to escape our silos. Claims are often made that specific standards do not fit the current use case, or that implementation is too difficult, or that something is wrong with how the standard is defined. This is not a useful habit to develop. In a world of lifelong learning we owe it to our students to ensure that the artefacts and data that they generate can be exported to other contexts. The student desire to learn beyond the LMS (Kitto et al., 2015) quickly forces us to recognise that the time spent to map data between different silos is well spent, and a new move is evolving (yet again) to try and standardise interoperable educational data (Griffiths, Hoel and Cooper, 2016).

What is the point in using the educational standards released by organisations like the IEEE,[2] ISO,[3] ADL[4] and IMS[5]? Many HE institutions do not insist that the products they build or purchase adhere to the various standards that are available, which means that these solutions often use their own in-house syntax and semantics when mapping out educational information. However, much can be gained with a careful application of these standards. For example, in the UK Jisc has implemented a national learning analytics infrastructure which is built upon the xAPI data standard (see https://www.adlnet.gov/research/performance-tracking-analysis/experience-api/). This enables the provision of an ecosystem of services all built off an underlying interoperable data format. It is important to realise that providing this kind of connectivity between datasets and IT infrastructure is non-trivial. To ensure a seamless student experience a large amount of work must be completed at the 'back end' of the systems to link them up, and following extant standards can make it far easier to both release data from its silos, and add new technology to the ecosystem of an institution down the track.

IT Couplings Should be Loose not Tight

Core to the work of building up a connected university is the infrastructure that enables data to move between different systems. Traditionally universities have made use of tight couplings between systems, for example, the Student Information System (SIS) is directly linked to the LMS to transfer data via a point integration. This makes for a fragile IT infrastructure where it is difficult to move to new IT solutions; changing a system (e.g. a LMS) constitutes a major undertaking. In contrast, modern service-oriented architectures allow for flexible and adaptive solutions to be built, where a university can swap infrastructure in and out as technology evolves, but the overarching user experience does not change.[6] Often, this makes use of an API which works as an intermediate layer providing user facing services (e.g. LA dashboards) with the data they need, regardless of what has changed in the back-end infrastructure. We believe that more universities should be following this path. The benefits will be even greater if they connect together in doing so, using *a university API derived from a universal standard*. This would enable different software vendors to interface with the same set of hooks, saving both universities and software providers from the substantial integration efforts that they currently have to undertake every time a new IT product is acquired.

Knowledge Sharing Should be Institutionalised and Supported by Infrastructure

Finally, the knowledge gained by various parts of a university is rarely shared in a widely accessible way. This means that even when pockets of best practice emerge their learnings are often unavailable to the rest of the institution. While seminars, events and informal meet-ups are all useful for the transmission of best practice, it is essential that universities start to provide ways to transmit knowledge when needed, just in time. The staff member who is trying to work out how to do something *right now* cannot wait until the end of year forum to find out how another group solved their problem. For example, as data warehouses are increasingly used across an institution, how many groups are consistently reinventing the wheel?

Internal web pages and wikis are frequently provided by institutions to help staff record information as required. Unfortunately, they are rarely kept up to date, and often result in redundant information that is factually incorrect and can even be conflicting. More modern knowledge repositories provide an excellent solution to this problem, but few universities make use of these best practice solutions. Tools such as Knowledge Repo (http://knowledge-repo. readthedocs.io/) enable groups in different organisational units to share knowledge across the entire institution using a service that aggregates code repositories and documents without duplication, but other solutions exist.

Regardless of the solution chosen, a connected university will only prioritise knowledge sharing if there is a genuine staff commitment to this process, and yet we rarely see this type of institutional citizenry recognised by KPIs or other awards. The connected university is one where people share knowledge because it is recognised as important, not one where they are told to do so. Senior management would do well to consider ways in which they can create a culture of knowledge sharing at their institution.

TOWARDS THE FUTURE

These recommendations are only the tip of the iceberg. Implementing connectedness learning across the lifetime of our students is a mammoth task. But as we discussed at the outset, the changing nature of work creates a strong imperative to do so if we are genuinely taking the interests of our students into account. But what benefits await a university that attempts this venture? Could it be worth the effort?

If data portability is taken seriously, then it would enable us to give our students access to Personal Data Stores (PDS) that they could take with them for life. They would be able to directly interface with employers using ePortfolios that are verifiable, and which contain directly accessible evidence of their evidence of their skills and capabilities. If these were implemented with a full consideration of the personal rights associated with the GDPR then our students would have ways to control access to that data. They would be able to create different views of their skills and capabilities for different potential employers. They would be able to update their PDS while training at work, and use it to get recognition of their prior learning if they decide to return to university. A PDS could be used to *personalise* the student experience, helping our students to select a pathway through a university system that suits them. Being able to offer this type of individual service to students is a key differentiator that many universities are currently working to deliver, but without the underlying connected data it will be very difficult to achieve.

CONCLUSIONS

Learning happens throughout a lifetime, and all universities would do well to recognise that they are only a part of the journey that each of their students have embarked upon. It is fast becoming essential for universities to provide *lifelong* connected learning, where our graduates can demonstrate their skills and competencies not just to potential employers, but to other HE providers as they attempt to navigate the changing nature of work. We have discussed the complexities associated with providing this level of service, pointing to key recommendations that have emerged from UTS as it attempts to deliver infrastructure capable of supporting this overarching goal. We welcome other institutions that are willing to connect with us on this journey.

ACKNOWLEDGEMENTS

We gratefully acknowledge support from the Australian Government Office for Learning and Teaching (OLT) and Graduate Careers Australia (GCA) in completing this work. The views in this chapter do not necessarily reflect the views of either body.

NOTES

1. See the Open University student privacy note as an example: http://www.open. ac.uk/students/charter/essential-documents/student-privacy-notice (accessed 18 January 2019).
2. http://www.ieeeltsc.org/.
3. https://www.iso.org/committee/45392.html.
4. http://adlnet.gov/.
5. https://www.imsglobal.org/.
6. See https://edutechnica.com/2015/06/09/flipping-the-model-the-campus-api/ for an introductory discussion of the power of this approach, along with the ongoing work by Kin Lane on university APIs at http://university.stack.network/, and the blog by Binghamton university which explains their API design: https:// developer.byu.edu/blog/method-madness-goals-and-design-decisions-university -api-specification.

REFERENCES

Bakharia, A., Kitto, K., Pardo, A., Gašević, D. and Dawson, S. (2016). *Recipe for success: Lessons learnt from using xAPI within the connected learning analytics toolkit.* Paper presented at the Proceedings of the sixth international conference on learning analytics and knowledge.

Bersin, J. (2018). HR Technology Disruptions for 2018: Productivity, Design, and Intelligence Reign. Retrieved on 7 May 2018 from http://marketing. bersin.com/HR-Technology-Disruptions-Report-Reg.html.

Bridgstock, R. (2019). Graduate Employability 2.0: Education for work in a networked world. In J. Higgs, G. Crisp and W. Letts (eds), *Education for Employability: The Employability Agenda* (pp. 268–282). Rotterdam: Sense-Brill Publishers.

Bryant, T. (2017). Everything depends on the data. *Educause Review.* Retrieved on 7 May 2018 from https://er.educause.edu/articles/2017/1/ everything-depends-on-the-data.

Buckingham Shum, S. and Crick, R. D. (2016). Learning analytics for 21st century competencies. *Journal of Learning Analytics*, *3*(2), 6–21.

Buckingham Shum, S. and Ferguson, R. (2012). Social learning analytics. *Journal of Educational Technology and Society*, *15*(3), 3–26.

Buckingham Shum, S. and Mckay, T. (2018). Architecting for learning analytics: Innovating for sustainable impact. *Educause Review*, *53*(2), 25–37.

Chakravorti, B. (2018). Trust in digital technology will be the internet's next frontier, for 2018 and beyond. *The Conversation US.* Retrieved on 7 May 2018 from http://theconversation.com/trust-in-digitaltechnology-will-be -the-internets-next-frontier-for-2018-and-beyond-87566.

Chen, B., Chang, Y.-H., Ouyang, F. and Zhou, W. (2018). Fostering student engagement in online discussion through social learning analytics. *The Internet and Higher Education, 37*, 21–30.

Colvin, C., Rogers, T., Wade, A., Dawson, S., Gašević, D., Buckingham Shum, S. and Fisher, J. (2015). *Student Retention and Learning Analytics: A Snapshot of Australian Practices and a Framework for Advancement.* Sydney: Australian Office for Learning and Teaching.

Committee for Economic Development of Australia. (2015). Australia's future workforce? Retrieved on 7 May 2018 from http://www.ceda.com.au/research-and-policy/policy-priorities/workforce.

Davenport, T. H. and Prusak, L. (1997). *Information Ecology: Mastering the Information and Knowledge Environment.* Oxford: Oxford University Press.

Dawson, S., Poquet, O., Colvin, C., Rogers, T., Pardo, A. and Gašević, D. (2018). *Rethinking learning analytics adoption through complexity leadership theory.* Paper presented at the Proceedings of the 8th International Conference on Learning Analytics and Knowledge.

Dey, F. and Cruzvergara, C. Y. (2014). Evolution of career services in higher education. *New Directions for Student Services, 2014*(148), 5–18.

Duch-Brown, N., Martens, B. and Mueller-Langer, F. (2017). The economics of ownership, access and trade in digital data. Retrieved on 7 May 2018 from https://ec.europa.eu/jrc/sites/jrcsh/files/jrc104756.pdf.

Echeverria, V., Martinez-Maldonado, R., Granda, R., Chiluiza, K., Conati, C. and Buckingham Shum, S. (2018). *Driving data storytelling from learning design.* Paper presented at the Proceedings of the 8th International Conference on Learning Analytics and Knowledge.

Ferguson, R. and Buckingham Shum, S. (2012). *Social learning analytics: Five approaches.* Paper presented at the Proceedings of the 2nd International Conference on Learning Analytics and Knowledge.

Ferguson, R., Macfadyen, L., Clow, D., Tynan, B., Alexander, S. and Dawson, S. (2014). Setting learning analytics in context: Overcoming the barriers to large-scale adoption. *Journal of Learning Analytics, 1*(3), 120–144.

Gibson, A., Kitto, K. and Willis, J. (2014). *A cognitive processing framework for learning analytics.* Paper presented at the Proceedings of the Fourth International Conference on Learning Analytics and Knowledge.

Gibson, D., Ostashewski, N., Flintoff, K., Grant, S. and Knight, E. (2015). Digital badges in education. *Education and Information Technologies, 20*(2), 403–410.

Granovetter, M. (1973). The strength of weak ties. *American Journal of Sociology, 78*(6), 1360–1380.

Griffiths, D., Hoel, T. and Cooper, A. (2016). Learning analytics interoperability: Requirements, specifications and adoption. Retrieved on 7 May 2018 from http://www.laceproject.eu/d7-4-learning-analytics-interoperability-req uirements-specifications-and-adoption/.

Hickey, D. T. and Willis, J. (2017). Where open badges appear to work better: Findings from the design principles documentation project. Retrieved on 7 May 2018 from http://www.badgenumerique.com/wp-content/uploads/ 2017/08/DPD-Project-Final-Report-Dan-Hickey-Willis-May-2017.pdf.

Jackson, D. and Bridgstock, R. (2018). Evidencing student success in the contemporary world-of-work: Renewing our thinking. *Higher Education Research and Development, 37*(5), 984–998.

Keevy, J. and Chakroun, B. (2015). Level-setting and recognition of learning outcomes: The use of level descriptors in the twenty-first century. Retrieved on 7 May 2018 from http://unesdoc.unesco.org/images/0024/ 002428/242887e.pdf.

Kitto, K., Buckingham Shum, S. and Gibson, A. (2018). *Embracing imperfection in learning analytics.* Paper presented at the Proceedings of the 8th International Conference on Learning Analytics and Knowledge.

Kitto, K., Cross, S., Waters, Z. and Lupton, M. (2015). *Learning analytics beyond the LMS: The connected learning analytics toolkit.* Paper presented at the Proceedings of the Fifth International Conference on Learning Analytics And Knowledge.

Kitto, K., Lupton, M., Davis, K. and Waters, Z. (2017). Designing for student-facing learning analytics. *Australasian Journal of Educational Technology, 33*(5), 152–168.

Kovanović, V., Joksimović, S., Waters, Z., Gašević, D., Kitto, K., Hatala, M. and Siemens, G. (2016). *Towards automated content analysis of discussion transcripts: A cognitive presence case.* Paper presented at the Proceedings of the Sixth International Conference on Learning Analytics and Knowledge.

Lai, E. R. and Viering, M. (2012). Assessing 21st century skills: Integrating research findings. Retrieved on 7 May 2018 from http://researchnetwork. pearson.com/wp-content/uploads/Assessing_21st_Century_Skills_NCME.pdf.

Lockyer, L., Heathcote, E. and Dawson, S. (2013). Informing pedagogical action: Aligning learning analytics with learning design. *American Behavioral Scientist, 57*(10), 1439–1459.

McPherson, S. (2017). What role can employers play in preparing young people for the future of work? Retrieved on 7 May 2018 from https://www. fya.org.au/2017/06/07/what-role-can-employers-play-in-preparing-young-people-for-the-future-of-work/.

Nowak, M. and Highfield, R. (2011). *Supercooperators: Altruism, Evolution, and Why We Need Each Other to Succeed.* New York, NY: Simon and Schuster.

Oliver, B. and Jorre de St Jorre, T. (2018). Graduate attributes for 2020 and beyond: Recommendations for Australian higher education providers. *Higher Education Research and Development*, *37*(4), 821–836.

Richardson, W. and Mancabelli, R. (2011). *Personal Learning Networks: Using the Power of Connections to Transform Education*. Bloomington, IN: Solution Tree Press.

Siemens, G., Dawson, S. and Lynch, G. (2013). *Improving the Quality and Productivity of the Higher Education Sector: Policy and Strategy for Systems-Level Deployment of Learning Analytics*. Canberra: Australian Government Office for Learning and Teaching.

Teasley, S. D. (2017). Student facing dashboards: One size fits all? *Technology, Knowledge and Learning*, *22*(3), 377–384.

Tsai, Y. S., Moreno-Marcos, P. M., Tammets, K., Kollom, K. and Gašević, D. (2018). *SHEILA policy framework: Informing institutional strategies and policy processes of learning analytics*. Paper presented at the Proceedings of the 8th International Conference on Learning Analytics and Knowledge.

15. Future connections: implications for connectedness strategy, pedagogy and capability in higher education

Ruth Bridgstock and Neil Tippett

The Connectedness Learning Approach sets out the institutional enabling strategies, pedagogic approaches, and individual capabilities that will enable learners to build, maintain and make the most of their social networks and relationships for success in life and career. As a practical exploration of the Connectedness Learning Approach in higher education, this volume has presented ten accounts of connectedness learning, spanning a broad cross-section of higher educational contexts. Together, these chapters demonstrate that there is no single way in which universities should support connectedness learning. Rather, connectedness learning requires a detailed understanding of students' needs and existing capabilities, along with the institutional context and strengths, through which the pedagogic approaches and wider enabling strategies that enhance connectedness capabilities can be designed and enacted.

CONNECTEDNESS CAPABILITIES: KEY FINDINGS

Connectedness capabilities represent the knowledge and skills that students require in order to build, maintain and make the most of their networks and social relationships for life and career. Given the centrality of these skills within the Connectedness Learning Approach, Chapters 3 through 5 of this volume explored the knowledge and use of social networks among students and recent graduates, finding that many had not yet developed the key capabilities required to connect professionally with others. Although there were promising signs in terms of students' social networking literacy and ability to create connections, the majority of students and graduates possessed significantly underdeveloped professional networks, even up to several years after graduation.

Exploring the concept of professional identities, in Chapter 3, Lupton, Oddone and Dreamson found that a major hurdle in encouraging students to develop and employ connectedness capabilities appeared to be their perception of themselves as a 'student' rather than as a 'professional'. Learning activities which aimed to encourage and develop students' connectedness capabilities tended to be treated as academic exercises which had little relevance to the professional context. There were, however, several students who exhibited strong digital professional identities, providing evidence of hands-on experimentation with their digital selves, and the ongoing development of their career identities, both of which were tested progressively with professional connections over time. This links back strongly to the extant theoretical literature surrounding career identity development (e.g. Holmes, 2013; Jackson, 2017; Tomlinson, 2017), which suggests that career identity development follows a cycle involving social experience followed by reflection (whether explicit or tacit). In higher education we hear many examples of this cycle breaking down, which would suggest that any form of connected career identity development needs to be supported from early on within the degree program, using well-promoted avenues and support through which students can revise and refine their identity.

In Chapter 4, de Villiers Scheepers, McIntyre, Crimmins and English found that while students had personal experience of using social media for social purposes, their professional connectedness capabilities tended to be at a foundational level. Their social networks were, as one might expect, largely comprised of family, friends and peers, with content being shared within these closed communities, but not beyond. Students were acutely aware of the value and importance of both career development learning and authentic learning experiences in establishing their professional identities, offering strong support for embedding these forms of learning into the curriculum to ensure positive student engagement. Attitudes towards connectedness learning differed according to whether participants had any prior career experience. School-leavers or those with part-time work experience tended to compartmentalise their student and professional lives, perceiving connectedness capabilities and the development of professional networks as being future orientated; something to be developed once their studies had been completed. In contrast, students with previous full-time employment displayed a greater awareness and willingness to embrace connectedness practices, taking opportunities to acquire marketable skills and update their knowledge and professional networks as they transitioned to new career pathways. This would suggest that previous career development learning, including that related to connectedness, is broadly generalisable, and can be translated across multiple settings and disciplinary areas.

In Chapter 5, Bridgstock, Jackson, Lloyd and Tofa explored the professional networks of recent graduates as they transitioned into professional employment. Although most participants possessed some level of social network literacy and ability to build their social networks, their connectedness capabilities remained underdeveloped, and it was only after four or five years of professional employment that the quality and quantity of their professional social networks improved. Having experienced the professional world of work, many graduates expressed a clear desire to improve their connectedness capabilities, particularly their social network literacy, networking capabilities, and capacity to use networks for career development. This finding could be taken to support the idea of universities offering post-graduation just-in-time career launch support and development programs for early alumni. However, incorporating connectedness learning into the curricula of degree programs offers the best way to give students a head-start in creating and using professional networks, whilst also ensuring they have reasonably well-developed career identities by the time of graduation. Connectedness capabilities differed between Creative Industries and Business graduates, and between domestic and international graduates. These findings reinforce the fact that connectedness learning needs to be specific to the needs of learners and their intended pathways.

Together, the findings from these three chapters offer several useful lessons which can guide educators. First, career identity development is a crucial journey for higher education learners, because identity determines how they will engage with future learning, how they will make career-related decisions, and whether/to what extent they will engage in career-building activities (including networking). A key way that career identities are developed is through connectedness – through exposure to professionals and others related to their possible future careers. As such, connectedness learning becomes a virtuous circle. Through exposure to professional connections, learners develop identities that make them more likely to engage in purposeful networking behaviour, which in turn strengthens their identities and enhances their employability.

Although students may have the capacity to build and engage with their networks, learning how to apply this knowledge within the professional context is crucial. Authentic learning experiences, which focus on real-world, complex problems and their solutions (Lombardi, 2007), can support students in converting their knowledge into practice. These experiences, which have been explored in detail in the second section of this volume, ensure that learning has real-world relevance, including exposing students to professional connections, and can support students in bridging the gap between their student and career identities.

Second, the varying levels of social networking literacy evident among students suggests that foundational learning opportunities should be provided to those who lack core connectedness capabilities. As Lupton, Oddone and Dreamson contend, the affordances of connectedness learning may not be fully exploited if students lack the capacity to initiate, manage and utilise their network connections. Students who already possess these skills are unlikely to benefit from any learning experiences pitched at a foundational level yet could offer the potential for peer forms of learning, whereby students share their knowledge and experience of professional networking and use this to enhance the connectedness capabilities of their peers. Thus, just as it is necessary to adapt connectedness learning to students and their intended pathways, it must also be tailored to their social networking literacy.

Third, if students are to learn how to use their connectedness capabilities effectively while at university, then they need to be given access to wider professional networks beyond the university so that they have the opportunity to develop, maintain and strengthen their own networks. Chapter 3 demonstrated that, even where students were able to demonstrate a high level of social networking literacy, without established networks and access to industry partners, there were few opportunities to put their learning into practice. For optimal outcomes, connectedness learning needs to be integrated into wider and deeper career development learning within the curriculum, including explorations of the world of work and reflective identity development, which requires social interaction and the development of professional networks.

The value of previous learning should be recognised, in particular, the connectedness capabilities and networks of students who have engaged in prior careers, or those with already established strong career identities. Educators should look for ways to acknowledge the resources and skills that prior experience can provide. In some cases, students are entering HE with highly developed connectedness capabilities and fully functioning professional networks, yet these are ascribed little importance in their additional learning. Most universities, even those with large non-traditional student populations, lack the mechanisms necessary to ascertain and recognise students prior learning, thus, as Chapter 5 suggests, some formal recognition of prior learning could be an important step in helping students leverage their existing skills while pursuing a new career.

CONNECTEDNESS PEDAGOGIES: KEY FINDINGS

The second section of this volume focused on the pedagogic strategies that universities can adopt to integrate connectedness into the learning experiences of their students, both within and outside the formal curriculum. Many of the pedagogic approaches outlined under the Connectedness Learning Approach can already be found in higher education learning and teaching, however, they are by no means thoroughly integrated, and their value for enhancing connectedness goes under-recognised. Chapters 7 through 10 offer practical examples of how the Connectedness Learning Approach can be taken up in a way that responds to the specific needs of different learners and different institutions.

In Chapter 7, Brown, Healy, Lexis and Julien demonstrated how the delivery of an employability module inside a third-year non-vocational Health Sciences course was able to support students in recognising the value and relevance of connectedness learning for the development of their career identities. In Chapter 8, Radoll et al. considered how pedagogies might be better informed through connecting with cultural and community perspectives. Using the Aboriginal 8 Ways of Learning (Yunkaporta, 2009) as a cultural lens, the chapter forged connections between Indigenous perspectives, contemporary pedagogies, and connectedness learning, identifying how HE learning and teaching can be better aligned with cultural and community values and perspectives. In Chapter 9, Goodwin et al. brought together the experiences of educators across four large and diverse arts and humanities capstone courses within one higher education institution to set out a roadmap for effective capstone experiences. From this collaboration, the authors described five principles which define effective and connected capstone experiences: *authentic*, *reflective*, *creative*, *celebratory* and *networked*. Lastly, in Chapter 10, Bedford and Bell explored a whole-of institution curriculum transformation model at the University of Wollongong, outlining the rationale for, and delivery of, a diverse range of pedagogic approaches that meet the needs of the learners, disciplines and professional contexts.

Although each chapter addressed a different HE context, there are several overarching themes which can be applied to any institution looking to embed connectedness learning within their curricula. Foremost is the need for connectedness learning to be delivered as part of a scaffolded approach where students' capability development is supported through a structured and timely incremental process which commences from the outset of the course. Students enter university with differing levels of social network literacy; some have extensive professional networks while others have little or no social networking experience. First-year activities could focus on developing foundational career identities and also developing a threshold level of social network literacy throughout the cohort. Foundational career identity development provides the fundamental 'why' for development of social network literacy, which then provides the 'how' for network development and the further development of career identity. Those with existing professional networks or well-developed social network literacies might feed their expertise into strengthening learning activities as part of a peer-learning approach. This initial engagement with connectedness learning would enable students to begin constructing their own professional networks within the university and learn to use these strategically to support their academic growth.

Upon these foundations, educators can look to provide intermediate-level 'broadening and deepening' learning opportunities such as work integrated learning or industry-led teaching, which expand students' abilities to use social networks for professional purposes. The whole-of-course progression culminates with the capstone experience, where students reconcile their learning experiences by demonstrating their capacity to apply their learning critically and creatively as they transition into the workforce. As Goodwin et al. suggest, an overarching whole-of-course process would require a carefully structured long-view towards curriculum design, with buy-in among all academics involved.

Scaffolded and progressive learning is reliant on the provision of appropriate, just-in-time learning activities. As such, the Connectedness Learning Approach does not focus on one specific pedagogy, but rather offers a suite of pedagogic approaches, each with different strengths, that can be used in concert to guide students' learning. Which pedagogies are used is dependent upon a number of individual learner, contextual, and disciplinary factors, and the four pedagogic chapters offer examples of how these approaches can be tailored to the individual context. Using a variety of pedagogies to thread connectedness learning throughout a whole degree supports students in realising the value of social networks and enables them to use their skills progressively to build and utilise their professional connections. Examining the outcomes for high school students who participated in a co-curricular social entrepreneurship program, Kerr, Wright and Barraud conclude in Chapter 12 that "students' connectedness capabilities were not developed from participation in one specific activity, but from a culmination of the learning experiences provided by the new, complex learning ecosystem".

Students also require access to the tools necessary to put their learning into practice. A common theme among the earlier chapters was the value of LinkedIn as a pedagogic tool. For many, LinkedIn is a pivotal means by which professionals can connect with others, as well as a means to develop connected professional identities. However, Bedford and Bell argue that just as a one size does not fit all with choice of pedagogic approaches, students should also be supported to engage with a "wide range of technologies, media, tools and platforms to learn, create and connect with others, both within and beyond the university". Using such tools does of course necessitate a consideration of the ethical and privacy implications associated with their use, but also the provision of professional learning and capacity building initiatives for staff to support them in adopting new tools, adapting new pedagogic approaches, engaging with industry, and leading connectedness learning approaches. With any alternative approach to learning, Radoll et al. note that teaching staff will require clear training and guidance in making the transition, and undoubtedly this will need to be accompanied by clear messaging from university leaders which explains the value and purpose of connectedness learning.

Consistent with the guiding principle that "learning should be authentic, occurring in real professional contexts and involving professional activities and interactions with professionals" the pedagogic chapters in this volume demonstrated the importance of authentic learning experiences in helping students translate and apply their knowledge outside of the university environment. The value of WIL activities in enhancing students' employability skills is well documented, and Goodwin et al. recommend that these experiences continue to be employed as a means of extending students' professional networks and connectedness capabilities. In their chapter, the authors suggest that while key capabilities of '*growing connections*', '*working with connections*' and '*developing social literacy*' could potentially be achieved in simulated learning environments, '*strengthening and maintaining connections*' and '*building a connected identity*' require authentic engagement with industry and community partners to be fully realised. In an era where online learning is ubiquitous, and universities are developing digital campuses and delivering fully-online programs, one might ask how learning that best occurs through face-to-face interaction with others (such as through WIL in the workplace, or strengthening connections through close collaborative projects) might be achieved? Through seeking increased efficiency of teaching and flexibility of delivery for learners, are we inadvertently increasing their isolation and limiting the development of a key set of capabilities?

Each chapter in this volume has taken a differing approach to partnerships: some focused on breaking down school or disciplinary boundaries within the university to create shared and networked learning experiences; others made use of careers or employability services to support students' transition into the workforce; and several looked beyond the university entirely, establishing links with industry and community stakeholders to ensure learning experiences were authentic and appropriate. Irrespective of who these partnerships involved, the industry specific knowledge they provided was invaluable in tailoring course content to service the development of learners' connectedness capabilities. Where partnerships extended beyond the university itself, opportunities were also provided through which students could begin forming their external professional networks, establishing their identities as a 'future professional' and no longer just a 'student'.

Further, as Chapter 8 suggested, authentic learning not only relies on input from industry stakeholders, but also the use of different cultural lenses and perspectives, which engage students with diverse ideas and new contexts. With specific consideration towards Indigenous ways of learning, Radoll et al. illustrate that cultural perspectives can help students reflect on and connect up their learning experiences, situating the knowledge and skills they have learnt within the broader social and cultural context. The authors suggest that this cultural authenticity can be achieved through progressively aligning university teaching across the whole curriculum and framing this process within broader historical and contemporary cultural frameworks to forge connections between students, universities and the communities in which they operate.

INSTITUTIONAL ENABLING STRATEGIES: KEY FINDINGS

In the final section of this volume we moved away from some of the individual approaches to connectedness learning to consider how degree programs, organisational areas and universities more broadly can work to build connections and provide cohesive learning experiences which support connectedness capabilities. As Bridgstock (2019) found in her analysis of the Australian HE sector, contemporary universities are not set up in a way that supports connected and networked learning. From an internal perspective, many HE institutions are filled with staff, programs and organisational areas working in isolation to each other; there is often little interaction or collaboration occurring between these silos. Furthermore, many universities also struggle to facilitate lasting and meaningful relationships with external partners, limiting the transfer and exchange of knowledge between the institution and the wider community. Assembling a wide suite of pedagogies is a necessary step in delivering a whole-of-institution connectedness curriculum, however, in supporting and enabling this process, universities must also channel significant effort into developing and leading sustainable strategies which break down the silos in learning and teaching to encourage greater networking and collaboration. Chapters 12 through 14 provided three examples of how higher education institutions have integrated these enabling strategies within and across differing contexts to support graduates' connectedness capabilities.

In Chapter 12, Kerr, Wright and Barraud recounted the experience of creating a university-school partnership to deliver a co-curricular social entrepreneurship program. Benefitting students and teachers alike through the connectedness opportunities that it offered, the development of a sustainable community of practice had spawned further opportunities for collaboration, both within and outside the university, exemplifying the value that connectedness could bring to an institution.

In Chapter 13, Hammer et al. created a cross-disciplinary team comprising educators and careers and employability staff to review programmatic quality in the Creative Arts and Engineering and enhance opportunities for students to connect with industry partners and promote their career identity. The authors found that intra-institutional collaboration enabled educators to reframe and reconceptualise the purpose of their learning and teaching activities, creating greater connections with students, industry, community and other disciplines, and also establishing a platform for future collaboration across and beyond the institution.

Lastly, in Chapter 14, Kitto et al. considered the technological, systemic and data considerations necessary for learners and also universities to become better connected. The authors suggest that universities have the capacity to provide graduates with lifelong connected learning, outlining a series of key recommendations including organisational architecture, IT infrastructure, data portability and institutional knowledge sharing, which will allow universities to fulfil their potential, and enable graduates to connect with others across a lifetime of learning.

Based on what we have learnt from these chapters, how can universities implement a whole-of-institution approach to connectedness learning? Undoubtedly, one of the most critical antecedents for any form of connectedness learning is the development of sustainable and meaningful partnerships, both within and beyond the university. This can be a challenging endeavour in large institutional bureaucracies, where entrenched hierarchical relationships, discrete divisions, and organisational areas competing for funding and KPIs can militate against clear communication and collaboration.

The formation of intra-university partnerships, specifically cross-disciplinary teams and communities of practice is evident in several chapters in this volume, whereby academics from different programs and schools have collaborated in developing and delivering a connectedness curriculum. In Chapter 9 we saw how the integration of disciplinary perspectives towards capstone experiences was integral in developing a series of guiding principles which could be applied more broadly, across and even beyond the institution. The knowledge provided by different partners enabled the authors to identify commonalities and differences between their approaches, establishing a platform from which disciplines, schools or courses can develop their own individual learning experiences, while at the same time providing learning opportunities which align with and are informed by other capstone experiences provided throughout the institution.

Another common approach to intra-university partnerships involved bringing in additional expertise, such as careers and employability staff, who were able to link learning and teaching approaches with graduate skill requirements. Hammer et al. found that incorporating careers and employability staff into program review and enhancement activities enabled career development activities to be more deeply embedded into program design processes. Furthermore, these staff were able to identify knowledge gaps and support faculty colleagues in areas where they lacked expertise.

As Brown et al. suggest, the creation of partnerships within the university is dependent upon all staff possessing a shared vision of students' needs and working in partnership to achieve this vision. Furthermore, Kitto et al. assert that collaborative activities also require cohesive and tightly-coupled systems which enable information to be easily transferred between organisational structures. As the authors contend, any approach to connectedness learning in which one partner maintains core responsibilities or decision-making capabilities over another is likely doomed to failure. An intra-institutional approach to learning therefore not only requires connectedness between staff to break down disciplinary silos, but also connected systems to enable the fluent transfer of information across differing institutional partners.

The formation of sustainable, equitable partnerships with industry and community outside of the university is also an important step in providing students with authentic learning experiences. The nature of these partnerships will vary depending upon student needs and institutional context. These might involve WIL experiences with industry partners, such as the school–university social entrepreneurship program in Chapter 12, or the alignment of learning and teaching with community values and perspectives, as shown in Chapter 8. What all of these partnerships require is that the institution itself has the capacity to identify and make strategic connections with those beyond its walls. As Bedford and Bell suggest, these connections create a 'pipeline' to support graduate employability, while simultaneously fostering "interdisciplinary discussion between key stakeholders to eliminate silos and improve efficacy and institutional uptake".

Consistent with the enabling strategies of *identifying, making and growing strategic extra-university connections*, and *strengthening and maintaining extra-university connections*, the partnerships explored within this volume were developed on the basis of sustainable and substantive collaboration over time. This approach is not without its challenges; namely the intensive effort required to facilitate these partnerships and develop and deliver an industry relevant curriculum. However, the value that they offer in terms of institutional connectedness was evident. For students, these connections implanted their learning within the real world. Direct interactions with industry figures provided inspiration and the drive to develop their own professional identity, but crucially, also gave them their first taste of connecting with others as a professional. Goodwin et al. found that networked learning not only enabled the development of disciplinary skills and industry connections, but also empowered the students in their study to independently seek out and extend their own professional communities. Inviting external stakeholders into the teaching space can also offer wider institutional benefits. As Hammer et al. found, connections with industry in the two programs they reviewed had created a platform for sharing good practice, and paved the way for a "more systematic, whole-of-discipline approach to industry connection and career development".

Finally, the chapters in this volume demonstrated the importance of senior leadership in enabling the implementation of connectedness learning across the institution as a whole. Any effective integrated and systemic approach to connectedness learning is contingent on strategic vision and leadership. The curriculum transformation program documented in Chapter 10 acts as an example of how this might be achieved. In their chapter, Bedford and Bell outline the overarching vision, design principles, themes and transformative practices which define the University of Wollongong's approach to graduate employability. Although clearly a lengthy and resource-intensive process, a whole-of-institution approach offers a consistent and communicable way to ensure all university stakeholders work towards the same goals, while permitting sufficient diversity and innovation in practice inside programs and different disciplinary areas.

CONNECTING WITH THE FUTURE: FUTURE-PROOFING THE UNIVERSITY THROUGH CONNECTEDNESS LEARNING

In the final section of this book, we turn to consider the future forces that will shape learners, learning, teaching, and the university, and the roles that connectedness can play in supporting higher education to navigate turbulent times ahead. We ask what will the learning needs of future students be, and what will universities need to offer them in order to meet those needs? In turn, what would a genuinely connected university look like, and how would it function? How can we start to 'future proof' our universities through connectedness learning?

It is hard to know exactly what the future will bring to higher education, however, it is fair to say that we can all expect to experience significant and ongoing change. This change is already happening. Technological advancements in automation and machine learning, big data, the Internet of Things, robotics, and increases in computer processing power are key drivers, and their impacts are likely to be felt even more significantly over coming years (Hajkowicz et al., 2016; Organisation for Economic Co-operation and Development, 2017). Technological progress is only one class of the change drivers that will impact the world in which our students will work and live (Bakhshi et al., 2017). Environmental sustainability concerns, urbanisation, increasing social inequality, demographic changes, and political instability can be added to the list of 'mega trends' that contribute to a complex and mutable future for us all.

These influences also ensure that the era of the single undergraduate degree, where all of the knowledge required for professional life is acquired in a single place over a single time period, is over. Lifelong learning is no longer something that is "voluntary and self-regulated" (Department of Education and Science, 2000). While significant self-regulation of learning is still required (possibly now more than ever), a lifelong commitment to the acquisition of new knowledge and capabilities has become essential. Some commentators have predicted the demise of entire occupational fields (accountants, lawyers, professional drivers, manufacturing workers), along with the creation of others (such as cybersecurity, social media marketing and robotic engineering – see Tytler et al., 2018), at a rate that has not been seen since the last Industrial Revolution. Certainly, with technological advancements and ongoing social/ environmental changes, the emphases of many job roles and the tasks people will undertake inside those roles are already changing and will continue to do so (Manyika et al., 2017). Cognitively and manually routine tasks and roles are already disappearing, and people are taking on more roles that require high level and specialised knowledge and skills, and emotional intelligence. Good quality, relevant and lifelong higher education is pivotal to the future of work.

Shifting labour markets, changes to labour policy and HR practice mean that people are more likely to need to reskill, change job roles more often, and hold multiple roles, including in the so-called 'gig' economy. As well as being recurrently tasked with acquiring new work and acquiring the capabilities required to be successful in that work, individuals in the gig economy bear much of the risk of employment and unemployment that would usually be taken on by employer firms. In order to protect themselves, they also need to learn and be prepared for changing and evolving HR practices and workforce regulations.

Ongoing higher education-based learning is increasingly central to employment and career development. It is also important to people's capacities to traverse and contribute meaningfully to an increasingly complex society. Higher education develops the capabilities that learners require in order to be informed and capable citizens, through the development of critical and digital literacies, and broader issues-based educational experiences beyond disciplinary learning. Ongoing social and environmental change means that learners benefit from continuing to be plugged in to the sensemaking and capability development facilitation that the university can provide. Learners become critically engaged 'citizen scholars', who are engaged in an ongoing way in applying their knowledge and skills for the betterment of society (Arvanitakis and Hornsby, 2016). Part of the role of the university becomes explicitly about supporting learners to make sense of, and know how to contribute to, the world over their lifespans. Connectedness learning can help them to do this.

It is clear that in the age of hyper-complexity and rapid change in which we live, there are strong positive implications for learners from ongoing access to the learning opportunities that universities can offer. As learners benefit from this learning, they contribute in a continuing way to the economy and society through their work and citizenship activities. Such a university maintains its connections with learners in a lifelong way, offering ongoing informal and formal learning opportunities to alumni, and providing ways to continue to connect inside and outside the university with researchers, teachers and learners who have access to valued and up-to-date information and capabilities. This picture is presented in striking contrast with lingering notions of Western universities as 'ivory towers', operating in a state of privileged seclusion and separation from the world.

The lifelong connections that the university seeks to foster are not just with its students. The connections are with a wide range of stakeholders. Thus, the university becomes a broker of learning, and hub of a global network of learners, teachers, researchers, industry and community representatives, and interested citizens who are engaged in ongoing learning and production of new knowledge, and sharing of that knowledge (Bridgstock, 2017). Rather than emphasising the static transfer of knowledge and 'content' in the industrial-age educational institution, in the learning broker/network hub university, the focus is on production of new knowledge through research and discovery, and also synthesis and sharing of knowledge that is relevant and useful to its networks, in dynamic and adaptable ways (Bridgstock, 2017). The university supports transformative learning of individuals and societies (Brennan, King, and Labeau, 2004), by engaging openly, and facilitating the ongoing pursuit of procedural and tacit knowledge in applied ways. People who are connected with the university learn from it and its associated network, and in turn the university and its associated network learns from them.

Barnett (2011, 2017) discusses the associated notion of the ecological university, which is engaged with deepening and widening its networks across society, a task which it performs in the interests of the world. He argues that the university is interconnected with seven ecosystems in which it is embedded: knowledge; social institutions (including politics); physical environment; economy; culture; learning; and human subjectivity. The university is influenced by, and in turn intentionally acts upon, the seven zones. Barnett argues that these ecosystems are not separate from the ecological university, but that they all flow into one another. He further suggests that even now when universities maintain some level of perceived independence from their ecosystems, that these still form a 'deep ecology' of the university that can be brought to the surface and strengthened through visioning, strategy and intentional networking activity.

It is relatively easy to propose a more connected university, and quite another matter to achieve it. Universities maintain the same basic organisational structures as their early Industrial Age counterparts. To a great extent they maintain strong institutional boundaries in order to manage risk and protect themselves from outside influences. These practices lead them to sacrifice agility and responsiveness (Doz and Kosonen, 2008). As Gibb and Haskins (2014) suggest, to achieve the kinds of connected dynamism and agility required as a future-capable institution, the university must be porous to learning from stakeholders at all levels of the organisation. It does this by creating a shared culture of trust and learning. Second, it must facilitate a flow of knowledge gained across horizontal and vertical boundaries of the university. This book starts to suggest how we might get there from here, but there is a significant journey ahead of us.

The overarching vision and direction around the connected university's ecosystems and enabling strategies and structures are set by the top level of the university (Gibb and Haskins, 2014), which undertakes a strategic assessment of the stakeholder environment and brings forward stakeholder futures and visions to identify ways forward together. This is how the top-level research, academic, and engagement priorities are determined. Such strategies are already emerging among universities, with higher education institutions building distinctive profiles and differentiating themselves on the basis of regional, community, international, pedagogic or research areas of focus. In the connected university, central units of the organisation perform integration, co-ordination and communication functions. Heads of School and Faculty Leaders are responsible for communication of top-level priorities, innovation scaling, support of risk-taking, formation of high-level strategic partnerships, and breaking down of silos and organisational boundaries in order to promote information and knowledge sharing.

The connected university also demands decentralisation of the ability and the freedom and support for staff inside Schools to reach out to stakeholders and work/learn with them, while their activities are co-ordinated and integrated across the institution. Academics may collaborate with engagement professionals employed by the university in order to facilitate connections with stakeholders. This distributed model is advantageous because of the demonstrated learning and innovation effects of informal networks and social interactions (Obstfeld, 2005). It also enhances the agility of the institution, and its capacity to learn from both within and outside organisational boundaries. Through a combination of top level strategic-enabling, distributed-engaged, and vertically integrated connectedness processes, the university can influence our society, culture and the economy in meaningful and important ways.

This book started with an affirmation of the individual value of learning from, and with, others to all aspects of life and career development. It finishes the same way, but at a grander scale. Just as students make meaning of what they are learning and learn who they are and what they can contribute to the world through connectedness, so, too, do our educational institutions, our businesses, our communities, and indeed our governments. Through fostering diverse connections and learning with these connections, we develop social cohesion. Social cohesion creates a sense of belonging and trust and works towards the wellbeing of all. In this way, connectedness learning may be one key way that we can ensure that we strengthen our society and foster our collective capability to navigate global challenges ahead.

REFERENCES

Arvanitakis, J., and Hornsby, D. J. (2016). *Universities, the Citizen Scholar and the Future of Higher Education*. New York, NY: Palgrave Macmillan.
Bakhshi, H., Downing, J., Osborne, M. A., and Schneider, P. (2017). *The Future of Skills: Employment in 2030*. London: Pearson and NESTA.
Barnett, R. (2011). The coming of the ecological university. *Oxford Review of Education*, *37*(4), 439–455.
Barnett, R. (2017). *The Ecological University: A Feasible Utopia*. London: Routledge.
Brennan, J., King, R., and Labeau, Y. (2004). *The Role of Universities in the Transformation of Societies: An International Research Project*. London: Association of Commonwealth Universities.
Bridgstock, R. (2017). The university and the knowledge network: A new educational model for 21st century learning and employability. In M. Tomlinson (ed.), *Graduate Employability in Context: Research, Theory and Debate*. London: Palgrave Macmillan.
Bridgstock, R. (2019). *Graduate Employability 2.0: Enhancing the Connectedness of Learners, Teachers and Higher Education Institutions. Final Report of the National Senior Teaching Fellowship*. Canberra: Department of Education and Training.
Department of Education and Science. (2000). *Learning for Life: Paper on Adult Education*. Dublin: Stationery Office.
Doz, Y. L., and Kosonen, M. (2008). *Fast Strategy: How Strategic Agility Will Help You Stay Ahead of the Game*. London: Wharton School Publishing.
Gibb, A. A., and Haskins, G. (2014). The university of the future: An entrepreneurial stakeholder learning organization?. In A. Fayolle and D. T. Redford (eds), *Handbook on the Entrepreneurial University* (pp. 25–63). Cheltenham, UK and Northampton, MA, USA: Edward Elgar Publishing.
Hajkowicz, S., Reeson, A., Rudd, L., Bratanova, A., Hodgers, L., Mason, C., and Boughen, N. (2016). *Tomorrow's Digitally Enabled Workforce: Megatrends and Scenarios for Jobs and Employment in Australia Over the Coming Twenty Years*. Brisbane: Commonwealth Scientific and Industrial Research Organisation.
Holmes, L. (2013). Competing perspectives on graduate employability: possession, position or process? *Studies in Higher Education*, *38*(4), 538–554.
Jackson, D. (2017). Developing pre-professional identity in undergraduates through work-integrated learning. *Higher Education*, *74*(5), 833–853.

Lombardi, M. M. (2007). Authentic learning for the 21st century: An overview. *Educause Learning Initiative*, *1*(2007), 1–12.

Manyika, J., Lund, S., Chui, M., Bughin, J., Woetzel, J., Batra, P. … Sanghvi, S. (2017). *Jobs Lost, Jobs Gained: Workforce Transitions in a Time of Automation*. San Francisco, CA: McKinsey Global Institute.

Obstfeld, D. (2005). Social networks, the tertius iungens orientation, and involvement in innovation. *Administrative Science Quarterly*, *50*(1), 100–130.

Organisation for Economic Co-operation and Development. (2017). *Future of work and skills*. Paper presented at the 2nd meeting of the G20 Employment Working Group, Hamburg, Germany.

Tomlinson, M. (2017). Forms of graduate capital and their relationship to graduate employability. *Education+Training*, *59*(4), 338–352.

Tytler, R., Bridgstock, R., White, P., Mather, D., McCandles, T., and Grant-Iramu, M. (2018). *100 Jobs of the Future*. Melbourne: Deakin University.

Yunkaporta, T. (2009). *Aboriginal pedagogies at the cultural interface*. Doctor of Education PhD thesis, James Cook University, Townsville, Qld.

Index

framework 101–2, 104, 105,
109, 115
careers
boundaryless careers 51–2
portfolio careers 51–2
social media career 54–5
Careers and Employability 221
celebratory capstone experience *see*
capstone, experience, celebratory
Clarke, J. A. 165, 166
Clarke, V. 34
client relationship management approach
183
co-curricular activities 94, 96, 199
communities of practice 2, 6, 25, 168–9,
191, 258
Community Development and
Engagement for Social Change
172
community-based participatory research
(CBPR) 124–5
connected identity 25, 43–4, 111
connected institution *see* connectedness,
institutional
Connected Intelligence Centre (CIC)
234, 236, 239
connected learning *see* Social
Entrepreneurship Project (SEP),
connected learning
connected learning community 193–4
connected universities *see* connectedness,
institutional
connectedness 1–3
capabilities 12–13
capacity building 14–15
for career development 5–6
connected identity, building 25
connections
digital social 73
future-proofing the university
260

growing connections 14, 25, 44,
108, 111
maintaining 44
strengthening 44
strong tie 3, 6, 25, 54, 65, 72,
73
weak tie 3, 6, 25, 44, 54, 62, 64,
71–2, 73, 95, 231
working with 44
connectedness capabilities 22, 250–53
building a connected identity 12, 14,
25, 26, 31, 42–3, 93, 107–8,
110, 112, 143, 191, 256
developing social network literacy
12, 14, 42–3, 110, 112, 143,
256
digital identity and 42–7
enabling strategies 13–14
for graduate employability 23–4
growing connections 14, 25, 43, 44,
108, 110, 111–13, 143, 256
graduates 74–6
and health 4
in higher education 7–10
importance 3–7
institutional 183–5, 240–44
institutional enabling strategies for
185–8
for learning 6–7
learning 96
community, connected *see*
Social Entrepreneurship
Project (SEP), connected
learning community,
developing
connected *see* Social
Entrepreneurship Project
(SEP), connected
learning
connectedness *see* curriculum
transformation,
connectedness learning

Analytics, Social *see* Social
  Learning Analytics
authentic *see* capstone, authentic
  learning
blended *see* connectedness
  pedagogy, blended learning
community, connected *see* Social
  Entrepreneurship Project
  (SEP), connected learning
  community, developing
connected *see* Social
  Entrepreneurship Project
  (SEP), connected learning
connectedness *see* curriculum
  transformation,
  connectedness learning
Connectedness Learning Approach
  see connectedness, learning,
  Connectedness Learning
  Approach
Connectedness Learning Roundtable
  see connectedness, learning,
  Connectedness Learning
  Roundtable
connecting with connectedness *see*
  curriculum transformation,
  connecting with
  connectedness learning
embedded connectedness learning
  see connectedness, learning,
  embedded
events 200
HybridLearning@ UOW *see*
  University of Wollongong
  (UOW), HybridLearning@
  UOW
Indigenous ways of *see* Indigenous
  ways of learning
informal *see* informal learning

journey map, student connected
  see Social Entrepreneurship
  Project (SEP) *see* student
  connected learning journey
  map
lifetime of *see* lifetime of learning
network, professional *see*
  professional learning network
  (PLN)
networks, personal *see* personal
  learning networks (PLNs)
peer *see* peer learning
problem-based *see* problem-based
  learning
professional *see* professional
  learning
progressive *see* progressive learning
recognition of prior *see* recognition
  of prior learning (RPL)
  process
scaffolded *see* scaffolded learning
self-manage(ment) *see*
  self-manage(ment) learning
self-regulation of *see* self-regulation
  of learning
service *see* service learning
social *see* social learning
student-centred *see* student-centred
  learning
valuable *see* valuable learning
work integrated *see* work integrated
  learning (WIL)
work-based *see* work-based learning
workplace *see* workplace learning
Learning Analytics (LA) 232–3
  learning journeys 36, 123, 170, 175,
  197, 235
Learning Management System (LMS)
  148, 217, 235, 236
lecture-tutorial model 91
Lee, N. 175
Liden, R. C. 78